War, Conflict and Human Rights

Theory and practice

Chandra Lekha Sriram,
Olga Martin-Ortega and
Johanna Herman

Routledge
Taylor & Francis Group

LONDON AND NEW YORK

First published 2010
by Routledge
2 Park Square, Milton Park, Abingdon, Oxon OX14 4RN

Simultaneously published in the USA and Canada
by Routledge
270 Madison Ave, New York, NY 10016

Routledge is an imprint of the Taylor & Francis Group, an informa business

Typeset in TimesNewRoman by
Keystroke, 28 High Street, Tettenhall, Wolverhampton
Printed and bound in Great Britain by
TJ International Ltd, Padstow, Cornwall

British Library Cataloguing in Publication Data
A catalogue record for this book is available from the British Library

Library of Congress Cataloging-in-Publication Data
Sriram, Chandra Lekha, 1971-
War, conflict, and human rights : theory and practice / Chandra Lekha Sriram,
Olga Martin-Ortega and Johanna Herman.
p. cm.
1. War. 2. Human rights. 3. Peace-building. 4. War–Case studies.
5. Human rights–Case studies. 6. Peace-building–Case studies.
I. Martin-Ortega, Olga. II. Herman, Johanna. III. Title.
JZ6385.S75 2009
355.02–dc22
2009001036

ISBN 10: 0–415–45205–8 (hbk)
ISBN 10: 0–415–45206–6 (pbk)
ISBN 10: 0–203–87474–9 (ebk)

ISBN 13: 978–0–415–45205–2 (hbk)
ISBN 13: 978–0–415–45206–9 (pbk)
ISBN 13: 978–0–203–87474–5 (ebk)

War, Conflict and Human Rights

War, Conflict and Human Rights is an innovative new interdisciplinary textbook combining aspects of law, politics, and conflict analysis to examine the relationship between human rights and armed conflict.

Making use of both theoretical and practical approaches, this book:

- examines the tensions and complementarities between protection of human rights and resolution of conflict – the competing political demands and the challenges posed by internal armed conflict;
- explores the scope and effects of human rights violations in contemporary armed conflicts, such as those in Sierra Leone, Sudan, the Democratic Republic of Congo, and the former Yugoslavia, as well as the "global war on terror";
- assesses the legal and institutional accountability mechanisms developed in the wake of armed conflict to punish violations of human rights law and international humanitarian law, such as the ad hoc tribunals for the former Yugoslavia and Rwanda, and the International Criminal Court;
- discusses continuing and emergent global trends and challenges in the fields of human rights and conflict analysis.

This book will be essential reading for students of war and conflict studies, human rights, and international humanitarian law, and highly recommended for students of conflict resolution, peacebuilding, international security and international relations, generally.

Chandra Sriram is Professor of Human Rights at the University of East London and Director of the Centre on Human Rights in Conflict.

Olga Martin-Ortega is Senior Research Fellow at the Centre on Human Rights in Conflict at the University of East London.

Johanna Herman is Research Fellow at the Centre on Human Rights in Conflict at the University of East London.

Contents

Maps

Boxes and tables

Boxes

Tables

About the authors

Chandra Lekha Sriram is Professor of Human Rights at the University of East London, School of Law, and Director of the Centre on Human Rights in Conflict (http://www.uel.ac.uk/chrc). She received her PhD in Politics in 2000 from Princeton University. Her research interests include human rights, conflict prevention, and peacebuilding. Her most recent book is *Peace as Governance: Power-Sharing, Armed Groups, and Contemporary Peace Negotiations* (Palgrave, 2008).

Olga Martin-Ortega is Senior Research Fellow at the Centre on Human Rights in Conflict. She received her PhD in Law at the University of Jaén, Spain. Her research interests include business and human rights, postconflict reconstruction, and transitional justice. She is author of the monograph *Empresas multinacionales y derechos humanos en derecho internacional* (Bosch, 2008).

Johanna Herman is Research Fellow at the Centre on Human Rights in Conflict. She received her MA in International Affairs from Columbia University, with a concentration in human rights. She has worked for a number of United Nations agencies and international nongovernmental organizations. Her research interests include peacebuilding, transitional justice, and human rights.

Carmen Draghici is the author of Chapter 9, "The 'global war on terror'." She was Leverhulme Visiting Research Fellow at the Centre on Human Rights in Conflict in 2008. She received her PhD in International Law and Human Rights from the University of Rome "La Sapienza." Her research interests include international protection of family rights, and counterterrorism and human rights.

How to use this book

War and other forms of armed conflict often give rise to massive human rights violations, and violent conflict is indeed often provoked by grievances that may include serious violations of human rights and international humanitarian law. Demands for accountability for human rights violations are common in countries emerging from conflict, and postconflict countries have deployed a variety of mechanisms to address these demands. Indeed, demands for accountability can pose obstacles to peace negotiations. However, these crucial connections between war and human rights lie at the intersection of international human rights law and international humanitarian law, and conflict analysis and resolution. The issues at stake are not merely theoretical ones; they are central to the work of practitioners in international politics and international law. The knowledge needed to address these issues is therefore interdisciplinary, being both legal and political. There is thus a need to develop expertise that is analytic as well as theoretical, and substantive knowledge of both politics and law.

The study of war, conflict, and human rights is a complex, interdisciplinary undertaking. Many students may have expertise in international human rights law but not in conflict analysis, or may be familiar with particular conflicts but not with the legal and institutional responses to those conflicts, and abuses committed during their waging. This book attempts to bridge those gaps by presenting a comprehensive approach to the interaction between conflict resolution and human rights. It is designed to support students in upper-division undergraduate and Master's-level courses in conflict resolution and in human rights, as well as in hybrid studies of both.

Structure of the book

Part I addresses the theoretical issues underlying conflict and human rights, examining critical debates, politics, and law. Chapter 1 lays out the relationship between war and human rights, establishing the interaction that underpins the rest of the analysis in this book. Chapter 2 surveys the literature on critical conflict analysis, conflict resolution, and postconflict peacebuilding. It addresses the broad debates over the root causes of conflict; different methods of conflict prevention, mitigation, and resolution; and the challenges of postconflict peacebuilding. Chapter 3 examines the history of human rights and key debates in the human rights literature. These debates include those between universalist and particularist approaches, between individual and group rights, and between political and economic rights. Chapter 4 presents the relevant law, specifically international human rights law and international humanitarian law, and examines the specific challenge of addressing violations of these obligations in internal, as opposed to international, armed conflicts, and the special problem of armed groups, including terrorist groups.

Part II moves from the theoretical to the concrete, examining serious internal conflict and attendant human rights violations in the context of five case studies. The first four of these involve specific countries that have recently reached agreements ending armed conflict, while the fifth involves the global community. The country case studies examine the respective peace negotiations, and the choices made within those negotiations. Students will be able to explore the opportunities that were available for accountability, and to think about the various possibilities, without being constrained by what ultimately happened. Chapter 5 examines the wars in the former Yugoslavia during the 1990s, and the resolution reached through the Dayton Accords. Chapter 6 examines the peace process in Sierra Leone, which experienced violent conflict over resources and poor governance, and serious violations of human rights, including forcible conscription of child soldiers, mutilation, torture, and massacres. Chapter 7 considers the peace process in the Democratic Republic of Congo, which also experienced violent conflict over resources and governance, and gross human rights violations perpetrated by internal forces as well as militaries and militias sent or supported by multiple neighboring countries. Chapter 8 addresses the process in Sudan, where a protracted conflict over resources, religion, territory, and human rights violations raged in the south until recently, with the conflict and demands changing character over time. Here the only accountability process under way is linked not to the recently completed peace agreements, but to an ongoing conflict in Darfur. Finally, Chapter 9 presents a different type of case study, examining conflict, armed groups, and human rights in the context of the "global war on terror."

Part III examines a range of accountability mechanisms that have been developed since the early to middle 1990s. Each chapter examines a different model of response to abuses linked to armed conflict: transnational, hybrid, and international. Chapter 10 discusses the ad hoc international criminal tribunals established for the former Yugoslavia and Rwanda in 1993 and 1994, respectively. Chapter 11 examines transnational methods of accountability, specifically the exercise of universal jurisdiction and transnational civil accountability. Chapter 12 addresses a relatively recent development in accountability – the hybrid or mixed tribunal – and discusses the operations of hybrid tribunals in Sierra Leone, East Timor, and Kosovo, and prospects for such a tribunal in Cambodia. Chapter 13 turns to the emerging practice of the International Criminal Court and its investigations and cases under way in the Democratic Republic of Congo, Sudan, Uganda, and the Central African Republic. Finally, Chapter 14 considers lessons learned from these cases, and prospects and challenges for the future.

Guidance for students and instructors

While the three parts of this volume differ in content and approach, guidance for students and instructors is provided throughout. A general glossary is provided at the end of the book, presenting key terms used in the human rights, international law, and conflict resolution literature. Whenever a key term is used for the first time in a chapter it is highlighted in bold so the reader will know that a definition is available in the glossary. To help guide class discussion and assist students in initiating future research, each chapter begins with an outline of key points highlighting the main debates and concepts addressed in that chapter, and concludes with a set of discussion questions and group exercises, as well as a list of further readings and official documents and sources. The country-specific chapters in Part II of the volume also include maps, key facts about the country or territory under discussion, and a list of key players to help guide students through the complex web of groups and institutions involved in the conflict concerned.

Acknowledgments

As with all large projects, this book owes its completion to many individuals and institutions. We are especially grateful to the School of Law of the University of East London for its ongoing support to the Centre on Human Rights in Conflict (http://www.uel.ac.uk/chrc), at which we are based within the university. We are also particularly grateful to Fiona Fairweather, Dean of the School of Law, for her active support in facilitating our work on a daily basis. Our management team within the school, and our international advisory group, provided us with vital guidance as well.

We thank our colleague Carmen Draghici, who was a Leverhulme visiting research fellow at the Centre on Human Rights in Conflict during 2008, for contributing Chapter 9, on human rights in the "global war on terror." We are also indebted to Jordi Palau Loverdos for his kind assistance in accessing information on the international crimes committed in Rwanda and the Democratic Republic of Congo, as presented in court before the Spanish Audiencia Nacional. The indictment order referred to in this book was made public by the Audiencia Nacional's Fourth Investigative Court on February 6, 2008.

Finally, we thank our editor at Routledge, Andrew Humphrys, for initiating discussions on this project, and offering encouragement and feedback throughout.

Chandra Lekha Sriram, Olga Martin-Ortega, and Johanna Herman

Part I

War and human rights

Critical issues

1   The interplay between war and human rights

Overview

This book examines key issues and debates regarding the connections between armed conflict and human rights, both theoretical and practical. It also examines the key legal sources and obligations in both **international human rights law** and **international humanitarian law**. And it does so from a grounded, real-world perspective, through in-depth case studies of particular countries involved in and emerging from armed conflict, paying attention to the specific human rights and conflict resolution challenges presented in each, and the compromises ultimately reached. The chapters in Part I examine in detail a wide range of human rights and accountability mechanisms that have been developed, each of which maps to one or more of the country case studies in Part II. This book thus examines an important set of issues that are directly located at the intersection of courses on human rights and international humanitarian law, and courses on conflict analysis and conflict resolution. The approach is explicitly hybrid, mixing disciplinary approaches, policy analyses, case studies, and legal analyses.

War, armed conflict, and human rights

The relationship between war and other violent conflict is complex and dynamic. As discussed later, violations of human rights can be both causes and consequences of violent conflict. Further, gross violations of human rights and violations of international humanitarian law can alter the course of conflicts, adding grievances and changing the interests of various actors, in turn making conflicts more intractable. Where this is the case, conflict resolution can become much more difficult, not least because many issues beyond the original "root causes" of conflict will be at stake, and because trust between the warring parties will be extremely low. Finally, demands for accountability will be made, whether by victims and relatives of victims, by local and international nongovernmental organizations, or by various international actors such as donor countries. The pursuit of legal accountability is often controversial, and is often resisted by one or more of the fighting parties; insisting upon legal accountability may impede negotiations or peace implementation. Nonetheless, there have been many attempts to pursue legal accountability while also making peace, and this book will examine many such cases.

These complex problems are both legal and political. Developing useful policy responses requires an understanding not only of international human rights and humanitarian law, but also of conflict dynamics and conflict resolution. We turn next, briefly, to the specific fields and disciplines of conflict analysis and resolution, human rights, and international humanitarian law, which will be developed in greater detail in subsequent chapters. We then address in greater detail the specific ways in which war and human rights violations may be intertwined, and the particular and competing demands and goals of conflict resolvers and human rights promoters.

Conflict analysis and causes of conflict

Conflict analysis, in theory and in practice, seeks to identify the "underlying" causes of conflict as well as to enable us to understand the dynamics of conflict once it is under way. In any given conflict there is always more than one cause, although some will be more salient in particular conflicts, as is discussed in Chapter 2. Causes of conflict can include mistrust or grievances based upon ethnic discrimination or preferential treatment; competition over resources, whether political or economic; demands for political autonomy or independence; allegations of corruption; and myriad claims regarding current or past human rights abuses. Attempts to resolve conflicts will need to address many or all of these underlying causes, which means that in conflict resolution processes, human rights abuses are but one concern among many. Those seeking to resolve conflict will be concerned with bringing all relevant parties to the negotiating table, including the possibility of defection by some, particularly "spoilers"; building confidence among parties; and addressing the many grievances that parties may have against one another. They may also be concerned with allocating future economic and political resources; guaranteeing security for all parties, particularly those that fear for their survival; rebuilding institutions of law and order; and addressing specific demands for justice to rectify past abuses. They may also be concerned with setting the stage for **peacebuilding** processes, often with a significant international presence, or with longer-term reconciliation and conflict transformation. Clearly, in many instances human rights are not the first topic of concern for conflict resolution experts or practitioners. However, as we will see, human rights violations and human rights protections are intimately linked to the patterns of contemporary conflict in a number of ways, meaning that contemporary efforts to end wars have been compelled to deal with human rights and humanitarian law obligations. Encounters between human rights advocates and conflict resolution experts have thus been necessarily uneasy, with each "side" viewing the priorities of the other as suspect.

Human rights violations as causes of conflict

Human rights violations can be both causes and consequences of conflict. We begin with the ways in which human rights violations can generate conflict, with some examples for illustration in Box 1.1. In the most general sense, grievances over the real or perceived denial of rights can generate social conflict. This may be the case where there is systematic discrimination, differential access to education or health care, limited freedom of expression or religion, or denial of political participation, whether based upon race, ethnicity, caste, religion, language, gender, or some other characteristic. These violations may seem relatively minor, particularly in comparison to some of the grave crimes examined later in this book, including **war crimes** and **genocide**, but they can still generate real grievances and social unrest. In functional polities, such grievances may be handled through relatively peaceful, constitutional means, whether through litigation in the courts or through legislative reform or administrative policy change. However, in weak, corrupt, abusive, or collapsed and collapsing states, such conflict is more likely to become violent. That violence may be merely sporadic, if serious, or it may give rise to more systematic opposition.

Box 1.1 **Conflict and human rights in practice: Northern Ireland, Kosovo, and Sierra Leone**

> In Northern Ireland the Catholic community claimed that they were the victims of systematic abuse and discrimination, and sought first to gain reforms through a non-violent civil rights movement. When that failed, they resorted to the use of violence, and the Irish Republican Army emerged. The sustained denial of fundamental rights, even in the absence of serious bodily harm, can thus promote violent conflict.
>
> In Kosovo the Kosovo Liberation Army claimed that it took up arms in response to real and anticipated ethnic cleansing efforts by the Serbs.
>
> In Sierra Leone the Civil Defense Forces emerged to protect local communities from the predations of both the government and Revolutionary United Front rebel forces.

Violent conflict may also emerge where there are more violent human rights abuses: illegal detention, extrajudicial execution, disappearances, **torture**, widespread killing, or even attempts at genocide. Where civilians have already been targeted by such violence, whether committed by the state or by **nonstate actors**, it is unlikely that peaceful resistance will have much effect, so it is yet more likely that affected individuals and groups will take up arms to defend themselves. In such situations, then, human rights violations are an important underlying cause of conflict, although seldom the only one. Once war has erupted, any serious attempt at conflict resolution will also have to address the underlying sources of the original conflict, including abuses of human rights. Otherwise, violence, particularly retaliation for past abuses, is likely to reemerge once third-party mediators, observers, or peacekeepers have departed.

Human rights violations as consequences of conflict

Alternatively, human rights abuses can emerge primarily as a result of violent conflict. A conflict may have been undertaken by the parties primarily out of concern to promote a political or ideological agenda, or to promote the welfare of one or more identity groups, or over access to resources. Examples abound: the leftist rebels in El Salvador ostensibly fought to redress the massive wealth imbalance in the country and the grinding poverty suffered by the majority, seeking land redistribution and a more egalitarian economic system. However, the conflict with the government that ensued generated vast human rights abuses, such as "disappearances," torture, illegal detention, and execution, mostly committed by the government. In Argentina, the alleged threat of communist subversion was used by the military junta to maintain its own power and engage in systematic disappearances and repression. Conflicts over access to resources, such as diamonds in Sierra Leone, timber in Liberia, coltan (a metallic ore) in the Democratic Republic of Congo, and oil in Sudan, have taken a great toll beyond the cost to human life on the battlefield, resulting also in wide-scale killing and displacement of civilians, and gross human rights abuses. By far the greater part of the harm in recent conflicts has been inflicted on civilians, either incidentally or, more frequently, deliberately in the pursuit of resources. Violations may include human rights abuses such as torture and disappearances, but also frequently include war crimes, **crimes against humanity**, and even genocide.

Human rights violations as both causes and consequences of conflict

Of course, human rights violations are usually both causes and consequences of conflict, intertwined among other factors. For example, in Sudan, causes of conflict have included concerns about religious repression, access to resources, and control of land, as well as the human rights violations themselves, incurred over the course of the multi-decade conflict. It would be incorrect to suggest that the north–south conflict was generated by attempts of the government in the north to impose *sharia* on the population of the south, who were largely Christian or animist. It would similarly be incorrect to argue that the conflict in Sudan was over access to oil alone. Rather, religious repression, discrimination and marginalization based on perceived racial distinctions and geography, and access to resources were at stake in that conflict, which reached a negotiated conclusion in 2005.

Human rights violations as transformers of conflict dynamics

Human rights violations are not only causes and consequences of violent conflict, however; they are also potentially transformative of conflicts and may make their resolution a greater challenge. Thus, conflicts that begin over resources, religion, or ethnic or territorial claims may, as they progress, create new grievances through the real and perceived violation of human rights by one or more parties. Further, such violations may reify divides in society, making it easier for leaders to mobilize people – civilian and armed – to violent action. In such mobilization it becomes easy to demonize the "other," whether rebel group or state actor, which in turn facilitates not merely killing on the battlefield, but also the commission of further human rights violations. The conflict may sometimes be transformed into one that is primarily about grievances, identity, and recrimination, even though other causes may have precipitated the original fighting. Further – and this is key from the perspective of conflict resolution – heightened mistrust and resentments make initial negotiations difficult, and may create impediments to long-term peacebuilding and reconciliation. Moreover, it is difficult to persuade people and groups who have abused one another to sit face to face and negotiate; even if leaders take that step, ordinary individuals might be reluctant to set aside grievances. This fundamentally changes the terrain of peacebuilding; victims, civil society, and other actors may demand redress of past abuses, even though such redress is likely to be resisted by some or all of the warring parties.

Human rights and accountability as demands during peace negotiations and postconflict peacebuilding

Human rights protections and accountability for past violations are usually among the demands that parties consider when negotiating the end to an armed conflict. However, these are not the only demands, as is discussed in Chapter 2. Human rights may emerge as a central concern in negotiations in a number of ways. First, the demand for accountability will likely be central for one or more parties at the negotiating table, with civil society, nongovernmental organizations, or the international community also pressing for some form of accountability beyond the negotiation table. The latter might take the form of prosecutions, lustration or vetting (removal or barring of abusers from certain public offices), **truth commissions**, or reparation. Any of these groups, and indeed some armed groups as well, might demand the restructuring and retraining of security forces so that they will respect human rights in the future. Yet simultaneously, individuals who have also been perpetrators of serious human rights violations, whether they are part of armed groups or the government, may fear imprisonment or, at the very least, loss of privileges through lustration, or public shaming through the release of a truth commission report. They may press for blanket amnesties or at least for their own protection. Thus, demands for accountability can be serious obstacles during negotiations. A variety of provisions may be built into a peace agreement, or the issue may be held in abeyance to be dealt with subsequently. Demands for accountability and the various mechanisms to address past abuses after conflict are examined in greater detail in Parts II and III of this volume.

Alternatively, human rights protections may also be central to a negotiating process, important in laying the groundwork for democratic development, and may be useful in confidence building. Thus, for example, in El Salvador's multiple rounds of negotiations, one of the first operational agreements, the San José Agreement, approved the creation of a **United Nations** (UN) human rights observer mission. The functioning of the mission not only meant that human rights were prioritized during the negotiating process, but also introduced a third party on the ground in the country. Many scholars argue that the presence of a third party – as monitor, guarantor, and stabilizer – is essential if **peace negotiations** are to succeed.

Human rights protections and accountability for past abuses are also often claimed to be essential to **peacemaking** and peacebuilding. Analysts and advocates have argued that addressing human rights violations is essential for restoring the peace and building **rule of law**, and in particular for demonstrating that a society is now on a different, nonviolent path. They have similarly argued that the absence of accountability may hamper long-term peacebuilding, because some former victims may seek vengeance, or the population more broadly may place little faith in postconflict institutions that have not addressed human rights abuses.

Conversely, the pursuit of accountability may hamper not only peace negotiations, but also peace implementation, where those who face accountability return to violence or threaten to return to violence. Thus, in El Salvador, for example, the impending release of the truth commission report, which would find the armed forces responsible for the vast majority of human rights abuses committed during that country's conflict, caused unrest in the military. In Argentina, a country emerging from a severe internal repression that never became an official armed conflict, the attempt to prosecute the former military leadership was greeted with five coup attempts.

Other issues covered by peace processes might not seem directly related to human rights but could have an important impact on demands for accountability and reconciliation processes. For example, peace negotiations and peace processes deal with the disarmament, demobilization, and reintegration of ex-combatants to guarantee that they do not return fighting. This may require a host of guarantees to parties that may be at cross-purposes with human rights protections, including **amnesty** but also other concessions to individuals or groups who may be responsible for grave violations of human rights or international humanitarian law. Thus, the 1999 Lomé Agreement in Sierra Leone granted a blanket amnesty, and guaranteed notorious rebel leader Foday Sankoh a position in government. Negotiations will address an array of contentious issues, such as land tenure or access to resources, and restructuring of and access to governance and political representation. Particularly where governance has been poor, corrupt, or undemocratic, some domestic and international actors will be interested in rebuilding, or building for the first time, key elements needed to establish the rule of law – transparent legislation, a functional judiciary and correctional system, and the like. Protection of human rights may be an important component of rule of law strategies.

Human rights concerns thus play a complex range of roles and have a complicated relationship to both peace negotiations and peacebuilding processes. The relationship is made more complex by the fact that specialists in the protection of human rights and specialists in conflict resolution form different communities, with different expertise.

Box 1.2 **The relationship between conflict and human rights**

- Human rights violations as causes of conflict
- Human rights violations as consequences of conflict
- Human rights violations as both causes and consequences of conflict
- Human rights violations as transformative of conflict dynamics
- Human rights and accountability as demands during peace negotiations and post-conflict peacebuilding

Advocating human rights and conflict resolution: different communities, different agendas

Rhetorically, the goals of those who seek to protect human rights and those who seek to promote conflict resolution are complementary: both seek to reduce human suffering, in particular to prevent physical harm and violence to individuals, largely civilians, by governments or nonstate armed groups. However, the two groups may prioritize goals or assess success differently, with conflict resolution advocates typically prepared to place less importance on human rights concerns, at least temporarily, while details of peace agreements are being resolved, as explained in Box 1.3. Human rights advocates, conversely, will generally focus upon the underlying grievances as causes of the conflict, or on the abuses that occurred during the conflict, and insist that conflict might reemerge if "justice" is not done. They may be less sensitive to the possibility that a demand for justice during peace negotiations might actually block conflict resolution.

Box 1.3 **Advocating human rights and conflict resolution: potential tension**

- Human rights advocates prioritize accountability, public reckoning, national human rights institutions, and the needs of victims, and will be wary of any outcome that involves negotiation with or amnesty for human rights abusers.
- Conflict resolution advocates prioritize reaching a settlement that can bring an end to violent conflict, and will be prepared to negotiate with and even consider amnesty for human rights abusers.

Not surprisingly, conflict resolution advocates will prioritize different goals than human rights advocates. The latter will be suspicious of amnesties, and promote legal accountability, the creation of human rights institutions, the needs of victims, and public discussion of past abuses. Conflict resolution advocates, as noted above, will be interested primarily in reaching a negotiated settlement, and may be willing to sacrifice some human rights concerns to that end. However, they are also concerned with creating a sustainable, long-term peace and reducing the risk of return to conflict, and thus have an interest in the rule of law, democratic governance, and, ultimately, many human rights protections. Thus, while the primary goals of the two communities may appear to be at odds, given the intertwined nature of human rights violations and war there may be a convergence to be identified, and each group of practitioners needs to be sensitized to the concerns of the other.

Relevant law

This book does not cover all obligations under international human rights law and international humanitarian law, as these are too vast to be addressed sufficiently here. The relevant legal obligations, developed in greater detail in Chapter 4, are primarily those that are closely tied to violent conflict as either causes or consequences. Further, the bulk of this book addresses situations in which violations of legal obligations are actually crimes, for which international, individualized criminal accountability is possible. These comprise a narrow set of violations, and are those for which postconflict regimes, or the international community, have prosecuted perpetrators.

The legal rights and obligations of greatest relevance here are the core international human rights documents, often referred to as the **International Bill of Rights**: the Universal Declaration of Human Rights (UDHR), the International Covenant on Civil and Political Rights (ICCPR), and the International Covenant on Economic, Social, and Cultural Rights (ICESCR). As we shall see in Chapter 4, these documents, where they do create obligations for states, do not create international crimes. The same is true of the Convention on the Elimination of Racial Discrimination in All Its Forms (CERD), the Convention on the Rights of the Child (CRC), and the Convention on the Elimination of Discrimination Against Women (CEDAW). Nonetheless, all of these documents articulate rights or obligations, the violation of which may serve to promote conflict, or result from conflict. Other human rights documents create more explicit obligations for states, and violations by individuals may be prosecutable crimes, as with the Convention on the Prevention and Punishment of the Crime of Genocide (the **Genocide Convention**) and the Convention Against Torture and Other Cruel, Inhuman, or Degrading Treatment or Punishment (the **Torture Convention**). Similarly, obligations under international humanitarian law, whether customary or based on treaty, may include **grave breaches**, known in common parlance as war crimes, for which individuals may be prosecuted. The key conventions of study here are the four **Geneva Conventions** of 1949 and their two additional protocols of 1977. Finally, the Rome Statute of the **International Criminal Court** defines three crimes for prosecution – war crimes, crimes against humanity, and genocide – and may eventually define a fourth over which it has jurisdiction, the crime of aggression.

Box 1.4 **Key international legal documents**

- International Bill of Rights:

  - Universal Declaration of Human Rights
  - International Covenant on Civil and Political Rights
  - International Covenant on Economic, Social, and Cultural Rights

- Convention on the Prevention and Punishment of the Crime of Genocide
- Convention Against Torture and Other Cruel, Inhuman, or Degrading Treatment or Punishment
- Four Geneva Conventions of 1949 and their two additional protocols of 1977
- Rome Statute of the International Criminal Court
- Convention on the Elimination of Racial Discrimination in All Its Forms
- Convention on the Rights of the Child
- Convention on the Elimination of Discrimination Against Women

Responses to human rights abuse

Given the complex relationship between conflict and human rights, and the competing demands articulated above, a number of responses to significant human rights abuse have been developed: the domestic, transnational, hybrid, and ad hoc and permanent international, as noted in Box 1.5 and discussed in Part III of this volume. Domestic responses to end armed conflict and simultaneously grapple with human rights abuses may include all of the measures already noted, ranging from amnesty to prosecution, alongside lustration, reparation, retraining of security forces, and development of national human rights mechanisms. Transnational responses, whereby abuses are addressed in a different country than that in which they occurred, are most commonly the case in the pursuit of criminal accountability, with the exercise of **universal jurisdiction**, but accountability may also be pursued through civil suits. Most criminal cases have been brought in a few European countries, such as Belgium and Spain, while most civil cases have been brought in the United States through the **Alien Tort Claims Act** (ACTA), or in the United Kingdom. Hybrid institutions for accountability have also been developed in recent years. These are tribunals created to function in the country where an armed conflict has occurred; they utilize not only domestic law and judges, but also a combination of domestic and international judges, prosecutors, and lawyers, and may rely on international human rights and humanitarian law or a combination of international and domestic law. There have been several such experiments to date – in Kosovo, East Timor, Sierra Leone, and Cambodia, although the latter is in its early stages. Finally, there are international responses, through international criminal tribunals. Historically, after World War II, prosecutions were undertaken in the Nuremberg and Tokyo Tribunals, but new international bodies began to emerge in the 1990s with the creation of two ad hoc tribunals for the prosecution of crimes committed during the war in the former Yugoslavia and during the genocide in Rwanda. More recently, the International Criminal Court has undertaken formal investigations of crimes committed in northern Uganda, the Democratic Republic of Congo, and Darfur, Sudan, and informal investigation of the situation in the Central African Republic. Each of these bodies is somewhat different; although many refer to the same core legal obligations, their mandates and competence vary significantly.

Box 1.5 **Accountability institutions and responses**

- Domestic transitional justice
- Regional courts
- Ad hoc international tribunals
- Permanent international tribunals
- Hybrid or mixed tribunals
- Universal jurisdiction
- Civil accountability

Internal armed conflicts

Many of the conflicts examined in this book share a unique feature: they are internal armed conflicts, although they often involve a cross-border dimension. The internal nature of many contemporary conflicts generates particular legal and practical difficulties. While international human rights law functions in times of war and peace, and applies consistently whether the conflict is internal or international, the same cannot be said of international humanitarian law. The latter operates only where an armed conflict occurs. In some instances of civil strife there may be genuine debate about whether an armed conflict is in fact occurring. Contemporary conflicts are seldom declared, and many low-intensity conflicts, while costly in lives and human rights violations, might not be treated as "wars." More important, however, international humanitarian law is traditionally dualistic, distinguishing between international and noninternational armed conflict. This, as we shall see, poses particular difficulty in pursuing accountability for armed groups engaged in internal armed conflict.

Key points

- The study of war and human rights is an interdisciplinary subject, involving knowledge of law, politics, and conflict analysis and resolution.
- Promotion of human rights and resolution of violent conflict are often viewed as being in tension by scholars and practitioners of each.
- The relationship between war and human rights is complex: human rights violations can underpin conflict, can emerge from conflict, and can transform conflicts already under way, and human rights accountability may be a critical demand within, but also an obstacle to, peace processes.
- Peace processes must not only address demands for accountability for past abuses, but also disarm combatants and reshape political processes and institutions of law and governance.
- A wide range of law exists that may be relevant in addressing human rights violations that arise during conflict, falling broadly under the rubrics of international human rights law and international humanitarian law.
- A wide range of responses to past abuses may be developed, through use of domestic courts or through international institutions and processes, including the International Criminal Court most recently.

- Nonstate armed groups play a critical role in contemporary armed conflicts and pose challenges to peace processes, but also complicate the application of international humanitarian law.

Discussion questions

- What is the general relationship between war and human rights?
- How might human rights violations engender conflict?
- How does conflict engender human rights violations?
- How does the evolution of conflict, and human rights violations, change conflict?
- How might the interplay of conflict and human rights violations and protections affect conflict negotiation, resolution, and peacebuilding?

Further reading

Bell, Christine, *Peace Agreements and Human Rights* (Oxford: Oxford University Press, 2003), chaps. 1, 2, 10, and app., "A Decade of Peace Agreements."

Crimes of War Project, http://www.crimesofwar.org/thebook/amnesty.html.

Human Rights Watch, *Human Rights and Armed Conflict* (2004), http://hrw.org/wr2k4, especially "Africa on Its Own," and "Right Side Up."

Lutz, Ellen, Eileen F. Babbitt, and Hurst Hannum, "Human Rights and Conflict Resolution from the Practitioners' Perspectives," *Fletcher Forum of World Affairs* 27, no. 1 (Winter–Spring 2003), http://fletcher.tufts.edu/chrcr/pdf/lutz4.pdf.

Mertus, Julie A., and Jeffrey W. Helsing, eds., *Human Rights and Conflict: Exploring the Links Between Rights, Law, and Peacebuilding* (Washington, DC: US Institute of Peace Press, 2006).

Parlevliet, Michelle, "Bridging the Divide: Exploring the Relationship Between Human Rights and Conflict Management," *Track Two* 11, no. 1 (March), http://ccrweb.ccr.uct.ac.za/archive/two/11_1/bridging.html.

Putnam, Tanya, "Human Rights and Sustainable Peace," in Stephen J. Stedman, Donald Rothchild, and Elizabeth Cousens, eds., *Ending Civil Wars: The Implementation of Peace Agreements* (Boulder: Lynne Rienner, 2002).

Official documents and sources

United Nations, *Report of the Independent Expert to Update the Set of Principles to Combat Impunity, Diane Orentlicher: Updated Set of Principles for the Protection and Promotion of Human Rights Through Action to Combat Impunity* (February 8, 2005), UN Doc. E/CN.4/2005/102/Add.1.

United Nations, *The Rule of Law and Transitional Justice in Conflict and Post-Conflict Societies: Report of the Secretary-General* (August 23, 2004), UN Doc. S/2004/616.

2 Conflict

Fundamentals and debates

Overview

After the end of the Cold War, internal conflicts proliferated significantly. Since then, collective efforts to prevent and resolve these conflicts have been a central focus for the international community. This chapter analyzes the characteristics and causes of contemporary armed conflicts, and how the international system copes with preventing and resolving them, as well as how it attempts to build durable peace afterward. This chapter examines the distinction between **peacemaking**, **peacekeeping**, and **peacebuilding**, and the historical evolution of these processes, as well as the main actors involved in **conflict prevention**, conflict resolution, and postconflict reconstruction, with special emphasis on the **United Nations** (UN) legal and institutional framework.

Today's conflicts

The international institutional architecture designed after World War II foresaw a system to prevent and resolve international disputes. It focused on conflict between two or more states, which had been the most common form until then. The end of the Cold War marked a significant change in the nature and development of armed conflicts, however, and therefore also in the strategies to prevent, resolve, and mitigate their effects. The 1990s saw a spectacular proliferation of internal armed conflicts. Since then, interstate wars have decreased in number to a mere few: the Gulf War in 1991, the wars between Ethiopia and Eritrea in 1998, the US invasions of Afghanistan and Iraq in 2001 and 2003, respectively, the war in the Democratic Republic of Congo, which involved some of its neighboring states (see Chapter 7), and the confrontation between Russia and Georgia in the summer of 2008.

Internal armed conflicts are different from interstate conflicts in many ways, and therefore their specific characteristics need to be considered when examining them. Whereas an interstate war involves two standing armies fighting each other, a civil conflict involves a government army or militia fighting one or more rebel organizations. These rebel organizations are referred to, in much of the conflict and legal literature, as nonstate armed groups. In civil wars, these groups seek a range of objectives, including secession from or control over the state or parts of its territory, as well as resource exploitation, as discussed in the country case studies in Part II of this book. It is rare that armed groups target only each other; the violence generated in internal armed conflicts is commonly – and devastatingly – directed at civilians as well, who often flee both internally and to other countries in search of security. Thus the repercussions of a civil war commonly extend beyond the borders of the territory in which it takes place, affecting security and economic development at the regional level and provoking destabilization, displacement, and human rights abuse.

Today, because of their capacity for destabilization and threat to human rights, civil wars are addressed within the international peace and security framework. Even so, the proliferation of civil conflicts has tested the competence of the **UN Charter** to prevent and resolve them, as discussed in Part III.

Characteristics and causes of conflict

Civil conflict can be categorized in a variety of ways according to cause. Generally, there is a confluence of several causes for a given conflict, even if one cause can be identified as more prominent. Frequently cited causes of conflicts include ideological issues, such as moral and religious differences; political issues; identity issues, such as ethnicity; distributional issues, such as control of and access to natural resources; and unmet human needs and human rights violations. These causes can be classified in different ways: in terms of proximity of the cause to the actual violence, and mobilization; in terms of insecurity, inequality, private incentives, and perceptions; and in terms of "greed" versus "grievance."

Structural, proximate, and mobilizing causes

Structural causes are deeply rooted problems that have the potential to provoke violent conflict. Many structural causes emerge from the nature of political regimes, including the relationship between the state and its citizens, the legitimacy of the government and the involvement of civil society in its election, and the state's willingness or capacity to provide basic services. Both overly weak and overly strong governments may create conflict-prone situations. Structural causes can include inequality, discrimination, absence or breakdown of the **rule of law**, unequal access to recourses and services such as education and health care, and poverty.

However, the presence of structural causes does not mean that a conflict will ignite. Conflict generally requires a proximate cause as well – a significant change in the situation, such as the emergence of individuals or groups who seek to change the status quo. Proximate causes, then, may differ from structural causes only by degree. Examples of proximate causes include loss of citizenship for certain groups; restriction of the rights of certain groups (e.g. the introduction of quotas for entrance to universities); restriction of access to certain places; restriction of religious expression; manipulation of government powers, including abuse of security forces; heightened corruption; and widespread human rights violations.

Still, even in these situations conflict may not necessarily occur. There generally needs to be a mobilizing cause too. These are causes that directly prompt the eruption of violence, such as the violent removal of a leader from office, electoral fraud, destruction of identity or religious symbols, and incitement of hatred or violence against a particular group of people.

Insecurity, inequality, private incentives, and perceptions

Insecurity

When the interests or agendas of two or more groups are at odds, such as over access to resources, political opinion, or religious beliefs, or when two or more groups perceive themselves as opponents because of ethnic or racial origins, there may arise what is sometimes called a *security dilemma*. In this scenario, actions taken by one group to increase its own security are seen by another group as threatening, provoking a competition for security that makes all groups less secure. The increased insecurity can have a range of consequences, from public disorder, to violence, to the collapse of the state, although the latter is rare as an end result. Conversely, the insecurity generated by the collapse of a state may also provoke a competition for security, which in turn may lead to violent conflict. Many of the conflicts that have proliferated since the 1990s have resulted from weak or collapsing states.

Inequality

Poverty is often cited as a cause of conflict. However, the countries in which violent conflicts have developed during the past decades, though they may have high levels of poverty, are also often home to a wealthy elite, and are often rich in natural resources. Thus, while poverty itself may be one of the underlying conditions that enable conflict, a structural cause, such as inequality, particularly horizontal inequality, is often what promotes the conflict. Horizontal inequality can be defined as differential access to specific goods across specific groups in a society, whether ethnic, linguistic, cultural, religious, or some other category of people. This access is not limited to economic resources, but may also include political resources, educational resources, and social status.

Private incentives

In some cases, leaders and would-be leaders mobilize specific sectors of the population, sparking confrontation and conflict. Some such leaders and their followers have legitimate security concerns, or are mobilized by specific grievances, but others have purely predatory intentions. In the latter scenario, the pursuit of private incentives, such as pursuit of political power (whether to obtain or maintain it) and economic gain (control over natural resources, including minerals and illicit crops), may promote conflict.

Perceptions

Perceptions can also mobilize conflict, if certain societal groups feel threatened by others. This is frequently the case where there has been a history of ethnic animosity. The perception of unequal treatment by the government, or of discrimination over access to power or resources, may mobilize groups and exacerbate the security dilemma, as actions taken by one group to increase its own security in such circumstances are likely to be viewed by other groups as threatening. In many cases, leaders and aspiring leaders manipulate perceptions for their own benefit.

As is illustrated in the country case studies in Part II, these causes are interrelated – they normally coexist and intersect – and in any given conflict it is difficult to identify one that has primacy over others. Conditions of inequality may exist, and in tandem with a history of ethnic violence, yet conflict might not ignite until leaders seek to manipulate perceptions and foment violence for their own ends. Equally, attempts to provoke violence may not work in the absence of a specific history of ethnic hostility, or where perceptions are more difficult to manipulate. The conflicts in the former Soviet bloc and in parts of Africa are examples of the interaction of such causes. Conflicts often emerge as weak states become repressive in an effort to retain power, or where there is competition among multiple groups for power or security in the absence of functional states. Inequality has been a common feature, but certainly perceptions of discrimination have been the proximate causes in conflicts such as those of the former Yugoslavia and Rwanda. Private incentives have played an important role in many contemporary conflicts especially in relation to access to natural resources, in Africa.

Greed versus grievance

An important debate in conflict analysis concerns the relative priority of "greed" and "grievance" as causes. Is it greed, such as the pursuit of control over economic or natural resources, or grievance, such as ethnic hatred or resentment over inequality or past abuses, that really underpins most conflicts? Some of the conflicts that arose after the end of the Cold War were depicted, particularly in the media, as motivated by "ancient ethnic hatreds." According to this analysis, conflicts both in former Soviet Union and Soviet bloc countries and in parts of Africa emerged because the end of bipolar control allowed the unleashing of historical ethnic resentment. This argument is rather simplistic, and does not take into account the broader range and interrelation of conflict causes discussed previously. While it is certainly the case that conflicts in the former Yugoslavia and Rwanda involved violence between ethnic groups, intermarriage among ethnic groups was common in Yugoslavia, particularly Bosnia-Herzegovina, and to a lesser degree in Rwanda, undermining claims that ethnic hatreds make peaceful coexistence impossible.

Conflict prevention

The term *conflict prevention* encompasses the range of activities taken to mitigate the risk of an imminent conflict, as well as those activities that seek to address deep-rooted causes that can lead to conflict in the future. Traditionally, in conflicts involving one or more states, the means for preventing a resort to violence involves diplomatic negotiations between the parties, sometimes with the involvement of a third, neutral party. The proliferation of internal conflicts has demanded new prevention activities outside this traditional framework of **diplomacy**. These preventive activities can be categorized as structural (long-term) and operational (short-term). Recently the **UN Secretary-General** introduced a third category: systemic prevention.

Structural versus operational prevention

The theory and practice of conflict prevention have been guided by the distinction between structural and operational prevention. Structural prevention refers to the activities undertaken to address the root causes of conflict, while operational prevention, also called direct prevention, comprises activities undertaken to reduce or eliminate more immediate sources of violence.

Structural prevention activities include poverty alleviation, reduction of corruption and inequality, reform of governance and institution-building programs, and reform of the security sector. Structural prevention, therefore, seeks to alleviate possible underlying causes of conflict where no conflict appears imminent.

Operational prevention seeks to address proximate and mobilizing causes of conflict, attempting to maintain stability and prevent grievances. These activities include provision of "good offices" by external actors; addressing sources of tension and friction before they lead to violence; meeting humanitarian needs, including access to basic resources such as food and water, and addressing immediate health needs; and even the use of targeted sanctions and military pressure. Targeted sanctions have been used in countries such as Angola, Sierra Leone, and Côte d'Ivoire.

Traditionally, structural prevention and operational prevention were undertaken by somewhat different sets of actors. Structural prevention was conducted by development and humanitarian actors, while operational prevention was conducted by security actors. UN prevention practice in the 1990s could be characterized in this way. However, research into the practice of conflict prevention shows that the distinction between structural and operational measures is often too rigid. Structural and operational activities and actors have complementary roles to play in addressing conflict prevention. Recent UN practice often involves actors from "security" and "development" agencies working together on similar types of prevention efforts.

Systemic prevention

In 2001 the then UN Secretary-General, Kofi Annan, developed a strategy to transform the United Nations culture from one of conflict reaction to one of conflict prevention, the latter comprising two categories: structural prevention and operational prevention. Later, Annan evolved the strategy further by adding a third category: systemic prevention. This third category refers to global measures to address the risk of conflict – measures that transcend particular states, including reduction of the illicit trade in small arms and light weapons, as well as the spread of nuclear, chemical, and biological weapons; reduction of environmental degradation; treatment of pandemic diseases such as HIV/AIDS; regulation of industries that are known to fuel conflict; and advancement of global development. Thus, while structural and operational preventive measures are conflict-specific, systemic measures have global scope. According to the Secretary-General, systemic initiatives, combined with ongoing, country-specific structural and operational preventive measures, increase the possibility of peace and reduce vulnerability to armed conflicts.

The 2007 Kenyan conflict illustrates a case in which prevention allowed violence to end before the conflict became intractable (see Box 2.1).

Box 2.1 **The 2007 Kenyan conflict**

In December 2007, fighting broke out in Kenya after a disputed general election. Both President Mwai Kibaki, who had been in office since 2002, and Raila Odinga, leader of the opposition, claimed to have won the election. A reported 1,500 people died in the fighting and 600,000 were displaced. The conflict was rooted in historical confrontations and inequality between the several ethnic groups, as well as systemic corruption, but the immediate trigger was the disputed election, exacerbated by violence between the Kalenjin and Kukuys. Immediately after the elections and the start of the conflict, the European Union and the United States pressured Kibaki and Obinga to end the fighting. Mediation was attempted by US envoy Jendayi Frazer and Ghanaian president John Kufuor, on behalf of the African Union, and assisted by four former African heads of state and the ambassadors from the United States, Britain, and France. In January 2008, former UN Secretary-General Kofi Annan took over the mediation. His intervention as mediator led to a power-sharing deal between the opposing parties, who in April 2008 formed a coalition government in which Kibaki would be the president and Odinga the prime minister.

Key actors in conflict prevention

There are a multiplicity of security and development actors who participate in conflict prevention, making coordination of their efforts difficult, especially when prevention actors are driven by competing political agendas.

Security actors are those that can exercise a certain degree of coercion. These include the United Nations, in particular the **UN Security Council**, and many **regional organizations** such as the European Union (EU), the **North Atlantic Treaty Organization** (NATO), the Organization for Security and Cooperation in Europe (OSCE), the Organization of American States (OAS), the **African Union** (AU), the **Economic Community of West African States** (ECOWAS), and the Association of Southeast Asian Nations (ASEAN). While some have played only a minimal role in conflict prevention to date, all have engaged in dialogue or collaboration with the United Nations.

Development actors include international financial institutions such as the World Bank and the International Monetary Fund (IMF), international agencies such as the United Nations Development Programme (UNDP), national development agencies such as the United Kingdom's Department for International Development (DfID) and the US Agency for International Development (USAID), and specialized nongovernmental organizations such as the International Committee of the Red Cross (ICRC). Other entities may also be involved in the prevention of specific conflicts, including the private sector and the media.

Among the international actors, however, perhaps the most important for conflict prevention is the United Nations, as conflict prevention is now understood to be one of its central missions. The main UN organ for coordinating conflict prevention efforts is the **Department of Political Affairs** (DPA). It provides political analysis and advice, and direct support for preventive diplomacy and "good offices." It plays a central role in monitoring and assessing global political developments; warning of potential crises before they break out; advising the UN Secretary-General on actions that could advance the cause of peace; providing support and guidance to UN peace envoys and political missions in the field; engaging member states directly through electoral assistance; and supporting interdepartmental relations and partnerships with other UN entities, regional organizations, and civil society. Box 2.2 lists the wide range of the UN bodies and agencies involved in these tasks.

Box 2.2 **UN bodies and agencies involved in conflict prevention**

- Security Council
- General Assembly
- Secretary-General and his Special Representatives and Envoys
- Department of Political Affairs (DPA)
- Department of Peacekeeping Operations (DPKO)
- United Nations Development Programme (UNDP)
- Office for the Coordination of Humanitarian Affairs (OCHA)
- Department of Economic and Social Affairs (DESA)
- United Nations High Commissioner for Human Rights (UNHCHR)
- World Food Programme (WFP)
- Food and Agriculture Organization (FAO)
- World Health Organization (WHO)

- United Nations Children's Fund (UNICEF)
- Department for Disarmament Affairs (DDA)
- United Nations Development Fund for Woman (UNIFEM)
- United Nations Educational, Scientific, and Cultural Organization (UNESCO)

Conflict resolution

The international conflict resolution system established after World War II, mainly within the UN framework, was primarily designed to address interstate wars, and thus inevitably it has experienced some difficulty adapting to intrastate conflicts. The UN Charter establishes a fundamental obligation for all member states to resolve their international disputes "by peaceful means in such a manner that international peace and security, and justice, are not endangered" (Article 2.3).

During the Cold War, many internal conflicts proliferated; however, the competition between East and West resulted in a stalemate, and the UN system was limited in its capacity to address internal as well as international conflicts. The end of the Cold War created new opportunities for the international community to promote resolution to civil wars. In the 1990s, peacemaking tools were further developed and new mechanisms created, and the number of actors involved in conflict resolution increased.

Actors

Traditionally, the primary actors involved in conflict resolution were the official actors, largely international governmental organizations and state representatives. However, more and more **nonstate actors** now participate in conflict resolution in different capacities and perform a range of functions, including strictly diplomatic efforts to bring parties together, providing humanitarian assistance, and mitigating the effects of conflict and preventing escalation.

Official actors

A central official actor is the United Nations. The UN's competence to participate in conflict resolution is confirmed in Chapters VI and VII of the UN Charter. These chapters outline the role of UN organs in the peaceful resolution of disputes that could endanger the maintenance of international peace and security. Chapter VI deals with peaceful settlement of disputes, while Chapter VII deals with responses to threats to peace, breaches of peace, and acts of aggression.

The main responsibilities in the UN Charter are those of the Security Council to call upon the parties to settle their disputes by peaceful means (Article 33.2), investigate any dispute or situation that might lead to international conflict (Article 34), and recommend appropriate responses (Articles 36.1 and 38). In the event of a threat to the peace, a breach of the peace, or an act of aggression, the Security Council decides on the measures that shall be taken to maintain or restore international peace and security (Article 39). Though use of force may be authorized if deemed necessary, softer measures such as economic sanctions and interruption of diplomatic relations are often the first recourse (Article 41).

In principle, UN peacemaking efforts are not intended to address civil conflicts through use of force, as such conflicts theoretically pose no threat to international peace and security. However, many civil conflicts have involved significant harm to civilians, and there have been demands for the use of force to protect them. While such humanitarian intervention remains hotly disputed by international lawyers, intervention has been justified on the basis of the threats to international peace and security that internal conflicts may pose. The UN has engaged in peacekeeping operations not originally envisaged by the UN Charter, for which there has been no clear, strictly legal basis. This is why the first operations of this kind were known as "Chapter VI1/2" operations, as they did not fall strictly under Chapter VI (peace-making) or Chapter VII (peace enforcement) of the UN Charter. Beyond peacekeeping, peacemaking may involve noncoercive actions by the UN Secretary-General through pro-vision of "good offices" to help parties resolve a conflict peacefully.

Recently, other intergovernmental organizations, in particular **regional organizations**, have participated in conflict resolution through both peacemaking and peacekeeping. Organizations such as NATO, the EU, the OSCE, the AU, and ECOWAS have participated in the resolution of conflicts in such places as the former Yugoslavia and Sierra Leone.

Unofficial actors

It is not just state representatives or intergovernmental organizations that are involved in conflict resolution. Other nongovernmental actors (also called informal intermediaries) include religious institutions, academics, former government officials, nongovernmental and humanitarian organizations, think tanks, and even businesses. These actors differ in their agendas, aims, and methods, but they generally attempt to provide an adequate environment for conflict resolution in which participants feel free to share their perceptions and needs and explore options for resolution, outside the more constraining governmental framework.

The participation of unofficial actors in conflict resolution and conflict prevention raises questions related to their accountability and the need to monitor their activities. In certain circumstances, well-intentioned individuals and organizations can do more harm than good when intervening in conflict zones. Among these organizations, there is growing concern about how to avoid unintended negative consequences when participating in conflict miti-gation, and this concern is increasingly taken into account in program and funding design.

Box 2.3 **"Do No Harm"**

Mary B. Anderson, a development economist and director of the Collaborative for Development Action, launched a project titled "Local Capacities on Peace" in 1995 to assist peace workers and organizations. It later became known as the "Do No Harm" project. In 1999 she published the book *Do No Harm: How Aid Can Support Peace or War*, in which she illustrated how aid that was intended to do good could end up doing harm. Anderson argued that aid actions directed at building peace in one area could reinforce divisions and conflict in another. She provided a framework for analyzing the impact of aid on conflict, which was implemented and tested in the field from 1997 to 2000 by different organizations. In 2000, Anderson's booklet *Options for Aid in Conflict: Lessons from Field Experience* was published, and at the request of donors and organizations involved in the implementation phase of "Do No Harm," the project began a "mainstreaming" strategy to disseminate the findings of the project widely throughout the aid community and to assist organizations in adapting the framework to their procedures. This project and the framework for analyzing the impact of aid on conflict have importantly influenced the way international donors now conduct their conflict prevention strategies.

Mechanisms

Diplomacy

Peace negotiation, mediation, conciliation, and arbitration are traditional conflict resolution methods. Official diplomacy is developed by official actors – international governmental organizations and states. It is referred to as "track one" diplomacy, while the interaction of nonstate actors and individuals is termed "track two" diplomacy.

Official actors are those that act in representation of a state, or with statelike authority. They engage with other states or statelike authorities to bring conflict to an end through diplomatic efforts. Therefore, track one diplomacy may take place bilaterally between two states, multilaterally among several states, and even regionally or globally through inter-governmental organizations. Bilateral diplomatic efforts between Russia and Estonia sought to solve the conflict of Russian-speaking minorities, while the OSCE High Commissioner on National Minorities held consultations not only with Estonia and Russia, but also with other Baltic states. The United Nations generally engages in track one diplomacy when developing its peacemaking activities, and its work has been described as "global" track one diplomacy. Such activities are considered to be an extension of the parties' own efforts. The Secretary-General is the lead UN actor in conducting conflict resolution diplomacy, acting personally or through special envoys and special representatives.

Track two diplomacy is also known as citizen diplomacy, multi-track diplomacy, back-channel diplomacy, and supplemental diplomacy. Track two diplomacy can be undertaken by private citizens or groups of individuals, as well as by representatives from conflicting parties. Activities can include the organization of interactive problem-solving workshops, such as the Inter-Tajik Dialogues organized to address the Tajik civil conflict. The Tajik discussions, which began in March 1993 in Moscow, involved a roundtable meeting of seven individuals from various factions to provide support to the official peace process.

Unofficial actors also engage in what is called "track three" diplomacy, or interventions at the grassroots level. These actions seek to build or rebuild relationships among ordinary citizens and change attitudes and perceptions of hostility. Examples include radio stations that broadcast programs dedicated to fostering peace and national reconciliation dialogue among groups, such as Radio Ijambo in Burundi, founded in 1995 by Search for Common Ground, a US-based nongovernmental organization; and activities that promote the inclusion of youth, such as the International Camp for Conflict Resolution, organized by the nongovernmental organization Seeds of Peace in the Middle East.

Diplomatic interventions include mediation and good offices, facilitation, fact-finding, and arbitration.

MEDIATION AND GOOD OFFICES

"Good offices" are a traditional means of conflict resolution in which parties to a conflict consent to the participation of a third party during peace negotiations. The third party must abstain from expressing any opinion on the merits of the controversy and from pushing the parties toward a single solution. Mediation, however, involves seeking the consent of the parties to evaluate the merits of their dispute and persuade them to adopt a specific solution. The line between these two methods can sometimes become blurred. Both require the consent of the parties involved in the conflict, are not imposed, and consist only of the provision of advice.

Traditionally, good offices and mediation were developed by a third party, in interstate conflicts normally a state, although the UN Secretary-General is authorized by Article 99 of the UN Charter to offer good offices. With the proliferation of internal conflicts and the end of the Cold War, the UN Secretary-General has increasingly offered good offices. The UN Secretary-General or his envoys and special representatives have provided their good offices on a case-by-case basis, and their role has evolved within peace processes. Parties must consent to the participation of the Secretary-General in the resolution of a particular conflict, and the Secretary-General's mandate might change during the process according to the needs of the parties, their level of trust, the effectiveness of other mediating actors, or the level of international support received.

FACILITATION

External actors engaged in facilitation can engage in a range of activities, from providing neutral facilities or transportation, to chairing negotiation sessions or meeting the parties separately to help them move discussions forward. The role of UN officials as facilitators changes according to the situation and the needs of the parties.

FACT-FINDING

Fact-finding enables external actors involved in conflict resolution to verify, authenticate, or investigate an incident that has given rise or might give rise to a dispute. The participation of an impartial actor is meant to legitimate the findings. Within the United Nations, such people are designated by the Secretary-General or the Security Council on the basis of reputation or expertise. The Office of the High Commissioner for Human Rights (OHCHR) can also engage in fact-finding. In Kenya (see Box 2.1) the OHCHR deployed a 21-day mission to investigate the violence and allegations of grave human rights violations that followed the December 2007 election. The mission found that the state appeared to have failed to take appropriate measures to prevent or stop the violence and the human rights violations.

ARBITRATION

Arbitration is a traditional method of conflict resolution in which an impartial third party, an arbitrator, is designated by relevant parties to issue a decision to resolve the conflict. The parties agree to be bound by the decision of the arbitrator. This mechanism of conflict resolution has been most common in interstate disputes, and the UN Secretary-General has not yet acted as an arbitrator, although as a result of the Secretary-General's peacemaking initiatives, parties may agree to submit their dispute to arbitration.

Peace negotiations

Contemporary conflicts seldom conclude with the military victory of one of the parties, but rather end through negotiated settlements between the state and one or more nonstate armed groups. The motive for participating in peace negotiation for each group varies, but their inclusion is essential in order to achieve complete, implementable peace agreements. Peace agreements often include provisions relating to the security of the groups involved; their disarmament, demobilization, and reintegration into society; their representation in new governmental structures, including their transformation into political parties; their insertion into new transitional governments and the security forces; territorial and resource distribution; and, increasingly, mechanisms of accountability for the human rights violations committed during the conflict. Agreements are frequently reached with the support of external parties, including their guarantees during the negotiation to support and monitor implementation. The cases presented in this book illustrate examples of conflicts terminated with peace agreements. The United Nations has been a key actor in monitoring and supporting the implementation of peace agreements since the end of the Cold War, through peacekeeping and peacebuilding missions.

Often the situation before and after implementation of peace agreements is so fragile that the international community opts to deploy foreign forces to monitor truces while diplomatic negotiations are taking place and monitor the protection of human rights. An example of a United Nations observer mission is the United Nations Observer Mission in Georgia (UNOMIG), established by Security Council Resolution 858 in August 1993 with a mandate to monitor and verify the cease-fire agreement between the Georgian and the Abkhaz sides of the conflict, and to oversee the safe and orderly return of refugees and displaced persons.

Peacekeeping

Peacekeeping is primarily conducted by the United Nations, although regional organizations have engaged in peacekeeping as well, as when a European Union police mission took over from the United Nations Mission in Bosnia and Herzegovina (UNMIBH) on January 1, 2003. In 2004, the African Union deployed its African Union Mission in Sudan (AMIS) to aid peacekeeping efforts in Darfur; AMIS was subsequently incorporated into the United Nations–African Union Hybrid Mission in Darfur (UNAMID).

To understand contemporary peacekeeping, it is important to understand its evolution since the adoption of the UN Charter, and particularly since the end of the Cold War. Since the 1990s, peacekeeping has evolved from an emphasis on interstate conflicts to encompass a wide range of operations. UN peacekeeping operations continue to increase in both number and complexity. In 2006 the UN was involved in 18 peace operations and 13 other field missions and offices, involving approximately 85,000 deployed personnel. By August 2007 the number had grown to over 100,000 personnel, excluding the highly complex UNAMID. The current annual budget for UN peacekeeping is approximately US$5.6 billion, representing half of 1 percent of global military spending. UN peacekeeping mission operate with personnel transferred by individual countries. In 2006, 110 countries provided uniformed personnel to UN peacekeeping missions, with the leading contributors being Bangladesh, India, and Pakistan, which together provide more than 40 percent of UN peacekeepers.

The United Nations has been involved in peacekeeping since its creation, but peacekeeping operations have evolved significantly since the end of the Cold War. The peacekeeping operations that developed between the end of World War II and the end of the 1980s are known as first-generation, classic, or traditional peacekeeping operations. They were designed to respond to interstate crises, the primary concern of the international community in the postwar period. These operations required the consent of the parties to the conflict, who allowed or invited the deployment of UN troops to monitor a truce, withdraw armed forces, or create a buffer zone during political negotiations. The UN forces were unarmed or lightly armed and adopted a neutral role; they could use force only in self-defense. Their primary objective was to serve as deterrents to renewed conflict. Examples of these first peacekeeping operations include the United Nations Emergency Force (UNEF) in the Sinai, which was sent to separate Israel and Egypt following the Franco-British-Israeli intervention in Suez in 1956; as well as the United Nations Peacekeeping Force in Cyprus in 1964 and the United Nations Transitional Assistance Group (UNTAG) in Namibia in 1989, the latter of which marked the transition between to the second generation of peacekeeping operations. In some cases, as in Cyprus, conflict was only delayed rather than resolved.

During the 1990s the so-called second generation of peacekeeping operations developed to address the proliferation of internal conflicts that began to emerge following the end of the Cold War. As with earlier operations, second-generation peacekeeping operations rely on the consent of the parties to a conflict, but they do not limit their engagement to traditional military functions; they also engage in policing and civilian tasks. Their main goal is not only to monitor peace arrangements, but also to achieve long-term settlements by confronting conflicts at their roots. These operations are also known as multidimensional operations, as they involve the implementation of complex, multidimensional peace agreements that seek to build the foundations of self-sustaining, durable peace and establish legitimate governments. This is done through developing the social, political, and economic infrastructure necessary to prevent future violence, which may include economic reconstruction, rebuilding of civil society, and reform of the security forces, judicial system, and electoral system. The civilian components of second-generation peacekeeping operations include policing functions, electoral monitoring and democratization activities, humanitarian relief, economic reconstruction and longer-term development work, civil engineering projects, the promotion, monitoring, and protection of human rights, and de-mining. Since the 1990s the operations under this second-generation model of peacekeeping have been particularly successful (as in Namibia [UNTAG] from 1989 to 1990, El Salvador [ONUSAL] from 1991 to 1995, Cambodia [UNTAC] from 1991 to 1992, Mozambique [ONUMOZ] from 1992 to 1994, and Croatia [UNCRO] from 1995 to 1996), and the growth of their civilian components has led to the creation of *peacebuilding* activities.

Peace enforcement

At the end of the Cold War the international community sought to extend its capacity to intervene in civil conflicts through enforcement action. These operations are also known as third-generation peacekeeping operations. Unlike prior generations, these operations do not necessarily have the consent of the parties to a conflict, and may proceed in the absence of a comprehensive peace agreement. Their mandate is based on Chapter VII of the UN Charter, which authorizes the Security Council to take necessary action to maintain or restore international peace and security (Article 42). Activities include low-level military operations to protect the delivery of humanitarian assistance, the enforcement of cease-fires, using force to persuade parties to settle the conflict by negotiation, forceful implementation of the terms of comprehensive peace agreements, and assistance in the rebuilding of so-called failed states. The use of force involved in these activities has led some commentators to refer to

Table 2.1 Ongoing UN peacekeeping operations through 2007

Operation	Start date
UN Truce Supervision Organization (UNTSO)	May 1948
UN Military Observer Group in India and Pakistan (UNMOGIP)	January 1949
UN Peacekeeping Force in Cyprus (UNFICYP)	March 1964
UN Disengagement Force (UNDOF)	June 1974
UN Interim Force in Lebanon (UNIFIL)	March 1978
UN Mission for the Referendum in Western Sahara (MINURSO)	April 1991
UN Observer Mission in Georgia (UNOMIG)	August 1993
UN Interim Administration Mission in Kosovo (UNMIK)	June 1999
UN Organization Mission in the Democratic Republic of Congo (MONUC)	November 1999
UN Mission in Ethiopia and Eritrea (UNMEE)	July 2000
UN Mission in Liberia (UNMIL)	September 2003
UN Operation in Côte d'Ivoire (UNOCI)	April 2004
UN Stabilization Mission in Haiti (MINUSTAH)	June 2004
UN Mission in Sudan (UNMIS)	March 2005
UN Integrated Mission in Timor-Leste (UNMIT)	August 2006
UN-AU Hybrid Mission in Darfur (UNAMID)	July 2007
UN Mission in the Central African Republic and Chad (MINURCAT)	September 2007

Note: See http://www.un.org/depts/dpko/list/list.pdf for a complete listing of all UN peacekeeping operations.

them as effectively "war-making." Landmark operations of this type include those in 1992 in Somalia (UNOSOM) and in Croatia, and Bosnia and Herzegovina (UNPROFOR), which also exposed the practical limitations of this approach.

UN peacekeeping operations are coordinated by the **Department of Peacekeeping Operations** (DPKO), whose mission is to assist the member states and the Secretary-General in their efforts to maintain international peace and security. Its functions are to plan, prepare, manage, and provide political and executive direction of peacekeeping operations. The DPKO is responsible for the implementation of UN Security Council mandates, which involves maintaining contact with the Security Council, the troops and financial contributors, and parties to the conflict, and engaging with other governmental and nongovernmental entities involved in peacekeeping efforts.

Postconflict reconstruction: peacebuilding

Since the end of the Cold War, peace operations have increasingly developed postconflict *peacebuilding* elements. Peacebuilding refers to the efforts of the international community to maintain a lasting peace in war-torn societies once initial peace has been achieved. Peacebuilding generally follows peacemaking and peacekeeping, but multidimensional peacekeeping operations contain significant peacebuilding elements. Even after conflicts are formally terminated, there remain risks that violence will resume during peacebuilding.

Peacebuilding ideally seeks to contribute to a so-called positive or participatory peace. A positive peace, contrary to a negative or sovereign peace, in which one of the factions is eliminated (a so-called peace of the grave), seeks to promote wider participation and participatory governance or democratic rule. Postwar states often suffer from weak or contested national identity, sometimes opposing ethnic identities, corrupted or destroyed state institutions, poverty and the absence of a substantial working class, and a civilian economy that has been looted or destroyed. Peacebuilding operations seek to address underlying economic, social, cultural, and humanitarian challenges in order to prepare for a more inclusive and competitive political system, with the aim of enabling a shared national identity, functioning state institutions, a significant middle class, and a growing economy. Peacebuilding operations also seek to develop stable constitutional and judicial means for dispute resolution, in order to avoid resort to force in the event of future disputes. The main aim of peacebuilding is thus to achieve a "sustainable" peace.

Peacebuilding includes a wide range of activities: monitoring cease-fires; demobilizing and reintegrating former combatants; helping organize and monitor elections of a new government; supporting democratic reform and improved governance, with particular focus on justice and security sector reform as well as restoration of the rule of law; assisting the return of refugees and displaced persons; enhancing human rights protection; and fostering reconciliation after past atrocities.

Peacekeeping and peacebuilding are inextricably linked. In 2001, in his report *No Exit Without Strategy*, the UN Secretary-General called for peacekeeping operations to include peacebuilding elements in their mandates in order to help dismantle the structures of violence and create the conditions conducive to durable peace and sustainable development. Most contemporary peacekeeping operations include these elements. The United Nations is the primary international actor involved in peacebuilding, but regional bodies have recently become increasingly involved in peacebuilding as well, just as they have in conflict prevention and peacekeeping. The complexity of contemporary missions has led to a so-called division of labor between the United Nations and other international actors. Thus, military tasks can be delegated, as in Afghanistan to NATO; the activities of specialized UN departments, funds, and agencies, such as the UNDP, can be shared with regional organizations, such as the OAS, the EU, and the OSCE; and financial institutions, such as the IMF, World Bank, and regional development banks, can address aspects of economic reconstruction. In this book we focus mainly on the UN system when addressing peacebuilding actors. Though most UN agencies are involved in one way or another in the implementation of peacebuilding programs, the primary responsibility for the coordination and direction of activities in the field lies with the DPA and DPKO.

Until recently, peacekeeping and peacebuilding operations lacked an overall strategic approach and coherence, even within the UN organs and bodies themselves. For example, some missions were under the supervision of the DPA and local peacebuilding support offices, such as the UN Assistance Mission in Iraq (UNAMI), the UN Mission in Nepal (UNMIN), and the peacebuilding support offices in Guinea-Bissau, the Central African Republic, and Tajikistan. These are relatively small operations compared with the peacekeeping missions administered by the DPKO, which also have a substantial peacebuilding component. Such missions include the UN Interim Administration Mission in Kosovo (UNMIK), the UN Organization Mission in the Democratic Republic of the Congo (MONUC), the UN Mission in Liberia (UNMIL), the UN Operation in Côte d'Ivoire (UNOCI), the UN Stabilization Mission in Haiti (MINUSTAH), the UN Mission in Sudan (UNMIS), and the UN Integrated Mission in Timor-Leste (UNMIT). The DPKO also directs and supports peacebuilding missions in Afghanistan, Burundi, and Sierra Leone.

To address this lack of coherence, the UN Peacebuilding Commission was created by agreement of the UN member states at the 2005 world summit. The Peacebuilding Commission is an intergovernmental advisory body designed to coordinate the actors and resources involved in postconflict reconstruction (see Box 2.4). The commission is supported by the Peacebuilding Support Office, within the UN Secretariat. This office also assists the Secretary-General in coordinating UN agencies in their peacebuilding efforts.

Box 2.4 **Peacebuilding Commission purposes**

Extract of UN General Assembly Resolution A/RES/60/180 (2005):

a) To bring together all relevant actors to marshal resources and to advise on and propose integrated strategies for post-conflict peacebuilding and recovery;
b) To focus attention on the reconstruction and institution building efforts necessary for recovery from conflict and to support the development of integrated strategies in order to lay the foundation for sustainable development;
c) To provide recommendations and information to improve the coordination of all relevant actors within and outside the United Nations, to develop best practices, to help to ensure predictable financing for early recovery activities and to extend the periods of attention given by the international community to post-conflict reconstruction.

During its first year of operations the Peacebuilding Commission focused on two countries, Burundi and Sierra Leone, where it engaged in developing comprehensive "integrated" strategies for coordinating peacebuilding activities. The main aim of these strategies is to guide government's engagement with all stakeholders in the country, and with the international community, during postconflict processes. In 2006 the UN Peacebuilding Fund was established to provide funding when other mechanisms are not available. It works closely with the Peacebuilding Commission to address the most immediate challenges in the early stages of peacebuilding. The fund is administered by the Peacebuilding Support Office.

Peacebuilding and accountability for past atrocities

As is discussed in more detail in Chapter 1, addressing the demands of victims of human rights violations and the reconciliation of societies that have been subjected to suffering during conflicts could also be considered part of the process of building sustainable peace. The range of processes and mechanisms through which such societies and the international community attempt to come to terms with a legacy of large-scale past abuse is known as postconflict accountability, often referred to as **transitional justice**. Transitional justice mechanisms are designed to provide accountability for the perpetrators, reparations for the victims, and reconciliation among the wider society. Transitional justice mechanisms include judicial mechanisms for individual prosecution, both national and international (addressed in Part III of this book): ad hoc tribunals, transnational tribunals, mixed or **hybrid tribunals**, and the **International Criminal Court**. Transitional justice mechanisms also include non-judicial mechanisms, such as traditional or customary conflict resolution methods, including traditional cleansing and reconciliatory ceremonies; truth commissions and national reparation processes, including symbolic processes such as changing street names and erecting monuments; and institutional reform, accompanied by vetting processes and dismissals of individuals who participated in repressive regimes or abuses of human rights.

Accountability and reconciliation are essential to peacebuilding. However, as is discussed in Chapter 1, even if the goals of accountability and conflict resolution may overlap significantly, there are also significant tensions, particularly with respect to the use of specific tools, including those described in this book. As is discussed in both Part II and Part III, the demands and processes of accountability can not only jeopardize the chances to achieve a peace agreement, but also destabilize the process of reconstruction and the chances for sustainable peace.

Key points

- Current conflicts vary significantly in nature and in the actors involved compared to the traditional interstate conflicts prevalent when the United Nations (UN) architecture for the prevention and resolution was designed.
- Understanding the root causes of conflicts is essential in order to design adequate conflict prevention and resolution policies.
- Security and development actors share the same ultimate goal of avoiding conflicts, but do not necessarily share the same priorities in specific conflicts; their priorities may sometimes even appear contradictory.
- The UN institutional framework provides the main apparatus for international peacekeeping and peacebuilding.

Discussion questions

- How can addressing potential structural causes of conflict help prevent conflict?
- What is the role of the UN Secretary-General in conflict mediation, both currently and historically, and what political constraints are involved?

Group exercise

Study the facts of the following two conflicts and compare them in terms of warring parties, structural and mobilizing causes, and conflict resolution options:

- the conflict between Russia and Georgia during the summer of 2008;
- the ongoing conflict in Colombia between the government and the Revolutionary Armed Forces of Colombia (Fuerzas Armadas Revolucionarias de Colombia [FARC]).

Further reading

Adebajo, Adekeye, and Sriram, Chandra, eds., *Managing Armed Conflicts in the 21st Century* (London: Frank Cass, 2001).
Anderson, Mary B., *Do No Harm: How Aid Can Support Peace or War* (Boulder: Lynne Rienner, 1999).
Call, Charles T., with Vanessa Wyeth, *Building States to Build Peace* (Boulder: Lynne Rienner, 2008).
Doyle, Michael W., and Nicholas Sambanis, *Making War and Building Peace* (Princeton: Princeton University Press, 2006).

Kaldor, Mary, *New and Old Wars: Organized Violence in a Global Era* (Stanford: Stanford University Press, 2001).

Paris, Roland, *At War's End: Building Peace After Civil Conflict* (Cambridge: Cambridge University Press, 2004).

Sriram, Chandra L., and Zoe Nielsen, eds., *Exploring Subregional Conflict: Opportunities for Conflict Prevention* (Boulder: Lynne Rienner, 2004).

Sriram, Chandra L., and Karin Wermester, *From Promise to Practice: Strengthening UN Capacities for the Prevention of Violent Conflict* (Boulder: Lynne Rienner, 2003).

Official documents and sources

European Union Conflict Prevention, http://ec.europa.eu/external_relations/cfsp/cpcm/cp.htm.

United Nations, *An Agenda for Peace: Preventive Diplomacy, Peacemaking, and Peacekeeping* (June 17, 1992), UN Doc. A/47/277–S/24111.

United Nations, *In Larger Freedom: Towards Development, Security, and Human Rights for All – Report of the Secretary-General* (March 21, 2005), UN Doc. A/59/2005.

United Nations, *No Exit Without Strategy: Security Council Decision-Making and the Closure or Transition of United Nations Peacekeeping Operations – Report of the Secretary-General* (April 20, 2001), UN Doc. S/2001/394.

United Nations, *Report of the Panel on United Nations Peace Operations* (August 21, 2000), UN Doc. A/55/305-S/2000/809.

United Nations, *The Rule of Law and Transitional Justice in Conflict and Post-Conflict Societies: Report of the Secretary-General* (August 23, 2004), UN Doc. S/2004/616.

United Nations Department of Peacekeeping Operations, http://www.un.org/depts/dpko/dpko/dpko.shtml.

United Nations Peacebuilding Commission, http://www.un.org/peace/peacebuilding.

3 Human rights
History and debates

Overview

Although the term "human rights" is used across the world in a way that suggests universal acceptance and understanding, the actual source of these rights and the implications of holding such rights are highly contentious. An understanding beyond the daily usage of the term is needed, one that examines competing claims and critiques and provides the context for discussion of the interplay between conflict and human rights.

The conventional account of human rights points to their emergence during the Enlightenment, and articulation in the declarations from the American and French Revolutions. The discourse from this period focuses on the goals of liberty and specific political and civil rights for individual citizens, with the backdrop of revolution leading to such claims being made against one's own state. Although specific countries may have outlined the concept of citizen rights in their own constitutions, it was only following World War II that the concept of rights evolved into international human rights as enshrined in the Universal Declaration of Human Rights. This particular narrative proves problematic, due to the focus on the individual and his or her rights, which has led to criticism that they are a Western concept rooted in a particular historical account and are therefore not appropriate to non-Western cultures and traditions, as the latter may put less emphasis on the individual. Even among those who accept the concept of individual rights, the content of such cannot be assumed, and there is ongoing debate over the importance of civil and political rights compared with social, economic, and cultural rights, which have historically been given less prominence.

The development of international human rights

The term "human rights" is so widely used today that it may seem to be common sense that these rights exist. Since first usage of the term in international law in the mid-twentieth century the concept of human rights has become so powerful that individuals, groups, and even governments identify with and use such rights for their own purposes. However, although the words "human rights" are used to call for or defend certain actions, there is little questioning of what they mean. Although human rights nongovernmental organizations make demands on governments to uphold the rights of individuals, the actual concept is seldom challenged. How did this idea of international standards for protection of human rights by national authorities emerge and become so established? If we recognize the high value that states place on the notion of national sovereignty, their acceptance of constraints on their behavior through human rights laws and mechanisms would seem contradictory, and it is to be expected that reaching agreements imposing such constraints would be difficult.

The content and widespread acceptance of international human rights standards emerged largely in the post-World War II period, following the atrocities that transformed human rights from a domestic matter into an international concern. The victorious Allies, meeting in Dumbarton Oaks to discuss and negotiate the formation of the international body that would become the **United Nations** (UN), stated that ensuring respect for human rights and fundamental freedoms would be one of its purposes. This was subsequently reflected in the preamble of the **UN Charter** with the words "We the Peoples of the United Nations . . . Determined to reaffirm faith in fundamental human rights, in the dignity and worth of the human person, in the equal rights of men and women and of nations large and small." This was the first time the words "human rights" were used in an international treaty. As one of the fundamental principles of the new organization, the protection of human rights paved the way for a new era. The **Nuremberg Charter**, followed by the Nuremberg trials, elaborated on the concept of **crimes against humanity** and led to the **Genocide Convention** (Convention on the Prevention and Punishment of the Crime of Genocide). The Genocide Convention was the first international treaty specifically focused on human rights.

These postwar events created momentum within the international community and laid the foundations of an international framework for human rights. This framework was enshrined in the source of **international human rights law**, the **International Bill of Rights**, which comprises the Universal Declaration of Human Rights (UDHR), the International Covenant on Civil and Political Rights (ICCPR), and the International Covenant on Economic, Social, and Cultural Rights (ICESCR). The drafting of the UDHR in 1948 signaled a change in the concept of human rights from the purely domestic to the *international*. During the drafting, representatives from across the world were consulted about how they conceived of human rights. This wide-ranging process resulted in a declaration, rather than placing specific obligations on states to uphold individual rights. Although some human rights advocates were disappointed that the UDHR was not a binding international treaty, the acceptance of the importance of human rights was demonstrated by the fact that 48 countries voted in the **UN General Assembly** to adopt the declaration, with no countries voting against (8 countries abstained).

Beyond the UDHR, there are treaties and conventions that create rights for individuals and also create obligations for states that ratify them. In comparison to the UDHR, the ICCPR and ICESCR were beset by delays as governments debated standards for an internationally binding treaty, and the impact of the Cold War made reconciling different ideas concerning human rights difficult. However, international conventions supplement the rights of the ICCPR and ICESCR with specific rights concerning the elimination of racial discrimination, discrimination against women, children, **torture**, and migrant workers. Within these international human rights treaties are a number of important distinctions. The content of each treaty addresses different types of rights and also provides different mechanisms through which to protect them. This means that not all human rights treaties can be enforced in the same way, as is explored further in Chapter 4.

The foundations for human rights claims

It is important to understand the underlying conceptualizations of human rights that form the foundations of the legal agreements discussed in Chapter 4. In particular, it is critical to understand the range of perspectives from different cultural and religious traditions in order to evaluate challenges and critiques. How we conceptualize human rights has wider implications in terms of which rights can or should be included or defended. How and why can the human rights treaties discussed above be justified?

The United Nations Human Rights Commission sought to develop a common basis for human rights through the drafting of the UDHR. This included commissioning the United Nations Educational, Scientific, and Cultural Organization (UNESCO) to consult with leading thinkers and writers from around the world by questionnaire. This exercise was an attempt to achieve a representative idea of how human rights were conceived by countries with cultural, religious, and political differences. The aim was to find roots for human rights in all cultures, to demonstrate that human rights transcended national boundaries and refute the idea that human rights were particular to Western history. Respondents such as René Cassin pointed to the Old Testament conception of rights, while others noted that Hinduism and Buddhism also protected fundamental freedoms and contributed rules of morality. Other thinkers, such as the Chinese philosopher Chung Shu-Lo, explored the contributions of Confucius, while the Indian poet and philosopher Hamayun Kabir commented on the influence of the Quran.

Although the UNESCO consultation does demonstrate that some concept of an objective moral standard can be found in all societies, human rights as conceived in the UDHR and subsequent human rights treaties originated in the Enlightenment period in Europe and America. Although we can point to similar ideas in other countries and at other periods, it is this particular development that led to the form that rights have taken today. The development of human rights is intrinsically tied to ideas of natural law and natural rights, which are specifically tied to Western philosophy and history.

The concept of natural law first appeared in ancient Greece and Rome, with the idea that a natural law exists beyond positive laws as decided by humans. This is a higher form of law (which can be conceived as coming from a creator or as something inherent in all humanity) and thus cannot be breached by human-made rules. This provided a form of moral code, insofar as men had a duty to follow natural law. The conceptualization of natural rights rather than just duties under natural law was articulated in the seventeenth and eighteenth centuries. With agitation for freedom of religion, particularly through the Protestant Reformation, the idea of natural law imposing duties on citizens, with no concomitant rights for them or obligations of the sovereign, began to be disputed. Natural law was recast as providing individuals with natural rights that were inherent within them, in the state of nature – before social rules were decided. Jean-Jacques Rousseau was a key proponent of such claims, arguing that man moves from the state of nature to civil society, governed by a sovereign but only with his consent (known as the *social contract*). Sovereignty of political authority stems from the consent of the governed, and they do not lose their rights in accepting the rule of a sovereign. John Locke further developed this concept in his discussion of the social contract, which enables individuals to hold rights against their government, including protection of private property. The political, social, and economic changes during this period were instrumental in allowing the concepts of individual rights and freedoms to evolve, with groups such as the Levellers in England campaigning for wider suffrage and religious toleration.

These ideas were highly influential in the American and French Revolutions, with the concepts forming the basis of the new republics. The American Declaration of Independence (1776) stated: "We hold these truths to be self-evident, that all men are created equal, that they are endowed by their Creator with certain unalienable Rights, that among these are Life, Liberty and the Pursuit of Happiness," while in France the Declaration on the Rights of Man and of the Citizen (1789) claimed that "men are born and remain free and equal in rights" and that "the aim of every political association is the preservation of the natural and

Table 3.1 The difference between natural law and the liberal conception of rights

	Natural law	*Liberal conception*
Account of human rights	Rights exist and are bestowed by a deity or inhere in humans	Rights are individual, largely civil and political
Sources of human rights	From a deity or from human nature	Universal and natural
Nature of human rights	Universal and natural	Rights are universal

imprescriptible rights of man." These declarations shaped the content of rights retained by the individual against the state, and the freedom of the individual became central to liberal thought in Western countries (Table 3.1). The concept of human rights then developed through the nineteenth and twentieth centuries, central to social struggles for universal suffrage, rights of women, slavery, labor rights, education, and economic welfare, until it achieved its centrality in the UDHR.

The problem of universality

Although the UDHR invokes the term "human rights," it does not define it. It is unlikely that the Allied drafters could have envisaged that human rights would develop into an international movement and that a set of legal obligations would emerge through agreements such as the **Torture Convention** (Convention Against Torture and Other Cruel, Inhuman, or Degrading Treatment or Punishment) or the Genocide Convention, culminating in some ways in the creation of the **International Criminal Court**. Despite the rapid growth of and widespread adherence to human rights agreements, they are still contested in some quarters, particularly by those who argue that human rights are culturally specific, and Western.

As discussed above, the concept of rights as elaborated in the UDHR does stem from the Western experience. Cultural relativists object that the concept of human rights does not transcend culture and thus should not be imposed on other societies that do not share the same outlook or history (an example is the idea that "Asian" values are different than Western values, as discussed later in this chapter). However, even those who do not accept the arguments of cultural relativists may recognize that different conceptions of the content of human rights exist, and that societies could function according to justifiable principles that do not invoke individual human rights. Consider the work of two authors, Steven Lukes and Michael Ignatieff. Lukes considers how society could use other philosophies to achieve the greater good, and ultimately demonstrates the uniqueness of human rights (see Box 3.1). Ignatieff does not deny that we can make a claim for human rights, but he sees them as political or a form of idolatry, and he thus supports a "thin" version of rights, which may not include all the rights that we would consider (see Box 3.2).

Box 3.1 **A world without human rights?**

A synopsis of Steven Lukes, "Five Fables on Human Rights," in Stephen Shute and Susan Hurley, eds., *On Human Rights: The Oxford Amnesty Lectures, 1993* (New York: Basic Books, 1994)

To understand the impact of human rights, it is helpful to imagine alternative ways that society could be organized without such an idea. Steven Lukes's essay "Five Fables on Human Rights" considers how other ideologies put forward by critics of human rights could be taken to their logical conclusion. He challenges readers to go beyond the recognized content of human rights and think about the actual concept, by presenting alternative worlds in which the principles of human rights are not accepted.

Utilitaria
Utilitarians believe in the greatest good for the greatest number. Therefore, the most important thing in Lukes's utilitaria is to measure what is good in order to calculate the costs of good and sacrifice and measure them against each other. Problems may occur where there are fundamental disagreements in what is understood as good. Also, such an outlook would mean that each individual could be asked to sacrifice for the greater good. This implies that it would probably be beneficial for the majority but bad for minorities.

Communitaria
Communitarians prize the connections, understanding, and relationships between individuals. They live according to evolving traditions and customs, which they identify, and identify with. In this world there are no universal principles; the community decides the rules. However, communitaria does not exist in a vacuum, and as new populations arrive, despite attempts by multiculturalism to recognize each new community's identity, problems still occur. The most difficult decision is how to determine which groups are included and how to deal with communities that have beliefs that are incompatible with each other. In addition, some beliefs and practices would not be challenged, as they are important to the group, although they may cause harm in practice to individuals.

Proletaria
In this world, there are no social classes and people identify with each other as human rather than as belonging to a particular community. There is no state, and society is purely egalitarian. Lukes points out that the problem is that there are no problems; it is a utopia that would be impossible to achieve in the real world. It is unlikely in any configuration that there would be no tensions over such issues as scarcity of resources or self-interest.

Why human rights? Lukes explains what human rights offer that these alternate possible societies cannot:

* Unlike utilitaria, human rights act as a restraint upon society – the good of the majority cannot be claimed at the expense of minorities.
* Unlike communitaria, human rights allow individuals to conform or deviate from specific practices according to their individual desire.
* Unlike proletaria, human rights acknowledge that human beings will be cruel and act in self-interest and have to deal with scarcity of resources, and protect individuals accordingly.

Box 3.2 **Human rights as politics and idolatry**

A synopsis of Michael Ignatieff, *Human Rights as Politics and Idolatry* (Princeton: Princeton University Press, 2001)

Michael Ignatieff criticizes the foundations used for human rights, such as natural law or religion, or claims about human nature or society. He criticizes human rights as either inherently political or engaging in idolatry, and thus argues that, at most, only a thin conception of human rights can be defended.

Human rights as politics
Ignatieff argues that human rights are implemented and enforced according to the political interests of states in the international community. He highlights various key problems. First, human rights activists and nongovernmental organizations from the West will often have a "Western agenda" and hold values and principles specific to their countries. Moreover, Ignatieff points to a more fundamental problem: that in this situation, claims based on the idea of human rights as "trumps" can lead to conflict between competing rights and be used to challenge the claims of others. Human rights can be used to halt political disputes by elevating the debate above interest or preference. According to Ignatieff, the assertion of rights to supersede another claim is a type of politics.

The solution is to engage in dialogue rather than competition over rights and other claims. Thus, for example, granting self-determination could destabilize a larger state or even a region. To uphold the right to self-determination could actually have a more severe impact than the denial of that right. Ignatieff would argue that because rights are politics, we must consider the consequence of rights, because they are not in fact all universal or "trumps" that can be applied to every situation. In addition, the international community makes a political decision in such a situation about whether to intervene or not. In sum, Ignatieff's argument of human rights as politics exposes flaws due to bias, the political nature of rights, and the practical implications of enforcing rights without thought to consequence.

Human rights as idolatry
Ignatieff believes that human rights have been separated from links to natural law and religion, and have become a "secular religion" built on the concept of human nature and dignity. Human rights advocates seek to depict human rights as universal because they are deemed innate in human beings. Ignatieff argues that this view of humanity as sacred is too disputed to be universal, as are religious claims, and that there is a need for a more widely accepted basis. His suggestion is to defend human rights on the grounds of what they do for human beings, which is defend human agency. This is a minimal theory of human rights, one that does not necessarily emphasize individual rights: if individuals find meaning in a community, then collective understandings of human rights may also be defensible.

If human rights cannot be defended as universal, an alternative could be to seek a consensus on human rights – basic norms that all can agree upon. Even if the underlying reasoning for specific norms differs – for example, some may use religious arguments against torture, whereas others may refer to human dignity – the agreed norm would still be the same. Nonetheless, it would be difficult to build such consensus in practice (the attempt to balance between universalism and multiculturalism is explored later in this chapter). In practice, it is possible for countries to accept the overall framework of a human rights agreement but make exceptions based on what is viewed as appropriate for their cultural contexts. States can make reservations to certain treaties, and some rights are derogable in states of emergency (although some abuses, such as torture, can never be permitted). Reservations to treaties are controversial; for example, although 178 countries have ratified or acceded to Convention on the Elimination of All Forms of Discrimination Against Women (CEDAW), some states have made reservations that could be seen as undermining the spirit of signing the treaty. Although reservations that contravene the object and purpose of CEDAW are prohibited under Article 28(2), countries from the Middle East and North Africa have made reservations to some provisions on the grounds that they are incompatible with *sharia* law or national legislation. These include reservations to Article 2 provisions condemning discrimination against women, Article 9 provisions on equal rights concerning nationality, and Article 16 provisions on marriage and family relations. This raises the question of whether it is better to have a widely ratified human rights instrument with many reservations, or a less widely ratified instrument but with fuller commitment from party states.

Challenges and disputes in human rights

Understanding the foundations of rights helps us understand the distinction between so-called first-, second-, and third-generation rights (see Box 3.3). First-generation rights (civil and political) seek to protect individuals against the state, while second-generation rights (economic, social, and cultural) allow the individual to make baseline welfare claims against the state. Third-generation rights involve claims about the need of the community for individuals to flourish. The struggle for equality in civil and political rights is well documented and is probably what most people associate with "human rights." However, within the field of human rights is an ongoing debate concerning the centrality of first-generation rights and the emphasis upon "individual" human rights.

Box 3.3 **The development of human rights**

First generation
Individual civil and political rights.

Second generation
Economic, social, and cultural rights. May attach to individual or groups.

Third generation
Group or community rights, which may include solidarity rights.

First vs. second-generation rights

After World War II there was a definite split between Western states, which promoted individual civil and political rights, and communist states, which argued that economic rights were crucial for achieving freedom. The United States sought to exclude economic rights from the UDHR, and was instrumental in separating the binding covenants, the ICCPR and ICESCR. The United States still has not ratified the ICESCR. Although, according to the Vienna Declaration on Human Rights, civil and political rights and economic, social, and cultural rights are indivisible and interrelated, they have been treated very differently and accorded different priorities.

Communist countries argued that they provided a better living environment for their citizens, which was essential for the securing of other rights, even though these states regularly engaged in abuse of civil and political rights. With the collapse of communism in the Soviet bloc, arguments for the primacy of economic, social, and cultural rights have fewer state supporters but this primacy still functions as a basis for a critique of liberal emphasis on individual civil and political rights. This separation can be understood as a distinction between positive rights, the duty to provide a baseline of welfare, versus negative rights, the duty to refrain from violating specific rights. Those who define human rights in terms of negative freedoms would argue that only civil and political rights can be upheld and that they provide the basis for freedom and protection of the individual. Proponents of economic, social, and cultural rights believe that the right to vote and freedom of expression have little meaning to people who live in poverty, are unemployed, or lack basic needs such as health and food.

This was famously elaborated by Amartya Sen in *Development as Freedom*, in which he argued that rights to subsistence are as crucial to freedom as are civil and political rights. Other theorists have demonstrated that critics of economic, social, and cultural rights use an artificial distinction between positive and negative rights, and that in fact economic, social, and cultural rights can be defined using this negative definition (see Box 3.4). Beyond these theoretical distinctions, the main obstacle for those who support economic, social, and cultural rights is how to implement them in practice. Such an argument, based on the premise of positive rights, means that governments are required to act to provide guarantees of subsistence or welfare. The difficulty with such requirements is that it is much harder to build a consensus to agree on the substance. The question of enforcement is even more difficult: there would be problems in defining and measuring a baseline as well as in determining penalties for failing to achieve the minimum standard. In terms of poverty or unemployment, these are structural problems, and interference in such political and social organization of a country would be vehemently resisted by a government, hence the refusal of the United States to sign the ICESCR.

Box 3.4 **The rights of homeless people**

A synopsis of Jeremy Waldron, "Homelessness and the Issue of Freedom," in Jeremy Waldron, *Liberal Rights: Collected Papers, 1981–1991* (Cambridge: Cambridge University Press, 1993)

"Without a home, a person's freedom is his freedom to act in public, in places governed by common property rules. That is the difference between our freedom and the freedom of the homeless."

In this essay, Jeremy Waldron addresses the question of homelessness and how it should be considered in relation to the concept of freedom. He argues that concerns about homeless people are usually classified under social and economic concerns, but actually the right to shelter is as important as other human rights such as freedom from torture and freedom of expression. In this way, freedom from homelessness is as much a human right as a civil right and a political right. He argues that although those who argue for the rights of the homeless or poor are often cast as arguing for a "positive" freedom, this can actually be considered a "negative" freedom.

Waldron begins by explaining that all societies have rules that divide property in the following way: property governed by private property rules, property governed by common property rules, and property governed by state property rules. The combination among each varies with the rules of each society. A homeless individual is someone who has no property governed by private property rules where he or she can reside safely, and Waldron argues that "the homeless person is utterly and completely at all times at the mercy of others."

Consequently, rules that formalize the distinction between public and private, banning private activities in public areas such as sleeping in subway tunnels and washing in public lavatories, affect the homeless, who must live their lives on common property. Waldron argues that the freedom to be somewhere and the freedom to do something are interconnected. An individual who is not free to be in any place is not free to do anything and therefore is not free. The homeless therefore depend on common property for the freedom to perform actions.

If we understand negative freedom as freedom from obstructions to an individual doing something, then a homeless person is not free to be in any place governed by a private property rule. Waldron argues that, therefore, demands for social and economic rights for the homeless are demands for negative, not positive, freedom. In this manner, private property rules restrict individual action just as legislation might restrict political freedoms such as those of speech or religion.

Waldron concludes by stating that a theory of human rights chooses actions that people should have the freedom to perform no matter what other restrictions there are on their conduct. The rights that should be secured for the homeless are not enshrined in a charter, but are preconditions to autonomy and as such should be valued.

As the human rights community debates the place of economic, social, and cultural rights within the broader framework of rights, treatment of these rights by the United Nations, human rights organizations, and nongovernmental organizations has evolved. The UN Human Rights Commission has appointed special rapporteurs on education, food, and health, and an expert on the right to development. There has been a broader movement on the development of rights-based approaches to work undertaken by UN agencies and aid agencies such as Oxfam. However, human rights organizations such as **Amnesty International** and **Human Rights Watch** have seldom engaged with economic, social, and cultural rights, in part because of their approach to advocacy. Their typical strategy is to find a specific violation, name and shame those responsible, and make simple policy recommendations, and this approach is easier to apply to violations of civil and political rights than to the more structural economic, social, and cultural rights. Nevertheless, several organizations that work only on economic, social, and cultural rights have recently emerged, as well as networks of activists, such as ESCR-Net. These developments demonstrate the evolution of debates about the importance of economic, social, and cultural rights.

Third-generation or group rights

Advocates of group rights argue that individuals suffer harm not only as individuals, but also due to their membership of a particular group. Further, individuals live and receive fulfillment in groups, and thus communities need protection through group rights. There are three types of claims that can be made under the rubric of group rights: collective, corporate, and solidarity.

Collective group rights

Individuals hold rights as individuals and also as members of groups. They come together to claim rights collectively, and collective claims may be more powerful in certain situations than an aggregation of individual claims. There are also some rights that cannot be exercised individually, such as the right to culture, which cannot be practiced by an individual on his or her own.

Corporate group rights

Corporate group rights are asserted when a group claims rights not as collective rights on behalf of individuals, but on the grounds that the group itself has rights and that it itself has moral standing. A key example of this might be indigenous peoples claiming specific land rights as a group.

Solidarity rights

Solidarity rights may be invoked on behalf of, essentially, all humanity, rather than on behalf of particular communities, or ethnic groups, or other self-identified groups. Instead, rights such as rights to development, the environment, and peace (see Table 3.2) are understood to be rights held collectively by all of humanity, such that their violation in any location undermines collective enjoyment of these rights.

The documents listed in Table 3.2 represent a range of obligations; some are asserted merely in declarations, while others are enshrined in treaties and conventions. In addition, the content between instruments differs; some assertions are of very general rights, while others indicate a more express requirement of states to actually secure those rights. Nonetheless, none of these rights are currently honored to any measurable extent. Beyond the question of enforceability, there are practical challenges. It is difficult to determine how to balance solidarist rights with other rights. For example, a situation could arise where solidarist rights come at the cost of rights for smaller groups, such as minorities or individuals. Would the right of everyone to peace be prioritized over a group's right to self-determination? This tension illustrates the difficulty of articulating rights in such a broad manner.

Table 3.2 Emerging solidarist rights

Right	Instruments	Description
Right of peoples	ICCPR and ICESCR	Rights of peoples to self-determination and to freely dispose of natural wealth and resources
Right to development	UN Declaration on the Right to Development, 1986	Right to development, also linked to self-determination
Right to environment	African Charter on Human and Peoples' Rights, 1981	Right to environment as a condition necessary for development
	Stockholm Declaration on the Human Environment, 1972	Right to quality of environment to permit a life of dignity
	World Charter for Nature, 1982	Enshrines respect for nature
Right to peace	Preamble to UN Charter	Goal of the United Nations is "to save succeeding generations from the scourge of war"
	UN General Assembly Declaration on the Preparation of Societies for Life in Peace, 1978	Inherent right of every nation and person to peace
	African Charter of Peoples' Rights, 1981	Right to international peace and security

Further objections to group rights may be raised. First, groups are not humans, but rather are entities made up of humans – so it is unclear how specific rights can be attached to them. Second, it is not necessarily the case that a group will better protect an individual, and it is unclear how a balance between individual and group rights could be determined. Furthermore, the corporate conception of group rights may threaten the individual by making it possible for the moral standing of the group to supersede the standing of individuals within the group. Beyond these objections, it may be asked whether separate group rights are necessary, since some first-generation and second-generation rights are already framed as collective rights, such as freedom of association.

Relativism and the "Asian values" debate

The UDHR is founded on the concept of human dignity, and the ICCPR and ICESCR state that human rights derive from the inherent dignity of the human person. The presumption is that every person has inalienable rights by virtue of being human, which she or he can claim against the state. However, as we have seen, non-Western countries have objected that such a concept of rights is not universal, and that elsewhere the concept of the individual and his or her relationship to community and society is quite different. This position is exemplified by the "Asian values" objection and debate.

The objection was first presented strongly in the 1990s by a number of political leaders, such as Lee Kuan Yew, president of Singapore. This school of thought gained support from adherents in Asian countries as well as from critics of the Western liberal conception of human rights elsewhere. In what may be seen as a simplification, but nonetheless one that found many supporters, Yew argued that Asian societies are culturally distinct, and in particular do not prioritize the individual in the way that Western societies do, but rather prioritize social goods such as order and security. Thus, for example, Yew claimed that discipline in Asian countries, such as corporal punishment, may seem to be at odds with international human rights standards, but is important to ensure order and security in Singapore. While Western society places great importance on the individual in structuring both economy and society, Yew and others argued that the importance of the individual is unique to the West. They claimed that Asian countries have a very different conception of economic and social organization, with the individual existing in the context of the family and wider community and society. Thus, advocates of Asian values sought to justify the prioritizing of the welfare state and social and economic rights over civil and political rights.

These claims were formally articulated in the Bangkok Declaration, adopted by several Asian states in 1993 (see Box 3.5). The Bangkok Declaration emphasized the importance of economic, social, and cultural rights, stated that the creation of international human rights norms should go hand in hand with endeavors to work toward a just and fair world economic order, and highlighted the importance of development and the environment. The declaration also stated that human rights should not be promoted through confrontation and the imposition of incompatible values, but rather that human rights must be considered in the context of a dynamic and evolving process of international norm-setting, bearing in mind the significance of national and regional particularities and various historical, cultural, and religious backgrounds.

Box 3.5 **Selected principles from the Bangkok Declaration**

Report of the Regional Meeting for Asia of the World Conference on Human Rights (Bangkok, March 29–April 2, 1993)

3. *Stress* the urgent need to democratize the United Nations system, eliminate selectivity and improve procedures and mechanisms in order to strengthen international cooperation, based on principles of equality and mutual respect, and ensure a positive, balanced and non-confrontational approach in addressing and realizing all aspects of human rights.

   . . .

8. *Recognize* that while human rights are universal in nature, they must be considered in the context of a dynamic and evolving process of international norm-setting, bearing in mind the significance of national and regional particularities and various historical, cultural and religious backgrounds.

9. *Recognize further* that States have the primary responsibility for the promotion and protection of human rights through appropriate infrastructure and mechanisms, and also recognize that remedies must be sought and provided primarily through such mechanisms and procedures.

10. *Reaffirm* the interdependence and indivisibility of economic, social, cultural, civil and political rights, and the need to give equal emphasis to all categories of human rights.

   . . .

18. *Recognize* that the main obstacles to the realization of the right to development lie at the international macroeconomic level, as reflected in the widening gap between the North and the South, the rich and the poor.

19. *Affirm* that poverty is one of the major obstacles hindering the full enjoyment of human rights.

20. *Affirm also* the need to develop the right of humankind regarding a clean, safe and healthy environment.

. . .

26. *Reiterate* the need to explore the possibilities of establishing regional arrangements for the promotion and protection of human rights in Asia.

These arguments have also been made outside Asia, with Islamic and African states raising similar objections. However, critics of these arguments would hold that objections raised by these states are really designed to justify repressive domestic measures, not as genuine criticisms of human rights. Although the Bangkok Declaration is a moderate document, it could provide some grounds for those who want to limit the effects of human rights in closed societies and repressive states. However, this objection does not mean that the relativist position (see Box 3.6) or Asian values should be ignored, as there are merits to concerns about the universality of human rights.

Box 3.6 Conceptions of cultural relativism

Elizabeth M. Zechenter, "In the Name of Culture: Cultural Relativism and the Abuse of the Individual," *Journal of Anthropological Research* 53 (Autumn 1997): 319–47

There is more than one type of cultural relativism, as explained by Elizabeth Zechenter:

- *Descriptive or weak relativism*. Cultures vary.
- *Normative or strong relativism*. There cannot be universal ethical or moral standards because these depend on culture.
- *Epistemological relativism*. Humans are shaped by their culture and there are no cross-cultural characteristics.

One possible solution would be to seek a middle ground. It may be feasible to recognize baseline rights, such as the right to life and the right to access justice, and also include the right to culture. This approach would recognize that the individual has some basic rights but also allow individuals to choose culturally specific practices important to them. However, in practice such a balance would be difficult to strike, particularly because it would be states that would seek to select which cultural rights should be promoted, and serious debates would arise about which cultural practices should be excluded as inconsistent with recognized basic rights. For example, if the right to life and the right to freedom from torture are among basic rights to be protected, culturally specific practices such as female genital cutting or amputation as punishment for stealing would be inconsistent with those rights, but societies with such practices would nonetheless seek to defend them as cultural rights.

Even engaging in dialogue about the subject is problematic. There is a risk of treating culture as static and unchanging. It would also be difficult to determine who has the right to represent any particular community. Vulnerable groups may be at risk where powerful groups seek to institutionalize inequality or abuse as culturally protected.

Critics will reject such claims of group rights and their relativistic underpinnings and advocate instead the rights of individuals above all. This is an ongoing debate that will prove controversial for the foreseeable future.

Feminist and gender critiques

Equality between men and women is enshrined in the Universal Declaration of Human Rights. However, in the early days of the development of the human rights movement, gender equality was not given the same prominence as the focus on civil and political rights or even race equality. The Convention on the Elimination of All Forms of Discrimination Against Women (CEDAW) was drafted only in 1979, nearly 15 years after the Convention on the Elimination of All Forms of Racial Discrimination (CERD), the ICESCR and ICCPR, and other treaties. A feminist critique of human rights emerged in the 1980s, arguing that a gendered perspective was needed in order to identify and address specific abuses not adequately addressed by the traditional human rights approach.

Feminists argue that the language and mechanisms of human rights enable structural gendered inequalities to exist, and that the emphasis on civil liberties ignores the possibility that some rights, such as freedom of religion, could be used to oppress women. One way to understand the challenge of protecting women's rights is to consider the distinction between public and private in international law. This distinction provides for state responsibility and in some instances for individual criminal accountability for abuses in the public sphere, such as torture, but does not address abuses in the private sphere, such as domestic violence, sexual violence, or infanticide. Although there are women who do suffer torture, for example as political prisoners, the position of women within families in many societies means that many abuses that they may face take place within the private sphere and as such are ignored by international human rights treaties. As with the critiques already outlined, this critique also challenges the liberal emphasis on civil and political rights. The feminist perspective is further complicated by efforts to account for the fact that women do not have the same experiences globally; their concerns may vary because of their economic standing personally or their location in a country that has specific economic difficulties or social norms, or because of additional dimensions such as race, membership in a particular group, and sexuality.

Economic, social, and cultural rights can provide one means to address structural inequalities whereby women are subject to abuses or suffer a particular burden because they are women. Women are more likely than men to be poor and to suffer malnourishment, and they tend to have less access to health services; this is sometimes referred to as the feminization of poverty. However, the distinction between public and private remains relevant, because women's domestic work within the family is not recognized as equal to the work carried out by men in the public sphere. Thus, invocation of Article 7 of the ICESCR to promote women's rights to just and favorable conditions of work, for example, would not be easy. Furthermore, as we have seen, claims to culture can in fact be detrimental to the position of women.

A gendered perspective on life and liberty has led to greater acknowledgment of women's rights. The Vienna Declaration and Programme of Action, an outcome of the World Conference on Human Rights in 1993, specifically called on governments and the United Nations to ensure the equal enjoyment by women of all human rights. It called for integration and cooperation within the UN system, including access to implementation procedures of the treaty-monitoring bodies and the use of gender-specific data. The declaration particularly stressed the importance of

> the elimination of violence against women in public and private life, the elimination of all forms of sexual harassment, exploitation and trafficking in women, the elimination of gender bias in the administration of justice and the eradication of any conflicts, which may arise between the rights of women and the harmful effects of certain traditional or customary practices, cultural prejudices and religious extremism.

That conference was followed by the World Conference on Women in Beijing in 1995, which issued a declaration that affirmed that women's rights are human rights and called for the prevention and elimination of violence against women and girls, the promotion and protection of all their human rights, and respect for international law to protect women and girls. The Beijing conference identified twelve areas of concern in its platform for action, including the "human rights of women." Three strategic objectives were put forth: (1) promote and protect the human rights of women, through the full implementation of all human rights instruments, especially the Convention on the Elimination of All Forms of Discrimination Against Women; (2) ensure equality and nondiscrimination under the law and in practice; and (3) achieve basic knowledge of the law among women. Progress on these objectives was assessed during a five-year review, and a ten-year review was carried out by the Commission on the Status of Women in March 2005, with member states reaffirming the declaration and its platform for action.

A number of key milestones in the recognition of sexual and gender-based violence against women are particularly relevant to conflict situations. The UN General Assembly's Declaration on the Elimination of Violence Against Women, in December 1993, defined violence against women as including violence in the family, violence in the general community, and violence by the state. States were asked to condemn violence against women and not invoke any custom, tradition, or religious consideration to avoid their obligations with respect to its elimination. Efforts to address the targeting of women during conflict proved decisive in the work of the **International Criminal Tribunal for Rwanda** (ICTR) and the **International Criminal Tribunal for the Former Yugoslavia** (ICTY) in prosecuting wartime rape and gender-related crimes. The Rome Statute of the International Criminal Court now recognizes rape and sexual violence as crimes against humanity and crimes of war. Crimes against humanity are defined to include rape, sexual slavery, enforced prostitution, forced pregnancy, enforced sterilization, or any other form of sexual violence of comparable gravity. Imposing measures intended to prevent births within a particular group can be considered **genocide**. The definition of **war crimes** also adopts a gendered perspective, including rape, sexual slavery, enforced prostitution, forced pregnancy, and enforced sterilization among acts that may constitute crimes.

Human rights and conflict

As is explored in Chapter 1, there are several intersections between human rights and conflict. Human rights can be both causes and consequences of conflict, and can also transform the nature of conflict. Debates over the universality or content of human rights can sometimes be manipulated in order to silence criticism when real violations happen. There are a range of ways in which denial of civil and political rights might provoke conflict. For example, if an election is not free and fair, political protests may escalate. If a group is systematically denied political access – to voting, to standing as candidates for elected office – it may protest in ways that might result in violence. Similarly, a group whose exercise of religion is infringed upon may protest, to the point of violence. Or, as occurred in February 2006 with the controversy over cartoons in Denmark that offended some Muslims, a group which feels that its religion has been slighted may protest, and that protest may become violent. Of course, such sporadic violence will not always escalate into broader civil conflict.

Although these grievances from denial of civil and political rights are well documented, denial of second- and third-generation rights can potentially provoke conflict, as discussed in Chapter 2. Protest may emerge over the denial of a wide range of economic, social, and cultural rights, such as over poor and insufficient provision for health, education, or housing. Or protest may arise where specific segments of the populace are particularly and systematically disadvantaged, whether intentionally or unintentionally, in their exercise of these rights. Such protest is mostly channeled peacefully through elections. But in dysfunctional states it might lead to more violent protest and conflict. If we consider revolutionary left-wing guerrilla movements in places such as Guatemala and El Salvador, for example, at least part of the reason they resorted to violence was that the state apparatus would not provide basic needs for the poor, and a wealthy elite had captured and controlled the state.

There are many violations that occur as consequences of conflict, with many internal conflicts targeting civilians as much as combatants. Abuses are not confined to the actual fighting; often children are abducted and forced to fight, or young girls are taken as "wives" to the combatants. Violence during conflict includes torture and killing of combatants as well as indiscriminate massacres and serious injury of civilians, with women and girls particularly targeted as victims of sexual violence. A much larger number will be internally displaced within the country in their escape from the fighting, or they may flee to neighboring countries. Often, the camps established for internally displaced persons and refugees are no more secure than their places of origin, and health, sanitation, and food provision are poor or nonexistent.

There have been a number of advances in promotion of rights related to conflict, particularly the recognition of gender-related violence, violence targeting children, and recruitment of child soldiers. The **UN Secretary-General** has appointed a Special Representative on Children and Armed Conflict, and the **UN Security Council** passed Resolution 1325 to acknowledge the impact of war on women and their role in conflict resolution and **peacebuilding**.

In any conflict, many basic human rights will be violated. The emphasis of this book is on the interplay between human rights and conflict, and deals largely with responses to gross violations of the right to bodily integrity; thus, the following chapters will not detail violations of CEDAW or the Convention on the Rights of the Child (CRC), for example. The focus here is those abuses that result in criminal punishment, particularly of the types of crimes that can now be prosecuted before the International Criminal Court, but that were punishable before the creation of this institution.

Key points

- Although the Universal Declaration on Human Rights declares that human rights are universal, there is no universally accepted definition of the content of human rights.
- There are many areas of contention within the field of human rights, including "group rights," feminist critique, and civil and political rights versus social, economic, and cultural rights.
- There is criticism concerning the implications of a "Western" interpretation of human rights.
- Human rights and conflict are inextricably linked. There are a range of ways in which denial of rights can lead to conflict, and numerous human rights violations occur as a consequence of conflict.

Discussion questions

- Should advocacy organizations such as Amnesty International concentrate more on economic, social, and cultural rights than on civil and political rights?
- If there are solidarity rights emerging on an international level, what might they be?

  - The right to development?
  - The right to a high-quality environment?
  - The right to peace?

  Upon whom are they binding?

  - States?
  - Individuals?
  - Public and private groups?

- What are the implications of a state making a reservation to an important article of a human rights treaty?
- Why was it so important for a feminist critique to use the phrase "women's rights are human rights"?
- Which human rights are most likely to be violated in a conflict situation?

Group exercise

Imagine that you are drafting a new international declaration on human rights.

- Write a list of five basic or core rights. Decide which economic, social, and cultural rights should be included, and which civil and political rights.
- Devise a strategy to decide what criteria a group must meet to be recognized, what rights it can be accorded, and how to determine when a group is restricting the rights of its members. Decide how you will mediate if conflicts emerge between groups.

Further reading

Cook, Rebecca, *Human Rights of Women: National and International Perspectives* (Philadelphia: University of Pennsylvania Press, 1994).

Donnelly, Jack, *Universal Human Rights in Theory and Practice* (Ithaca, NY: Cornell University Press, 2003).

Dunne, Tim, and Nicholas J. Wheeler, *Human Rights in Global Politics* (Cambridge: Cambridge University Press, 1999).

Ignatieff, Michael, *Human Rights as Politics and Idolatry* (Princeton: Princeton University Press, 2001).

Ishay, Micheline R., *The History of Human Rights: From Ancient Times to the Globalization Era* (Berkeley: University of California Press, 2004).

Kymlicka, Will, *Multicultural Citizenship: A Liberal Theory of Minority Rights* (Oxford: Oxford University Press, 1996).

Lukes, Steven, "Five Fables on Human Rights," in Stephen Shute and Susan Hurley, eds., *On Human Rights: The Oxford Amnesty Lectures, 1993* (New York: Basic Books, 1994).

Sen, Amartya, *Development as Freedom* (Oxford: Oxford University Press, 2001).

Steiner, Henry J., Philip Alston, and Ryan Goodman, *International Human Rights in Context: Law, Politics, Morals*, 3rd edn. (Oxford: Oxford University Press, 2008).

Waldron, Jeremy, "Homelessness and the Issue of Freedom," in Jeremy Waldron, *Liberal Rights: Collected Papers, 1981–1991* (Cambridge: Cambridge University Press, 1993).

Zechenter, Elizabeth M., "In the Name of Culture: Cultural Relativism and the Abuse of the Individual," *Journal of Anthropological Research* 53 (Autumn 1997): 319–47.

Official documents and sources

Bangkok Declaration on Human Rights (1993).

Charter of the United Nations (UN Charter) (1945), http://www.un.org/aboutun/charter/.

Convention Against Torture and Other Cruel, Inhuman, or Degrading Treatment or Punishment (Torture Convention) (1984), http://www.hrweb.org/legal/cat.html.

Convention of the Elimination of All Forms of Discrimination Against Women (1979), http://www.hrweb.org/legal/cdw.html.

Convention on the Elimination of All Forms of Racial Discrimination (1965), http://www.fletcher.tufts.edu/multi/texts/bh490.txt.

Convention on the Prevention and Punishment of the Crime of Genocide (Genocide Convention) (1948), http://www.hrweb.org/legal/genocide.html.

International Covenant on Civil and Political Rights (1966), http://www.hrweb.org/legal/cpr.html.

International Covenant on Economic, Social, and Cultural Rights (1966), http://www.hrweb.org/legal/escr.html.

Status of ratifications of key human rights instruments, http://www.unhchr.ch/pdf/report.pdf.

Universal Declaration of Human Rights (1948), http://www.un.org/overview/rights.html.

Vienna Declaration and Programme of Action (1993), UN Doc. A/CONF.157/23.

4 Humanitarian and human rights law in armed conflict

Overview

This chapter discusses the legal instruments that may be used to respond to serious human rights violations during war or political violence, specifically the key rights and obligations established by both **international human rights law** and **international humanitarian law**. While these two sets of rights and obligations share superficial similarities, their sources, purposes, applicability, and content differ. International human rights law recognizes rights for individuals and obligations for states, and applies whether an armed conflict exists or not. International humanitarian law establishes rights for individuals and obligations for both states and individuals, and applies where armed conflict exists, but differently depending upon whether the conflict is international or noninternational. Obligations under both international human rights law and international humanitarian law are contained in treaties and customary law. By signing an international human rights treaty, states assume the responsibility to respect, protect, and promote the human rights of individuals under their jurisdiction. In contrast, customary law binds all states, regardless of whether they have signed any international document agreeing to human rights obligations.

Rights and obligations under humanitarian and human rights law

International human rights law and international humanitarian law establish distinct types of rights and obligations, and not all breaches of obligations have the same legal consequences for states, or even for individuals. Simply stating that an individual or group of individuals have rights does not necessarily mean that such persons can act to enforce them, or have them enforced by a third party. There are various mechanisms to ensure that obligations are upheld, ranging from the monitoring of specialized bodies, including human rights courts established by treaties, to legal accountability for individuals, including international prosecutions.

Declarations of individual rights

The Universal Declaration of Human Rights (UDHR) is a document that simply asserts rights. It describes the rights vested in all individuals, but is understood to be a declaration and as such is not legally binding, although it is now considered part of customary international law. While the UDHR declares a set of rights, it does not indicate who, if anyone, has specific obligations to protect those rights. The UDHR's section on duties applies only to persons and is extremely general. Finally, the UDHR creates no enforcement or monitoring mechanisms, in part because it creates no specific obligations.

Treaties and conventions may create rights for individuals as well as vest the obligation to protect these rights in states that are signatory to those agreements

The International Covenant on Civil and Political Rights (ICCPR) and the International Covenant on Economic, Social, and Cultural Rights (ICESCR) are such conventions. These two instruments, together with the UDHR, constitute what is known as the **International Bill of Rights**. Other rights are contained in other specialized conventions, such as the Convention on the Elimination of All Forms of Racial Discrimination (CERD), the Convention on the Rights of the Child (CRC), and the Convention on the Elimination of All Forms of Discrimination Against Women (CEDAW), discussed in Chapter 3. These conventions also support the establishment of monitoring bodies (see Table 4.1) to which signatory states are required to report on the measures they have taken to protect the enumerated rights. However, violation of these rights and obligations by a state does not have significant further consequences beyond, perhaps, international condemnation. The state cannot be sued in any court by any victim, and while one state might sue another before the **International Court of Justice**, such suits are unlikely, because few states would be affected by internal breaches by another state, and thus would have no grounds to bring a case.

Table 4.1 Core human rights treaties treaty-monitoring bodies

Treaty	Monitoring body
Convention on the Elimination of All Forms of Racial Discrimination (CERD) (December 21, 1965)	CERD
International Covenant on Civil and Political Rights (ICCPR) (December 16, 1966)	CCPR
International Covenant on Economic, Social, and Cultural Rights (ICESCR) (December 16, 1966)	CESCR
Convention on the Elimination of All Forms of Discrimination Against Women (CEDAW) (December 18, 1979)	CEDAW
Convention Against Torture and Other Cruel, Inhuman, or Degrading Treatment or Punishment (CAT) (December 10, 1984)	CAT
Convention on the Rights of the Child (CRC) (November 20, 1989)	CRC
International Convention on the Protection of the Rights of All Migrant Workers and Members of Their Families (ICRMW) (December 18, 1990)	CMW

Treaties and conventions may articulate rights for individuals, and impose obligations upon states

Instruments such as the European Convention on Human Rights, the Inter-American Convention on Human Rights, and the African Charter for Human and Peoples' Rights create institutions that can not only monitor compliance, but also adjudicate violations. A few relevant cases identifying state abrogations of obligations of human rights in the context of conflict have been adjudicated by the inter-American and European courts, but this book focuses on mechanisms that more extensively and directly address abuses during conflict, largely by imposing international criminal accountability.

Treaties and conventions may obligate states not merely to protect rights, but also to prevent and punish violations

Such obligations are enshrined in the **Torture Convention** (Convention Against Torture and Other Cruel, Inhuman, or Degrading Treatment or Punishment) and the **Genocide Convention** (Convention on the Prevention and Punishment of the Crime of Genocide). Even between these two conventions, however, there are important distinctions. The Torture Convention imposes obligations upon states in their own territories, or in territories over which they have control. The Genocide Convention creates obligations that are more universal: states must prevent and punish the act of **genocide**, but nowhere in the convention is there a territorial requirement, essentially giving rise to **universal jurisdiction** (discussed in greater detail in Chapter 11). According to universal jurisdiction, states can exercise extraterritorial jurisdiction over certain acts in the absence of a territorial nexus. This is particularly important when considering human rights violated during conflict, since states may be unwilling or unable to carry out prosecutions on their own territory. Notwithstanding the differences between the language of the Torture and Genocide Conventions on territoriality, over time **torture** has come to be viewed as a crime over which all states can exercise jurisdiction. Similarly, violations of some provisions of the four 1949 **Geneva Conventions** may constitute what are referred to as **war crimes**. These are known as **grave breaches**, and are also part of customary international law. Individuals found to have violated grave breaches provisions may be subject to criminal prosecution.

Instruments that obligate states not only to respect and protect human rights, but also to prevent and punish violations, may give rise to individual accountability through creating categories of international crime. Thus, violations of these conventions may therefore result not merely in a breach by a state, but also in a crime by an individual, who can be tried in a domestic tribunal or an international court. It is important to understand that while the Torture and Genocide Conventions define identifiable crimes, which may therefore be punished, the bulk of human rights law articulates rights that states are bound not to infringe upon, or upon which they may infringe only in specific, narrow circumstances. Thus, in many instances a violation of a human rights agreement may not be a crime unless it is defined as such in domestic law. However, a state might still be found to have violated a treaty and suffer sanction from the international community.

International humanitarian law, by contrast, places more extensive obligations upon states, and articulates rules that states must apply to their officials and combatants, as shown in Table 4.2.

Substantive human rights obligations

Here we focus on the three documents that comprise the International Bill of Rights – the UDHR, the ICCPR, and the ICESCR – as well as the Genocide and Torture Conventions. Other treaties are excluded from extensive discussion in this book because they are less frequently invoked in postconflict jurisprudence considering human rights violations. However, this does not mean that the rights enshrined in these other treaties, such as those concerned with elimination of racial discrimination and protection of women and children, are not frequently affected by conflict, and do not deserve protection during conflict and redress afterward.

Table 4.2 Rights, duties, enforcement, and accountability under humanitarian law

Instrument	Level of rights	Duties	Measures for enforcement	Criminal punishment or accountability
Universal Declaration of Human Rights	Specific rights for individuals	No clear duties imposed on states	None	None
ICCPR and ICESCR	Specific rights for individuals	States have duties to provide	None	None
Genocide Convention	No specific rights for individuals	States prevent and punish, with no territorial limitations	Between states at the International Court of Justice	Individual criminal accountability
Torture Convention	No specific rights for individuals	States prevent and punish domestically	Monitored by the Committee Against Torture; states can bring suits against each other at the International Court of Justice	Individual criminal accountability
European Convention on Human Rights and American Convention on Human Rights	Specific rights for individuals	States have duties to provide	Systems include courts to adjudicate disputes and violations	None
Rome Statute	No specific rights for individuals	States punish crimes or extradite to court	By states against individuals	Individual criminal accountability

International treaties and customary international law obligations

The ICCPR

The ICCPR establishes largely individual rights, ranging from protection of bodily integrity to freedom from discrimination, as shown in Box 4.1.

Box 4.1 The ICCPR

- Physical integrity of the individual, including protection against torture, arbitrary arrest, and arbitrary deprivation of life
- Procedural fairness when an individual has been deprived of liberty by a government: provisions on arrest, trial procedure, and conditions of imprisonment
- Equal protection: protections against discrimination along racial, religious, gender, or other lines
- Freedom of belief, speech, and association
- Right to political participation

The ICESCR

The ICESCR also enshrines rights for individuals, but its emphasis is upon economic rights such as the right to work, and cultural rights such as the right to engage in one's culture, as shown in Box 4.2. The ICESCR and the ICCPR are necessarily interdependent, although not all countries that have ratified the former have also ratified the latter.

Box 4.2 **The ICESCR**

- Right to work, and to enjoyment of just and favorable conditions of work, such as fair wages and equal pay, safe working environment, equal opportunity for promotion, and the right to form trade unions
- Right to social security, including social insurance
- Special measures of protection for the family and for children
- Right to an adequate standard of living, including food, clothing, and housing
- Right to enjoyment of the highest attainable standard of physical and mental health
- Right to education, including the provision of compulsory primary education free of charge for all
- Right to take part in cultural life, to benefit from scientific progress, and to benefit from any moral or material interests emerging from productions of which one is the author

The Torture Convention

The definition of torture is articulated in Article 1 of the Torture Convention (see Box 4.3), and includes the infliction of both physical and mental suffering, for a variety of ends, committed by an official or a person acting in an official capacity. As discussed in Chapter 9, on human rights and the "global war on terror," despite the relatively straightforward language of the convention there has been dispute over its definition of torture.

Box 4.3 **The Torture Convention, Article 1**

For the purposes of this Convention, torture means any act by which severe pain or suffering, whether physical or mental, is intentionally inflicted on a person for such purposes as obtaining from him or a third person information or a confession, punishing him for an act he or a third person has committed or is suspected of having committed, or intimidating or coercing him or a third person, or for any reason based on discrimination of any kind, when such pain or suffering is inflicted by or at the instigation of or with the consent or acquiescence of a public official or other person acting in an official capacity. It does not include pain or suffering arising only from, inherent in or incidental to lawful sanctions.

Under the convention, states are not merely obliged to refrain from engaging in such activities, but are further obliged to prevent acts of torture on their territory; criminalize torture and punish such acts; not extradite or otherwise deport individuals to locations where they could be tortured; and extradite those accused of torture to other countries seeking to punish acts of torture, on appropriate request.

The Genocide Convention

The definition of genocide is articulated in Article 2 of the Genocide Convention (see Box 4.4), and includes two broad components: the intent to destroy a particular group, and the commission of specific acts in support of that intent. As discussed in Chapter 8, in the context of the situation in the Darfur region of Sudan, acts that fall merely within the definition of acts do not suffice where evidence of intent cannot be found.

Box 4.4 The Genocide Convention, Article 2

In the present [Genocide] Convention, genocide means any of the following acts committed with intent to destroy, in whole or in part, a national, ethnical, racial or religious group, as such:

(a) Killing members of the group;
(b) Causing serious bodily or mental harm to members of the group;
(c) Deliberately inflicting on the group conditions of life calculated to bring about its physical destruction in whole or in part;
(d) Imposing measures intended to prevent births within the group;
(e) Forcibly transferring children of the group to another group.

States are not merely obliged to refrain from the commission of genocide; they are also required to punish and prevent it, and to that end the convention requires that states commit to a number of specific measures. First, states are obliged to punish persons responsible for genocide, and to enact the legislation necessary for such punishment. Such legislation can be applicable to the commission of genocide anywhere in the world, not only to acts that take place on the territory of states that have signed the convention. States are also obliged to extradite suspects when appropriate – for example, if they are unable to prosecute, or if another state offers a more appropriate forum.

Crimes against humanity

Crimes against humanity initially formed part of customary international law but were later formally codified in the Rome Statute of the **International Criminal Court** (ICC) (see Box 4.5). Crimes against humanity make up a unique category. They are distinct from international humanitarian law in that the presence of armed conflict is not necessary, and in that they emerged not through international agreement, but through custom, as *jus cogens* obligations carrying greater weight than many human rights obligations. They have now been firmly established in jurisprudence, ranging from rulings of the Nuremberg Tribunal to those of the ad hoc tribunals for the former Yugoslavia and Rwanda. Crimes against humanity involve specific acts undertaken in the context of a widespread or systematic attack on the civilian population. Such acts may include murder, extermination, enslavement, deportation, imprisonment, torture, rape, sexual slavery, persecution, disappearances, and apartheid.

Box 4.5 The Rome Statute, Article 7

1. For the purpose of this Statute, "crime against humanity" means any of the following acts when committed as part of a widespread or systematic attack directed against any civilian population, with knowledge of the attack:

    (a) Murder;
    (b) Extermination;
    (c) Enslavement;
    (d) Deportation or forcible transfer of population;
    (e) Imprisonment or other severe deprivation of physical liberty in violation of fundamental rules of international law;
    (f) Torture;
    (g) Rape, sexual slavery, enforced prostitution, forced pregnancy, enforced sterilization, or any other form of sexual violence of comparable gravity;
    (h) Persecution against any identifiable group or collectivity on political, racial, national, ethnic, cultural, religious, gender as defined in paragraph 3, or other grounds that are universally recognized as impermissible under international law, in connection with any act referred to in this paragraph or any crime within the jurisdiction of the Court;
    (i) Enforced disappearance of persons;
    (j) The crime of apartheid;
    (k) Other inhumane acts of a similar character intentionally causing great suffering, or serious injury to body or to mental or physical health.

Substantive international humanitarian law obligations

It is important to distinguish international human rights law from international humanitarian law, as the two bodies of law have distinct purposes and histories, even though violations of international humanitarian law are often charged along with violations of human rights, in cases brought before domestic, international, or hybrid courts. While the purpose of international human rights law is to articulate the rights of humans, with an emphasis upon individual rights, the purpose of international humanitarian law is to regulate behavior in armed conflict. While this purpose is broadly humanitarian – to prevent abuses by armed forces of prisoners of war, civilians under occupation, and injured combatants – international humanitarian law aims to regulate conflict rather than protect rights. While laws regulating war have existed for centuries, the impetus for contemporary international humanitarian law was Henri Dunant, founder of the precursor to the International Committee for the Red Cross, who was supposedly so appalled by the excesses he witnessed at the Battle of Solferino in June 1859 that he began campaigning for stricter regulation.

We explore here the substantive obligations established by international humanitarian law. But we do not address much of the international humanitarian law predating the 1949 Geneva Conventions, because many key principles are subsumed in the 1949 agreements and their two additional protocols (see Box 4.6), or are customary law.

Box 4.6 The Geneva Conventions

The four Geneva Conventions of 1949
First Geneva Convention: treatment of sick and wounded in the armed forces
Second Geneva Convention: treatment of sick and wounded at sea
Third Geneva Convention: treatment of prisoners of war
Fourth Geneva Convention: protection of civilians

The two additional protocols of 1977
Protocol I: protection of victims of international armed conflicts
Protocol II: protection of victims of noninternational armed conflicts

What is the content of international humanitarian law, and what are its legal sources? In fact, it emerges from a range of sources, beginning with custom, and including the 1899 Hague Conventions, the four 1949 Geneva Conventions, and the two 1977 additional protocols to the Geneva Conventions. International humanitarian law regulates the behavior of combatants in armed conflict and variously sets forth rules for the treatment of prisoners of war, sick and wounded combatants, and civilian populations, particularly in circumstances of occupation.

For the purposes of this book, the Geneva Conventions, specifically the grave breaches that constitute war crimes and may call forth individual criminal accountability, are of most relevance. The drafters of the conventions specifically avoided creating a category of "war crimes": instead, they identified a list of "grave breaches" for which individual responsibility may be imposed. A comprehensive list of grave breaches can be found among the website sources listed at the end of this chapter, and includes willful killing, torture, willfully causing great suffering or serious injury to body or health, extensive destruction or appropriation of property not justified by necessity, compelling a prisoner of war or civilian to serve in the armed forces of a hostile power, willfully depriving a prisoner of war or protected person the rights of a fair trial, unlawful deportation, transfer, or confinement of a protected person, and hostage-taking. There are a range of prohibitions in Article 3 of each of the four Geneva Conventions, known as **Common Article 3** (see Box 4.7), that prohibit similar acts in all conflicts, whether internal or international. However, the traditional regulations of international humanitarian law differ in international and noninternational armed conflicts, although the Rome Statute essentially eliminates this distinction for signatory states. The Geneva Conventions and international humanitarian law generally regulate the conduct of armed conflict, and therefore are not applicable in the absence of conflict.

Box 4.7 Common Article 3 of the Geneva Conventions

In the case of armed conflict not of an international character occurring in the territory of one of the High Contracting Parties, each Party to the conflict shall be bound to apply, as a minimum, the following provisions:

(1) Persons taking no active part in the hostilities, including members of armed forces who have laid down their arms and those placed "hors de combat" by sickness, wounds, detention, or any other cause, shall in all circumstances be treated humanely, without any adverse distinction founded on race, colour, religion or faith, sex, birth or wealth, or any other similar criteria.

To this end, the following acts are and shall remain prohibited at any time and in any place whatsoever with respect to the above-mentioned persons:

(a) violence to life and person, in particular murder of all kinds, mutilation, cruel treatment and torture;
(b) taking of hostages;
(c) outrages upon personal dignity, in particular humiliating and degrading treatment;
(d) the passing of sentences and the carrying out of executions without previous judgment pronounced by a regularly constituted court, affording all the judicial guarantees which are recognized as indispensable by civilized peoples.

(2) The wounded and sick shall be collected and cared for.

An impartial humanitarian body, such as the International Committee of the Red Cross, may offer its services to the Parties to the conflict.

The Parties to the conflict should further endeavour to bring into force, by means of special agreements, all or part of the other provisions of the present Convention.

The application of the preceding provisions shall not affect the legal status of the Parties to the conflict.

Individuals who violate international humanitarian law under the grave breaches provisions (see Box 4.8) can be held to account in a domestic court of their state of nationality (see Chapter 10), in a domestic court of a third state (not party to the conflict) under universal jurisdiction (see Chapter 11), in a hybrid tribunal (see Chapter 12), and in the International Criminal Court (see Chapter 13).

Box 4.8 Grave breaches of the Geneva Conventions

First Geneva Convention, Article 50
Grave breaches to which the preceding article relates shall be those involving any of the following acts, if committed against persons or property protected by the

convention: wilful killing, torture, or inhuman treatment, including biological experiments, wilfully causing great suffering or serious injury to body or health, and extensive destruction and appropriation of property, not justified by military necessity and carried out unlawfully and wantonly.

Note: The grave breaches provisions of the Four Geneva Conventions, and of Additional Protocol I of 1977, are not identical. For comparisons, see the analysis provided by the International Committee of the Red Cross at http://www.icrc.org/web/eng/siteeng0.nsf/iwplist 133/1c2779ae80bf68ccc1256es90043580c.

While international human rights law begins with the rights of individuals, and may in a few circumstances be specifically enforceable, or in some cases create a category of crimes, such as torture or genocide, international humanitarian law sets forth limitations on the conduct of armed conflict, and identifies specific obligations whose breach may constitute crimes. This distinction is complicated, and has been blurred somewhat with the codification of war crimes provided by the Rome Statute of the International Criminal Court: the ICC includes war crimes, crimes against humanity, and genocide among the crimes subject to its jurisdiction, thus combining violations of international humanitarian law and violations of international human rights law. However, commission of torture is not included as a separate crime in the statute, although it is a proscribed act within the definition of war crimes and crimes against humanity.

Critical challenges

Armed groups and terrorist organizations

The problem of armed groups

As the international community has become more concerned with addressing internal armed conflict, the difficulty of addressing nonstate armed groups has grown in salience and importance. Since the events of September 11, 2001, dealing with nonstate armed groups categorized as terrorists has become the top priority for the United States, the **United Nations** (UN), and many of the world's governments. Yet neither political nor legal strategies yet seem up to the challenge of addressing these groups, which, while not state actors, pursue largely political goals through armed force.

There is thus an apparent gap between law and practice regarding the human rights obligations and accountability of nonstate armed groups. International human rights and humanitarian legal conventions that impose duties upon states regarding the conduct of conflict largely apply to states that are party to those conventions; these legal standards, even where they have reached the status of customary international law, are traditionally understood to regulate state activities in armed conflict. At the same time, conduct of states has been limited regarding the use of repressive measures through a host of human rights instruments, such as the Torture Convention. It is important to note that this body of law does not just preclude states' engagement in such abuses, whether in time of war or not, but also enables or requires the establishment of procedures for punishing individuals responsible for such abuses. Thus, it is not merely states, but also individuals, that are limited in their exercise of certain forms of violence. Individual responsibility has been further extended through the creation of ad hoc criminal tribunals, the establishment of the International Criminal Court, and the exercise of universal jurisdiction.

Regulation and control of nonstate armed groups, by comparison, remain relatively underdeveloped. The constraints placed upon states that are party to a host of international human rights and humanitarian treaties seldom apply to such groups. At the same time, individual criminal accountability does not apply to groups, but only to their members; nor is it either feasible or wise that criminal accountability should be extended to groups as groups. Responding to abuses by nonstate armed groups is increasingly important, given the prevalence of internal armed conflict since the end of the Cold War. This is compounded by the spillover effects of the movements of armed rebel groups and militias, and the phenomenon of cross-border terrorism. The result is that key players in contemporary domestic and international security remain relatively unregulated and unaddressed by international human rights or humanitarian law. This is particularly the case, as we shall see, because of the distinctions made in traditional international humanitarian law between international and noninternational armed conflicts.

The Rome Statute of the ICC resolves some of these issues by essentially eliminating the distinction between international and noninternational armed conflicts, making the acts prohibited by Common Article 3 of the Geneva Conventions war crimes. However, the ICC's jurisdiction is only over natural persons, and it can only impose individual criminal responsibility. There is no possibility of punishing groups, be they armed groups, corporations, or anything other than natural rather than legal persons.

Nonstate armed groups, and indeed terrorist organizations and activities, are not a new phenomenon. However, the rapid increase in internal armed conflicts since the end of the Cold War, as well as the rise of global terrorism and counterterrorism activities exemplified by Al-Qaida and the US global "war on terror," have sparked debates about the efficacy of both human rights law and international humanitarian law in regulating and punishing activities by nonstate armed groups, whether criminal or not.

Human rights violations and nonstate actors

Because the provisions of Common Article 3 and Additional Protocol II refer to activities in situations defined as armed conflict, they can encompass and regulate armed groups as well as states. However, the same cannot be straightforwardly said for human rights obligations. In human rights treaties, generally it is states that undertake to protect certain rights or refrain from violation of them. Treaties are driven by state consent, and speak to the relationship between the state and its citizens. Therefore, at least traditionally, armed groups do not have specific obligations under human rights agreements, such as the ICCPR, the CRC, CEDAW, and others. However, the desirability of applying human rights treaties to armed groups has increasingly come to the fore, supported, in part, by former UN Secretary-General Kofi Annan. However, while individual members of groups may be subject to punishment for violations, groups as groups are not subject to punishment or sanction of the sort related to state responsibility. The reason for this is relatively straightforward, deriving from the nature of the international legal order and the premium placed upon state sovereignty. States create international law, and traditionally were viewed as the only creators and subjects of international law. Nonetheless, states will generally reject any claim by bodies other than states, particularly armed groups that challenge the power or legitimacy of states, for standing under international law. To say that such groups have obligations, like states, under this body of law would appear to accord them greater legitimacy.

The provisions of the Torture Convention illustrate well the challenges of applying the terms of some human rights law to **nonstate actors**, not only where groups themselves are not subject to the provisions of the law, but also where some element of state action is required in order for a crime to have been committed. Traditionally, this has been the understanding of the Torture Convention. Why is this the case? Consider the language in Article 1 of the convention (see Box 4.3), which defines torture as suffering "inflicted by or at the instigation of or with the consent or acquiescence of a public official or other person acting in an official capacity." This provision would appear to require state action, but has more recently been understood to include the acts of those who exercise effective control over a territory, as was the case with Bosnian Serb leader Radovan Karadzic during the conflict in the former Yugoslavia (see Chapters 5 and 10). In a civil suit against Karadzic, a US court rejected his defense that obligations under international law regarding genocide, crimes against humanity, war crimes, and torture did not apply to him because he was not a state official. Instead, the court found that he was subject to suit in the United States under the **Alien Tort Claims Act** (see Chapter 11), because he had exercised effective control over the territory of Srpska during the time of the alleged acts were committed, even though he was not a state official (see Box 4.9).

Box 4.9 Kadic v. Karadžić

Kadic v. Karadžić : Opinion of 2nd Circuit re: Subject Matter Jurisdiction
UNITED STATES COURT OF APPEALS FOR THE SECOND CIRCUIT
Docket Nos. 94-9035, -9069, Decided: October 13, 1995

The plaintiffs-appellants are Croat and Muslim citizens of the internationally recognized nation of Bosnia-Herzegovina, formerly a republic of Yugoslavia. Their complaints, which we accept as true for purposes of this appeal, allege that they are victims, and representatives of victims, of various atrocities, including brutal acts of rape, forced prostitution, forced impregnation, torture, and summary execution, carried out by Bosnian-Serb military forces as part of a genocidal campaign conducted in the course of the Bosnian civil war. Karadžić, formerly a citizen of Yugoslavia and now a citizen of Bosnia-Herzegovina, is the President of a three-man presidency of the self-proclaimed Bosnian-Serb republic within Bosnia-Herzegovina, sometimes referred to as "Srpska," which claims to exercise lawful authority, and does in fact exercise actual control, over large parts of the territory of Bosnia-Herzegovina. In his capacity as President, Karadžić possesses ultimate command authority over the Bosnian-Serb military forces, and the injuries perpetrated upon plaintiffs were committed as part of a pattern of systematic human rights violations that was directed by Karadžić and carried out by the military forces under his command. The complaints allege that Karadžić acted in an official capacity either as the titular head of Srpska or in collaboration with the government of the recognized nation of the former Yugoslavia and its dominant constituent republic, Serbia.

However, while human rights agreements generally only articulate state obligations, even if broader obligations may be interpreted, international humanitarian law does deal with the obligations and violations of nonstate actors in more detail.

International and noninternational armed conflicts

Proscribed violations in internal conflict

As we have seen, the Geneva Conventions and their additional protocols define proscribed conduct in war regarding the treatment of both civilians and combatants. Violation of any of the grave breaches provisions of the Geneva Conventions may constitute a war crime.

However, traditional international humanitarian law has had difficulty addressing acts that might otherwise be war crimes when they are committed in the context of noninternational, or internal, armed conflict. First, the grave breaches provisions of all four Geneva Conventions apply only in international armed conflicts. States that are party to the conventions undertake to criminalize and punish these grave breaches, but not in *noninternational* armed conflicts. The only provisions that would apply to internal conflicts, then, are those of Common Article 3 (see Box 4.7), which articulates proscribed acts in conflict of a noninternational character, but does not explicitly require states to make them criminal, nor does it call such acts "grave breaches," the terminology used in the conventions elsewhere to enumerate acts that constitute war crimes.

Legitimate combatants in internal conflict: beneficiaries of protection

Addressing abuses in internal conflict is made more complex insofar as the Geneva Conventions recognize combatants in internal conflict as legitimate combatants, and thus subject to protections of prisoner of war status, *only* if they satisfy a number of criteria (see Box 4.10). These include being a member of the state's armed forces, without further qualification, whereas the standard is set significantly higher for irregular or internal opposition forces, be they rebel groups or militias.

Box 4.10 Article 4 of the Third Geneva Convention

A. Prisoners of war, in the sense of the present Convention, are persons belonging to one of the following categories, who have fallen into the power of the enemy:

2. Members of other militias and members of other volunteer corps, including those of organized resistance movements, belonging to a Party to the conflict and operating in or outside their own territory, even if this territory is occupied, provided that such militias or volunteer corps, including such organized resistance movements, fulfil the following conditions:

    (a) That of being commanded by a person responsible for his subordinates;
    (b) That of having a fixed distinctive sign recognizable at a distance;
    (c) That of carrying arms openly;
    (d) That of conducting their operations in accordance with the laws and customs of war.

Opposition groups often will not fulfill these criteria, which are not imposed upon state armed forces. The standards for armed groups to be considered prisoners of war, subject to protections of the convention, are higher. However, this standard is relaxed in Additional Protocol II of 1977 (see Box 4.11), relative to noninternational armed conflict. Similarly, this protocol recognizes the possibility of armed groups being directly bound by its terms.

Box 4.11 **Additional Protocol II to the Geneva Conventions, Article 1**

1. This Protocol, which develops and supplements Article 3 common to the Geneva Conventions of 12 August 1949 without modifying its existing conditions of application, shall apply to all armed conflicts which are not covered by Article 1 of the Protocol Additional to the Geneva Conventions of 12 August 1949, and relating to the Protection of Victims of International Armed Conflicts (Protocol I) and which take place in the territory of a High Contracting Party between its armed forces and dissident armed forces or other organized armed groups which, under responsible command, exercise such control over a part of its territory as to enable them to carry out sustained and concerted military operations and to implement this Protocol.
2. This Protocol shall not apply to situations of internal disturbances and tensions, such as riots, isolated and sporadic acts of violence and other acts of a similar nature, as not being armed conflicts.

Of most interest here is that the protections of the protocol, prohibiting the harms previously enumerated by Common Article 3, now apply in internal armed conflict, even if the armed group in question *does not* have a distinctive emblem or carry arms openly. Rather, the provisions apply to armed groups exercising control over territory and responsible command, and having the capacity to implement the protocol. This more relaxed standard might be of use in more fully ensuring the application of the content of international humanitarian law in internal armed conflicts. One area in which Additional Protocol II may set a higher standard than Common Article 3 is in its definition of conflict itself: Common Article 3 requires the presence of armed conflict, while Additional Protocol II offers a stringent definition, excluding much violence as no more than internal disturbance. Similarly, Common Article 3 does not set any requirement of effective control over territory for armed groups in order for them to be subject to its terms, while Additional Protocol II does.

As we will see in Chapter 10 when examining the work of the **International Criminal Tribunal for the Former Yugoslavia** (ICTY), this distinction between international and noninternational armed conflict can be problematic.

International criminal accountability

Key principles

International criminal accountability may be imposed in a range of national or international venues, as discussed later in this book, and with reference to one or more of the treaties outlined in Box 4.1. Regardless of venue or substantive law, however, a number of key principles have been established in practice.

First, for crimes of international concern such as genocide and crimes against humanity, the defense of superior orders is not accepted. The **Nuremberg Charter** (Charter of the International Military Tribunal) established the tribunal to try crimes committed by Germans during World War II. As the Nuremberg Charter explicitly states: "the fact that the defendant acted pursuant to an order of his government or of a superior shall not free him from responsibility, but may be considered in mitigation of punishment." The defense of duress may be acceptable in limited circumstances, and is allowed by the Rome Statute, Article 31(1)(d), in situations where the harm to others sought to be avoided by the person who committed the crime was far greater than the crime he or she actually committed.

The principle of command responsibility, according to which superiors are responsible for actions of their subordinates, also applies. The ad hoc ICTY required three elements in the *Čelebiči* case: superior–subordinate relationship, mental element or intent, and failure to act to prevent or punish violations.

In order to commit the crimes in question, defendants must have *mens rea*, a mental state involving intent to commit the crime. Defendants may raise defenses of mistake of fact, or mistake of law, meaning that they had not intended to commit a crime, but the defense of mistake of law is limited to situations where an element of the crime involves a legal evaluation.

General principles of criminal law found in most domestic criminal systems apply in international criminal law. Thus, the accused is presumed innocent until proven guilty. The principle of nonretroactivity also applies. Thus, the principles of *nullem crimen sine lege* (no crime without law) and *nulla poena sine lege* (no punishment without law) apply.

As with domestic law, group criminal accountability is generally not recognized under international law, in part because of due process concerns. While the Nuremberg Tribunal recognized the concept of joint criminal enterprise, it was not to be used to convict an individual in the absence of evidence of individual responsibility. There was even discussion of providing for jurisdiction of the ICC over not just natural persons – human individuals – but also legal persons – groups, corporations, and the like. This provision, however, was not included in the final draft of the Rome Statute.

Finally, in recent decades, judicial decisions and international agreements such as the Rome Statute of the ICC have progressively limited claims of immunity from prosecution by reason of official status. Before the ICC, no claims of official immunities may be invoked, and the same appears to be the case before any international court. Before domestic courts, sitting heads of state and high-level officials may invoke immunity while in office, but may not raise it as a defense once they have left office.

Specific institutions

Part III of this book examines specific institutions and processes that may impose sanctions upon individuals for the violations of law discussed here. It is important to understand that while it is the state that undertakes the obligations enumerated under international human rights and humanitarian law, the actual crimes addressed are crimes committed by individual persons that call for individual criminal accountability. Thus, an individual may face accountability for grave breaches of the Geneva Conventions, or for the commission of crimes against humanity, or genocide, or torture. A state cannot be similarly prosecuted.

This does not mean that a state cannot be held to account; after all, it is the state that undertakes these obligations. A state may be sued for actions that violate its obligations under relevant conventions, or that violate customary international law. Such a suit would occur before the International Court of Justice (ICJ), the key judicial organ of the United Nations system, if the Court has jurisdiction, or by another supranational court. As is discussed in Chapter 7, the Democratic Republic of Congo brought cases against Rwanda and Uganda before the ICJ for violations of human rights and humanitarian law. In December 2005 the case against Uganda reached a substantive judgment, while in early February 2006 the ICJ dismissed the case against Rwanda for lack of jurisdiction.

Key points

- There are many types of international human rights law and international humanitarian law.
- Some law creates no rights or obligations, while some law makes it possible to bring criminal charges against individuals.
- International humanitarian law imposes obligations primarily upon states, and distinguishes between international and noninternational armed conflicts.
- Individual criminal accountability may be imposed in a range of institutions.

Discussion questions

- What are the key distinctions between international human rights law and international humanitarian law? How do they vary in terms of purpose and subjects, and applicability?
- What are the key human rights protections that may be of interest during armed conflict? How might these rights be affected by conflict?
- Discuss the conventions and custom that together compose international humanitarian law. What do they regulate, and how do they work?
- Upon whom are international humanitarian law obligations imposed? States or individuals?
- Is the following statement correct? Why, or why not? While international bodies have addressed accountability of individual leaders of armed opposition groups, they have so far largely ignored the accountability of the groups in favour of the accountability of individual members.
- Consider the distinction between international and noninternational armed conflicts in key documents, and its effect upon what acts may be criminalized. Is this distinction evolving?

Further reading

Aksar, Yusuf, *Implementing International Humanitarian Law: From the* Ad Hoc *Tribunals to a Permanent International Criminal Court* (London: Routledge, 2004).

Andreopoulos, George, "The International Legal Framework and Armed Groups" (2003), http://www.armedgroups.org/images/stories/pdfs/andreopoulos_paper2.pdf.

Capie, David, and Pablo Policzer, "Keeping the Promise of Protection: Holding Armed Groups to the Same Standards as States" (2003), http://www.armedgroups.org/images/stories/pdfs/keeping%20the%20promise%20of%20protection.pdf.

Greenwood, Christopher, "A Critique of the Additional Protocols to the Geneva Conventions of 1949," in Helen Durham and Timothy L. H. McCormack, eds., *The Changing Face of Conflict and the Efficacy of International Humanitarian Law* (The Hague: Kluwer, 1999).

Nino, Carlos S., "The Duty to Punish Past Human Rights Violations Put into Context: The Case of Argentina," *Yale Law Journal* 100 (1991): 2619–41.

Orentlicher, Diane, "Settling Accounts: The Duty to Prosecute Human Rights Violations of a Prior Regime," *Yale Law Journal* 100 (1991): 2537–618.

Paust, Jordan J., M. Cherif Bassiouni, Michael Scharf, Jimmy Gurul, Leila Sadat, Bruce Zagaris, and Sharon A. Williams, *International Criminal Law* (Durham: Carolina Academic Press, 2000).

Ratner, Steven R., and Jason S. Abrams, *Accountability for Human Rights Atrocities in International Law and Practice* (Oxford: Oxford University Press, 2001).

Sassoli, Marco, "Possible Legal Mechanisms to Improve Compliance by Armed Groups with International Humanitarian Law and International Human Rights Law" (2003), http://www.armed groups.org/images/stories/pdfs/sassoli_paper.pdf.

Sriram, Chandra, "Achieving Accountability for Non-State Armed Groups" (2003), http://www.armed groups.org/images/stories/pdfs/sriram_paper.pdf.

Steiner, Henry J., Philip Alston, and Ryan Goodman, *International Human Rights in Context: Law, Politics, Morals*, 3rd edn. (Oxford: Oxford University Press, 2008).

Wippman, David, and Matthew Evangelista, eds., *New Wars, New Laws? Applying the Laws of War in 21st Century Conflicts* (Ardsley, NY: Transnational, 2005).

Zegveld, Liesbeth, *Accountability of Armed Opposition Groups in International Law* (Cambridge: Cambridge University Press, 2002).

Official documents and sources

Additional Protocols to the Geneva Conventions (1977):

    Additional Protocol I, http://www.unhchr.ch/html/menu3/b/93.htm.

    Additional Protocol II, http://www.unhchr.ch/html/menu3/b/94.htm.

Convention Against Torture and Other Cruel, Inhuman, or Degrading Treatment or Punishment (Torture Convention) (1984), http://www.hrweb.org/legal/cat.html.

Convention on the Elimination of All Forms of Discrimination Against Women (1979), http://www.hrweb.org/legal/cdw.html.

Convention on the Elimination of All Forms of Racial Discrimination (1965), http://fletcher.tufts.edu/multi/texts/bh490.txt.

Convention on the Prevention and Punishment of the Crime of Genocide (Genocide Convention) (1948), http://www.hrweb.org/legal/genocide.html.

Convention on the Rights of the Child (1989), http://www.hrweb.org/legal/child.html.

Geneva Conventions (1949):

    First Geneva Convention, http://fletcher.tufts.edu/multi/texts/bh238.txt.

    Second Geneva Convention, http://fletcher.tufts.edu/multi/texts/bh239.txt.

    Third Geneva Convention, http://fletcher.tufts.edu/multi/texts/bh240.txt.

    Fourth Geneva Convention, http://fletcher.tufts.edu/multi/texts/bh241.txt.

International Covenant on Civil and Political Rights (1966), http://www.hrweb.org/legal/cpr.html.

International Covenant on Economic, Social, and Cultural Rights (1966), http://www.hrweb.org/legal/escr.html.

Status of ratifications of key human rights instruments, http://www.unhchr.ch/pdf/report.pdf.

Universal Declaration of Human Rights (1948), http://www.un.org/overview/rights.html.

Part II
Contemporary conflict
Critical cases

5 The former Yugoslavia

Map 5.1 Former Yugoslavia, 1991

Source: Adapted from the PCL Map Collection, University of Texas Libraries, the University of Texas at Austin, http://www.lib.utexas.edu/maps/europe/former_yugoslavia.jpg.

Overview

The conflicts in the former Yugoslavia have been complex and have occurred both within states and between states since the end of the Cold War, after which many nation-states within the former Soviet Union and across Eastern Europe began to fragment. As a result, several successor states emerged, partially along the lines of the former Yugoslavia's administrative division into a number of republics, and also along ethnic lines (see Box 5.1 for key facts on Yugoslavia). Conflicts between 1991 and 1995 largely in the territory of what are now Bosnia and Herzegovina, and Croatia, sparked international outrage, intervention by the **United Nations** (UN) and the **North Atlantic Treaty Organization** (NATO), and eventually the creation of the first international **war crimes** tribunal since the Nuremberg and Tokyo Tribunals, the ad hoc **International Criminal Tribunal for the Former Yugoslavia** (ICTY). The 1999 conflict in Kosovo sparked a three-month bombing campaign by NATO in Serbia, and led to the creation of a UN interim administration in the province.

Box 5.1 **Key facts: Yugoslavia in 1991**

Geography

Location: Balkans, neighboring Albania, Austria, Bulgaria, Greece, Hungary, Italy, Romania

Disputes: Kosovo's status; the official name of Macedonia disputed by Greece

Area: Total area 255,800 km², land area: 255,400 km², water area: 400 km²

Natural resources: coal, copper, bauxite, timber, iron ore, antimony, chromium, lead, zinc, asbestos, mercury, crude oil, natural gas, nickel, uranium

People

Population: 23,976,040, growth rate 0.6%

Nationality: Yugoslav

Ethnic groups: Serb 36.3%, Croat 19.7%, Muslim 8.9%, Slovene 7.8%, Albanian 7.7%, Macedonian 5.9%, Yugoslav 5.4%, Montenegrin 2.5%, Hungarian 1.9%, other 3.9% (1981 census)

Religions: Eastern Orthodox 50%, Roman Catholic 30%, Muslim 9%, Protestant 1%, other 10%

Languages: Serbo-Croatian, Slovene, Macedonian (all official); Albanian, Hungarian

Literacy: 90% (male 96%, female 84%) age 15 and older can read and write (1981 census)

Government

Country name: Socialist Federal Republic of Yugoslavia (SFRY)

Government type: Federal republic; four of six republics have noncommunist governments

Capital: Belgrade

Administrative territorial divisions: Six republics: Bosnia and Herzegovina, Croatia, Macedonia, Slovenia, and Serbia; two nominally autonomous provinces within Serbia: Kosovo and Vojvodina

Independence: December 1, 1918; independent monarchy established from the Kingdoms of Serbia and Montenegro, parts of the Turkish Empire, and the Austro-Hungarian Empire; SFRY proclaimed November 29, 1945

Economy

Gross national product: US$120.1 billion, per capita US$5,040; real growth rate 6.3% (1990)

Unemployment rate: 16% (1990)

Source: Central Intelligence Agency, *World Factbook*,
http://www.theodora.com/wfb1991/yugoslavia/yugoslavia_people.html,
http://www.theodora.com/wfb1991/yugoslavia/yugoslavia_economy.html,
http://www.theodora.com/wfb1991/yugoslavia/yugoslavia_geography.html.
(last accessed December 2008)

This chapter examines the historical background of the conflict in the former Yugoslavia, human rights violations as both causes and consequences of conflict, the **international humanitarian law** and **international human rights law** applicable to the abuses committed, and prospects for accountability. Chapter 10 discusses the ICTY in greater detail.

Background to the conflict

The former Yugoslavia was the result of the unification of the Kingdom of Serbs, Croats, and Slovenes in 1918. While each population resided across the territory, and intermarriage existed, Serbs comprised the majority in the areas now known as Serbia, Croats in the areas now known as Croatia, and Slovenians in the areas now known as Slovenia. The territory now known as Bosnia-Herzegovina was mixed, but with a majority Bosnian Muslim population. Albanians resided largely in the territory now known as Kosovo, with a Serb minority. In 1929 the unified country became known as Yugoslavia. During World War II, Germany sought to occupy the territory. It faced resistance from paramilitary groups, but also found allies in Croatia in the Ustache (a Croatian ultranationalist organization), which engaged in ethnic cleansing and expulsion of Serbs, Gypsies, and Muslims. With the defeat of the Germans and Croatian collaborators, Josip Broz Tito took control of Yugoslavia, a federation of six republics: Serbia, Montenegro, Croatia, Bosnia and Herzegovina, and Slovenia. He established a communist regime, which endured after his death in 1980, independent of the Soviet Union and held together by authoritarian rule. In 1989, Slobodan Milošević became president of the Serbian Republic, within Yugoslavia, and began calling for Serbian domination of the country. This ultranationalism sparked separatism, and ultimately the violent breakup of the state along ethnic lines. The conflict in the former Yugoslavia was largely although not purely based upon ethnicity or religion, with political leaders using identity and historical grievances to stoke conflict. The three largest ethnic groups in the country (see Box 5.1), Serbs (composing about 36 percent of the population), Croatians (about 20 percent), and Muslims (largely Bosnian Muslims, about 9 percent), were far less integrated by the end of the conflict, and longer-term resentment and mistrust continue.

Conflict in Bosnia-Herzegovina and Croatia

In 1991, Croatia, Slovenia, and Macedonia declared independence from Yugoslavia, followed in 1992 by Bosnia and Herzegovina. The remaining republics of Serbia and Montenegro declared a new republic, the Federal Republic of Yugoslavia (FRY), in April 1992. While the FRY rejected Croatia's declaration of independence, Milošević initially reached a pact with Croatian leader Franjo Tudjman to partition Bosnia and Herzegovina into Serb- and Croat-controlled regions. The independence of Macedonia and Slovenia came relatively peacefully (as did Montenegro's independence in 2006), at least by comparison to the wars that ensued in Croatia and Bosnia and Herzegovina. In the latter regions, Serbia under Milošević promoted violent military campaigns, through support to local nationalist groups, to create a "Greater Serbia."

Bosnia and Herzegovina followed its declaration of sovereignty in October 1991 with a declaration of independence from the former Yugoslavia on March 3, 1992, following a referendum boycotted by ethnic Serbs. The Bosnian Serbs – supported by neighboring Serbia and Montenegro, led by Milošević – responded with armed resistance aimed at partitioning the republic along ethnic lines and joining Serb-held areas of Bosnia and Herzegovina to form a "Greater Serbia." They were led by Radovan Karadžić and his army chief, Ratko Mladić, who like Milosevic would later be indicted by the International Criminal Tribunal for the Former Yugoslavia for alleged involvement in war crimes and atrocities, in particular the massacre in Srebrenica. In Croatia, Croatian Serbs resisted Croatian independence and engaged in fighting with the support of Serbia. Bosnian forces and Croatian forces fought not only the Serb forces in their territories, but occasionally also each other, creating a three-way, albeit asymmetrical, conflict. The atrocities, involving targeted killing and widespread abuse of civilians of different ethnic groups, were committed by the major parties to the conflict, but in significantly greater numbers by Serb forces against Croat and Bosniak civilians. While these acts might have been characterized as **genocide**, they were termed "ethnic cleansing" by the international community. In March 1994, Bosniaks and Croats signed an agreement creating the joint Bosniak/Croat Federation of Bosnia and Herzegovina, ending fighting between these two parties.

Conflict continued in these territories, with intense international pressure to reach a peaceful, negotiated settlement. The **UN Secretary-General** appointed a personal envoy, Cyrus Vance, in October 1991, to seek a resolution. On February 15, 1992, despite objections by many in Serbia, the Secretary-General recommended to the **UN Security Council** the establishment of the UN Protection Force (UNPROFOR). This plan was approved in a **UN Security Council resolution**, Resolution 743 of 1992. The expectation at the time was that this would be an interim measure while a cease-fire was secured. However, the fighting endured, with atrocities, massacres, and targeting of civilians frequent and the UN force unable to halt them, given a relatively weak mandate. The UN force designated three original protected areas: Eastern Slavonia, Western Slavonia, and Krajina, with others to follow. However, despite increases in the size and mandate of UNPROFOR by the Security Council, it was unable to halt much of the violence and targeting of civilians, with the most notable failures being its inability to prevent the massacre of Srebrenica and the siege of Sarajevo.

International efforts at mediation promoted numerous peace plans, but all were doomed to fail. However, international pressure increased, and finally, on November 21, 1995, in Dayton, Ohio, the warring parties signed a peace agreement. The Dayton Accords (see Box 5.2) retained Bosnia and Herzegovina's international boundaries and created a multiethnic, democratic government with a rotating presidency. The peace agreement also recognized two entities within that state: the Bosniak/Croat Federation of Bosnia and Herzegovina, and the Bosnian Serb-led Republika Srpska (RS).

Box 5.2 The Dayton Accords

General Framework Agreement for Peace in Bosnia and Herzegovina
The Republic of Bosnia and Herzegovina, the Republic of Croatia and the Federal Republic of Yugoslavia (the "Parties"),

Recognizing the need for a comprehensive settlement to bring an end to the tragic conflict in the region,

Desiring to contribute toward that end and to promote an enduring peace and stability,

Affirming their commitment to the Agreed Basic Principles issued on September 8, 1995, the Further Agreed Basic Principles issued on September 26, 1995, and the cease-fire agreements of September 14 and October 5, 1995,

Noting the agreement of August 29, 1995, which authorized the delegation of the Federal Republic of Yugoslavia to sign, on behalf of the Republika Srpska, the parts of the peace plan concerning it, with the obligation to implement the agreement that is reached strictly and consequently,

Have agreed as follows:

Article I

The Parties shall conduct their relations in accordance with the principles set forth in the United Nations Charter, as well as the Helsinki Final Act and other documents of the Organization for Security and Cooperation in Europe. In particular, the Parties shall fully respect the sovereign equality of one another, shall settle disputes by peaceful means, and shall refrain from any action, by threat or use of force or otherwise, against the territorial integrity or political independence of Bosnia and Herzegovina or any other State.

. . .

Annex 6: Agreement on Human Rights

Chapter One: Respect for Human Rights

Article I: Fundamental Rights and Freedoms

The Parties shall secure to all persons within their jurisdiction the highest level of internationally recognized human rights and fundamental freedoms, including the rights and freedoms provided in the European Convention for the Protection of Human Rights and Fundamental Freedoms and its Protocols and the other international agreements listed in the Appendix to this Annex.

Conflict in Kosovo

The conflict in Kosovo involved efforts by Serbia to consolidate control over Serbs in the territory of the former Yugoslavia where they were in the minority. Serbs had been present in what is now Kosovo since the seventh century, but the territory did not fall under Serbian rule until the thirteenth century. Following defeat by the Ottomans in the Battle of Kosovo in 1389, large numbers of Turks and Albanians moved to Kosovo, and Albanians became the dominant ethnic group in Kosovo; this battle served as a symbolic tool for Serb nationalists such as Milošević to invoke in stoking the fires of nationalism during the 1990s. Serbia regained control over Kosovo from the Ottoman Empire in 1912. Following the creation of the Yugoslav government under Tito, Kosovo was recognized as an autonomous province within Serbia, and was given progressively greater powers. Kosovo was granted near-republic status in the 1974 Yugoslav constitution. Nonetheless, Albanian nationalism, including riots and demands for independence, increased in the 1980s. Serbs in Kosovo complained that they were being mistreated, and such claims were exploited by Serb nationalist leaders such as Milošević. Serbia passed a new constitution in 1989 that limited Kosovo's autonomy. In 1991, Kosovo Albanian leaders held a referendum in which Kosovo declared itself independent. Serbia responded with repressive measures, and Ibrahim Rugova, a moderate ethnic Albanian leader, established a parallel unofficial government, seeking to resist this repression peacefully, but without success. In response, Kosovo Albanians created the Kosovo Liberation Army (KLA) in 1995 and began fighting to oust Serb control. Both the US and the Yugoslav governments viewed the KLA as a terrorist organization due to its attacks on Serb targets, including police and civilians. The KLA also established a political wing, headed by Hashim Thaçi, who would become the prime minister of Kosovo when it declared independence in 2008. Serbia responded with a counterinsurgency campaign that entailed massacres and massive expulsions of ethnic Albanians by Serbian military, police, and paramilitary forces.

Attempts at negotiation culminated in the Rambouillet Accords in 1999, which set forth principles of interim self-government for Kosovo, enshrined principles of nondiscrimination and self-determination, and promised the right of return, protection of humanitarian assistance, and a halt to the use of force. The Rambouillet agreement was ultimately rejected by Milošević. NATO initiated a three-month bombing campaign in Serbia, beginning in March 1999, and Serbia was forced to withdraw military and police forces in June 1999. UN Security Council Resolution 1244 (1999) (see Box 5.3) placed Kosovo under a transitional administration, the UN Interim Administration Mission in Kosovo (UNMIK), until Kosovo's final status could be resolved. The resolution recognized Serbia's territorial integrity, with UNMIK engaged in actual governance of Kosovo. In 2001, UNMIK set out a constitutional framework that established Kosovo's provisional institutions of self-government and began to devolve responsibilities to it. In late 2005 the UN initiated proceedings to determine Kosovo's future status. Negotiations held intermittently between 2006 and 2007 failed to reach a compromise between Serbia's insistence on its territorial integrity, with significant autonomy for Kosovo, and the Kosovo Albanians' demand for full independence. On February 17, 2008, Kosovo declared its independence from Serbia. To date, Kosovo has been recognized a sovereign state by some 40 countries, including many European nations, but not by Serbia.

Box 5.3 **UN Security Council Resolution 1244**

UN Doc. S/RES/1244 (June 10, 1999)

. . .

3. Demands in particular that the Federal Republic of Yugoslavia put an immediate and verifiable end to violence and repression in Kosovo, and begin a complete verifiable phased withdrawal from Kosovo of all military, police and paramilitary forces according to a rapid timetable, with which the deployment of the international security presence in Kosovo will be synchronized;

4. Confirms that after the withdrawal an agreed number of Yugoslav and Serb military and police personnel will be permitted to return to Kosovo to perform the functions in accordance with annex 2;

5. Decides on the deployment in Kosovo, under United Nations auspices, of international civil and security presences, with appropriate equipment and personnel as required, and welcomes the agreement of the Federal Republic of Yugoslavia to such presences;

. . .

7. Authorizes Member States and relevant international organizations to establish the international security presence in Kosovo as set out in point 4 of annex 2 with all necessary means to fulfil its responsibilities under paragraph 9 below; establish the international security presence in Kosovo as set out in point 4 of annex 2 with all necessary means to fulfil its responsibilities under paragraph 9 below;

. . .

10. Authorizes the Secretary-General, with the assistance of relevant international organizations, to establish an international civil presence in Kosovo in order to provide an interim administration for Kosovo under which the people of Kosovo can enjoy substantial autonomy within the Federal Republic of Yugoslavia, and which will provide transitional administration while establishing and overseeing the development of provisional democratic self-governing institutions to ensure conditions for a peaceful and normal life for all inhabitants of Kosovo.

The fall of Milošević

Milošević's grip on power was first loosened in disputed elections in 2000; he was forced to resign amid mass protests. In 2001 he was arrested by the FRY government on charges of corruption, embezzlement, and abuse of power. However, he had also been indicted by the ICTY (see Chapter 10) on charges of crimes relating to the wars in Bosnia and Herzegovina and in Kosovo. He died in tribunal custody in March 2006.

Box 5.4 **Key players in the former Yugoslavia**

Individuals

Radovan Karadžić: Founder of the Serbian Democratic Party in Bosnia and Herzegovina and first president of Republika Srpska. In ICTY custody.

Slobodan Milošević: President of the Serbian Republic within Yugoslavia, and then of the Federal Republic of Yugoslavia (Serbia and Montenegro). Died in 2006.

Ratko Mladić: Chief of staff of the Army of Republika Srpska during the Bosnian conflict of 1992–5. In hiding.

Ibrahim Rugova: Moderate Kosovar political leader.

Hashim Thaçi: Leader of the KLA's political and subsequently prime minister of Kosovo.

Franjo Tudjman: Leader of the Croatian Democratic Union; declared Croatian independence 1991. Died in 1999.

National armies

KLA: Kosovo Liberation Army.

International and regional missions

UNMIK: UN Interim Administration Mission in Kosovo.

UNPROFOR: UN Protection Force.

Other actors

ICJ: International Court of Justice.

ICTY: International Criminal Tribunal for the Former Yugoslavia.

NATO: North Atlantic Treaty Organization.

Human rights violations in the former Yugoslavia

Human rights violations as underlying causes of conflict

Domestic grievances

Past abuses, even historically remote ones, were invoked by various sides to the conflict as justifications, among others, for fighting. Serb forces inside and outside Serbia justified their fighting against Croatian forces in part by invoking the memory of abuses by the Nazi-allied Croatian Ustache. Milošević also justified the support provided to Serb forces in Bosnia and Herzegovina, and fighting in Kosovo, as being in the defense of Serb minorities, who, according to Milošević, were being discriminated against and attacked, or were at risk of such treatment. Milošević's rhetoric surrounding the need to fight in Kosovo, and indeed in Bosnia as well, repeatedly harkened back to the 1389 battle that established Ottoman control, and his nationalist rhetoric was seen as ushering in repression by Serbs of various minorities. Kosovar Albanians took up arms under the banner of the KLA on the grounds that they were being abused by the regime in Belgrade, and were in danger of suffering ethnic cleansing. However, their struggle against repression from Belgrade also involved attacks on the Serb minority in Kosovo. Bosniak and Croat forces fought separately and together to defend against Serb military attacks, and attacks targeted specifically against civilians, which were viewed as ethnic cleansing.

These invocations of discrimination, abuses, and threats to survival were based on a mixture of truth and conveniently deployed mythmaking. In many instances, most evidently in assaults by Serb forces in Bosnia and Herzegovina and in Kosovo, abuses were currently taking place, perhaps offering the greatest justification for resort to force. Where historical grievances were invoked, however, the human rights justification for force appeared somewhat more remote.

Internal or international conflict?

Was the conflict in the former Yugoslavia an internal or an international (transborder) conflict? It was in fact both, and its character changed over time, although precisely when may be disputed. At the outset, the conflict was largely internal in character. However, with the declarations of independence by Croatia and Bosnia-Herzegovina, the war became internationalized. These declarations were rapidly recognized by a few states; EU recognition of Croatia came in January 1992, and Croatia, Slovenia, and Bosnia and Herzegovina were admitted into the United Nations as member states in May 1992. By this date they were clearly independent states and the conflicts were potentially both internal (purely Bosnian Serb, Croat, and Muslim forces fighting in the territory of Bosnia-Herzegovina, and purely Croatian Serb and Croat forces fighting in the territory of Croatia) and international (conflicts between Bosniak and Croat fighters, and material support from the FRY to Croatian and Bosnian Serb forces fighting in Bosnia-Herzegovina and Croatia). Characterization of the conflict as internal or international may shape the applicable law.

Human rights violations emerging from and transforming the conflict

A wide range of atrocities took place during the conflicts, the majority of which were perpetrated by Serb forces in Croatia and Bosnia-Herzegovina, although Bosniak and Croat forces also engaged in abuses. Similarly in Kosovo, Serb forces appear to have been responsible for the majority of abuses, with the KLA far from innocent of abuses itself. In both conflicts, violence by state and **nonstate actors** targeted civilians, forcing them to flee as part of a strategy of ethnic cleansing. Methods included massacres of civilians, **torture**, disappearances, rape and forced impregnation, and bombardment of population centers having no evident military value. We focus here upon three specific sets of events: the siege of Sarajevo, the massacre at Srebrenica, and the 1998–9 violence in Kosovo, which led to the NATO bombing campaign.

The siege of Sarajevo

The siege of Sarajevo, the capital city of Bosnia and Herzegovina, by Serb and Bosnian Serb forces is classed as the longest siege in modern conflict, lasting from April 1992 until February 1996 and outlasting the signature of the Dayton Accords. An estimated 12,000 were killed, 85 of whom were civilians. The siege also forced many to flee, a depopulation that reduced the size of Sarajevo to just over 60 percent of its former size. The siege involved massive shelling upon the city, as well as a campaign of sniper attacks designed to terrorize civilians. The city was blockaded, preventing necessities such as food, medicine, water, and electricity from reaching it. The shelling targeted government buildings, hospitals, UN facilities, markets, and even civilians standing in line for water.

The massacre at Srebrenica

The town of Srebrenica was designated a "safe area" by UN Security Council Resolution 819 in 1993, in response to the systematic attacks on civilians by Serb paramilitary forces. Despite this designation, siege of the town and violence against its civilians continued, with Serb forces capturing Srebrenica in July 1995. The violence reached its pinnacle with the massacre, in July 1995, of an estimated 8,000 Bosniak men and boys by a unit under the command of Mladić. This was the largest massacre of civilians in Europe since the end of World War II, and, with its specific targeting of men and boys of a single ethnic group, was viewed by many as genocide. The small Dutch contingent of UN peacekeepers was unable to halt either the fall of Srebrenica or the massacre. In addition to their removal and massacre of the men and boys, Serb forces engaged in widespread rape of women, although, under a UN-brokered agreement, some women were evacuated to government-held territory.

The 1998–9 violence in Kosovo

As part of their counterinsurgency campaign, Serbian forces engaged in widespread violence against civilians and civilian property in Kosovo. They committed mass rapes of women, engaged in forced disappearances, and undertook efforts at ethnic cleansing and forced migration of populations. A massacre by Serb forces in Račak sparked Western condemnation and intensified diplomatic efforts and threats. By March 1999, Serbian authorities had initiated an ethnic cleansing campaign of forced population movement on a massive scale. Ethnic Albanian refugees and **internally displaced persons** were driven from their homes by Serbian forces at gunpoint, with many loaded onto trains and other vehicles and expelled from Kosovo. Serbian forces drove out the majority of Kosovar Albanians from urban areas such as Djakovica. Those who were kept behind were used as human shields, compelled to accompany Serbian forces as protection against NATO airstrikes; Serbian forces also disguised themselves as nongovernmental workers to avoid being targeted by NATO aircraft. In addition, Serbian forces coerced many refugees into signing statements saying that they were leaving the province of their own free will, seized identity and property documents, and destroyed civilian property. Police systematically looted, destroyed, and burned villages, and shot livestock, with the apparent goal of depopulating certain regions, especially the villages near the border with Albania. According to the **UN High Commissioner for Refugees** (UNHCR), approximately 850,000 people fled to neighboring countries, and hundreds of thousands were internally displaced. KLA forces also engaged in attacks on ethnic Serbian civilians as well as in plunder, including the looting of an Orthodox Serb monastery.

NATO forces have also been accused of violating international law for the manner in which they conducted the bombing campaign. High-level flight plans increased the risks of misdirected bombs hitting civilian targets, and indeed there were a number of nonmilitary targets, including the Chinese embassy in Belgrade and a prison. NATO also targeted what it termed "dual-use" sites, such as a state-controlled television tower. These attacks have been condemned by some human rights advocates as failing to distinguish between military and civilian targets. So too has the use of cluster munitions, some of which remain on the ground unexploded and have led to civilian deaths long since the conflict ceased. Two cases were brought before the **European Court of Human Rights** regarding the effects of cluster munitions: *Behrami and Behrami v. France* and *Saramati v. France, Norway, and Germany*. However, the Court deemed the cases inadmissible because the acts in question were considered acts of the UN, not of individual states. Serbia also attempted to bring a case before the **International Court of Justice** (ICJ) against all NATO member states in 1999, claiming that they had violated obligations under the **UN Charter** limiting use of force. However, the Court found that it lacked jurisdiction and the case was unable to proceed.

Applicable law and possible subjects of legal accountability

State responsibility for genocide

Under international law, states are obligated to take measures to prevent genocide. While many of the atrocities that occurred in the former Yugoslavia were loosely termed "ethnic cleansing," some could constitute genocide or war crimes. Chapter 10 deals in greater detail with the jurisprudence of the International Criminal Tribunal for the Former Yugoslavia, established to consider individual criminal responsibility for particular acts committed during the conflicts there. However, states may also be responsible for breaches, such as failure to prevent genocide. Bosnia-Herzegovina brought a case against Serbia before the ICJ, alleging both Serbia's responsibility for genocide and its failure to prevent genocide in the context of attacks on a variety of civilian targets. In its application, filed in March 1993 as the conflict raged, Bosnia-Herzegovina alleged:

> Not since the end of the Second World War and the revelations of the horrors of Nazi Germany's "Final Solution" has Europe witnessed the utter destruction of a People, for no other reason than they belong to a particular national ethnical, racial, and religious group as such. The abominable crimes taking place in the Republic of Bosnia-Herzegovina at this time can be called by only one name: genocide.

The application referred to plans to create a "Greater Serbia" and the siege of Sarajevo as evidence of genocidal intent and action. The Court's final judgment encompassed a range of atrocities that had not yet occurred at the time of the original application, including the Srebrenica massacre.

In February 2007 the ICJ held that the acts committed in Srebrenica constituted genocide (see Box 5.5).

Box 5.5 International Court of Justice judgment in relation to Srebrenica

"The Court concludes that the acts committed at Srebrenica falling within Article II *(a)* and *(b)* of the Convention were committed with the specific intent to destroy in part the group of the Muslims of Bosnia and Herzegovina as such; and accordingly that these were acts of genocide, committed by members of the VRS in and around Srebrenica from about 13 July 1995."

Source: *Updated statute of the International Criminal Tribunal for the Former Yugoslavia* (February 2008), http://www.un.org/icty.

However, while the ICJ found that Serbia was responsible for its failure to take measures within its power to prevent the genocide (e.g., controlling its proxy Bosnian Serb leaders), it did not find that Serbia was directly responsible for the commission of genocide. It did find, though, that Serbia was obligated to cooperate with the ICTY and transfer to the court all those who had been indicted by it but were still hiding in Serbia or Republika Srpska within Bosnia-Herzegovina.

International humanitarian law

Applicable law is a critical issue in considering possible responses and individual criminal accountability for the crimes committed in the former Yugoslavia. Determining what international humanitarian law applies is complex, because the conflicts and abuses that occurred in the context of the breakup of the state require determining whether, at any given time, the conflict was internal or international. As is discussed in Chapter 4, under conventional and customary international law, particularly the **Geneva Conventions** of 1949 and their additional protocols of 1977, the characterization of a conflict as internal or international affects whether commission of **grave breaches** (or war crimes) can be considered. The statute of the ICTY, as established by the UN Security Council, included grave breaches of the Geneva Conventions and of customary international humanitarian law, suggesting that the Council viewed the conflict as international. However, at the time of some of the violations in Bosnia-Herzegovina, the independence of breakaway states was being contested internationally; and in the case of Kosovo it was not recognized at all. Thus, grave breaches provisions might not apply where the conflicts are treated as internal. A final obstacle is that if some of the successor states were not internationally recognized during a portion of the conflict, they could not be considered parties to the conventions. However, given that the content of the Geneva Conventions is now considered customary law, key provisions would continue to apply. Should grave breaches provisions apply, potential violations could be found with respect to attacks upon civilians and civilian property.

International human rights law

The situation is clearer with respect to applicable human rights law. Clearly, ***jus cogens*** proscriptions of genocide and torture applied to all participants in the conflicts, even if Serbia and Montenegro were not parties to the relevant conventions at the time of the conflicts. The judgment of the ICJ discussed previously confirms this assessment. Finally, **crimes against humanity** could potentially be identified in these conflicts, as those in both Bosnia-Herzegovina and Kosovo involved widespread and/or systematic attacks upon the civilian population.

However, a further complication was that, regardless of the status of states that had newly declared themselves independent, many of the accused perpetrators were not state officials. The **Torture Convention** criminalizes torture by state officials, creating the possibility that leaders of nonstate political groupings and paramilitary forces, such as Radovan Karadžić and Ratko Mladić, might evade responsibility. These were critical issues to be addressed by the ICTY, as discussed in Chapter 10.

Key points

- The conflicts in the former Yugoslavia have been complex, involving multiple belligerent parties and dissolution of the state.
- The conflicts have involved mass atrocities attributable to both state and nonstate forces.
- The shift from internal to international conflict may affect the applicability of certain international humanitarian law.
- The conflicts have led to the creation of the first international war crimes tribunal since World War II.

Discussion questions

This complex conflict raises critical questions regarding applicable law and appropriate subjects of legal proceedings. The purpose of this discussion is to consider what types of institutions might have been established to address any of the possible crimes identified through the previous discussion, not to discuss the proceedings actually under way in the ICTY (discussed in Chapter 10), nor those conducted before transnational mechanisms elsewhere (discussed in Chapter 11) or before hybrid mechanisms (discussed in Chapter 12). The questions posed here are hypothetical, in the sense that they do not take into account where individuals have actually been charged, or the death of Milošević.

Determining accountability

There may be practical difficulties in identifying specific perpetrators, or when considering prosecution of senior state or nonstate actors; demonstrating their connection to and responsibility for specific events can be problematic. Further, the distinction in international humanitarian law between international and noninternational conflict could affect when war crimes can be said to have occurred, and which actors might be held responsible.

- What law should apply in considering abuses in the former Yugoslavia? Be specific about which human rights treaties and which elements of international humanitarian law apply.
- What specific crimes can be identified, given these bodies of law? Bear in mind whether the conflict was international or noninternational at the time.
- Who might be charged for any of these crimes? Clarify the connections to the potential actors.

Prospects for addressing violations

Selection of institutions

Selecting appropriate institutions for addressing violations can be made more difficult by the fact that the country in which the crimes occurred became several countries, and by the fact that, in the case of Serbia and to a lesser degree Bosnia and Croatia, nationalists still hold significant political power.

- What are the pros and cons of establishing an international tribunal for this situation?
- Could or should domestic prosecutions be pursued in any of the new states emerging from the breakup of Yugoslavia?
- Could the International Criminal Court have jurisdiction over any of the events discussed here?

Balancing human rights and security

Because nationalists continue to hold significant power in successor states to Yugoslavia, attempts to prosecute anyone, and particularly top political leaders, might have the potential to destabilize a fragile peace agreement.

- What potential for disruption was or is present in the prosecutorial pursuit of powerful political figures?
- What charges might be brought, if any, against officials responsible for NATO's bombing campaign?

Dealing with the regional dimension

The breakup of the former Yugoslavia may have regional dimensions in two senses: first, in that an internal armed conflict became an international, regional conflict; and second, in that it had the potential to destabilize the wider Balkans and Europe.

- When would you argue that the conflict became international?
- Are there crimes that cannot be prosecuted because the conflict had not yet become international when those crimes were committed?
- Are some prosecutions likely to be hampered by the dissolution of the state into several states? How or why?

Group exercise

Form two groups. The first group should argue for a strategy of domestic justice, addressing the following questions:

- What are the advantages of domestic justice?
- Which particular events would you address?
- Whom would you hold accountable?
- How would you manage security threats?
- What are the obstacles to applying particular laws?
- How would the elements of prosecutions, **truth commissions**, and vetting work together? What could be the problems?
- How would a lack of regional accountability affect the situation?

The second group should argue for strategy of international justice, addressing the following questions:

- Whom should international justice pursue?
- What are the advantages of international justice?
- What are the challenges of international justice?
- What are the similarities and differences between the conflict in the former Yugoslavia and other situations?

Box 5.6 **Yugoslavia timeline**

1918	Kingdom of Serbs, Croats, and Slovenes created.
1929	Kingdom renamed Yugoslavia.
1945	Yugoslavia becomes a communist nation under the tight control of Josip Broz Tito.
1980	Death of Tito.
1989	Slobodan Milošević becomes president of the Serbian Republic; initiates ultranationalist rhetoric and revision of the Yugoslav constitution to reduce Kosovo's autonomy.
1991	Slovenia and Croatia declare independence.
1992	*January*: Macedonia declares independence; European Union recognizes Croatia.
	April: Bosnia and Herzegovina declare independence; Serbia and Montenegro form the Federal Republic of Yugoslavia with Milošević as leader.
	May: Croatia, Slovenia, and Bosnia-Herzegovina admitted to the United Nations as member states.
1992	UNPROFOR established.
1992–6	Siege of Sarajevo.
1993	International Criminal Tribunal for the Former Yugoslavia created.
1995	Srebrenica massacre.
1995	Dayton Accords signed.
1995	Kosovo Liberation Army formed.
1998–9	Intensified fighting between KLA and counterinsurgency Serb forces deployed by Milošević in Kosovo.
1999	NATO bombing campaign in response to Serb attacks in Kosovo.
2000	Milošević steps down.
2001	*April*: Milošević arrested and charged with corruption, embezzlement, abuse of power.
	June: Milošević handed over to the ICTY.

2003	New state, a federation of Serbia and Montenegro, replaces the former Yugoslavia.
2006	*March*: Milošević dies in ICTY custody.
	May: Montenegro holds a referendum in favor of independence.
	June: Montenegro becomes a UN member.
2008	Kosovo declares independence, and is recognized by 40 states but not made a member of the United Nations.
2008	Radovan Karadžić arrested and handed over to the ICTY.

Further reading

Anthony D'Amato, "Peace vs. Accountability in Bosnia," *American Journal of International Law* 88 (1994): 500–6.

Glenny, Misha, *The Fall of Yugoslavia* (London: Penguin, 1996).

Human Rights Watch annual reports, http://www.hrw.org.

International Crisis Group reports, http://www.crisisweb.org.

Meron, Theodor, "International Criminalization of Internal Atrocities," *American Journal of International Law* 89 (1995): 554–7.

Ramet, Sabrina P., *Thinking About Yugoslavia: Scholarly Debates About the Yugoslav Breakup and the Wars in Bosnia and Kosovo* (Cambridge: Cambridge University Press, 2005).

Rich, Roland, "Recognition of States: The Collapse of Yugoslavia and the Soviet Union," *European Journal of International Law* 14, no. 1 (1993): 36–65.

Shawcross, William, *Deliver Us from Evil: Peacekeepers, Warlords, and a World of Endless Conflict* (New York: Simon and Schuster, 2000): chapters 2 and 6.

Silber, Laura, and Alan Little, *The Death of Yugoslavia* (London: Penguin, 1995).

Official documents and sources

International Court of Justice, *Application of the Convention on the Prevention and Punishment of the Crime of Genocide (Bosnia and Herzegovina v. Serbia and Montenegro)*, Judgment of February 26, 2007, http://www.icj-cij.org/docket/files/91/13685.pdf.

United Nations, *Report of the Secretary-General Pursuant to General Assembly Resolution 53/35: The Fall of Srebrenica* (15 November 1999), UN Doc. A/54/49.

United Nations Department of Peacekeeping Operations sites for UNPROFOR and other related missions, http://www.un.org/depts/dpko/missions.

United States Department of State human rights country reports, http://www.state.gov.

Updated Statute of the International Criminal Tribunal for the Former Yugoslavia (February 2008), http://www.un.org/icty.

6   Sierra Leone

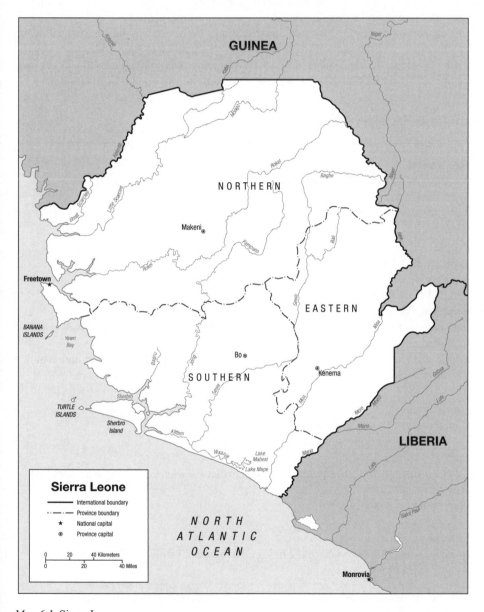

Map 6.1 Sierra Leone

Source: Adapted from the PCL Map Collection, University of Texas Libraries, the University of Texas at Austin, http://www.lib.utexas.edu/maps/africa/sierra_leone_pol_2005.jpg

Overview

The conflict in Sierra Leone resulted in the deaths of tens of thousands, and a significant number of the population fell victim to the worst forms of human rights abuses, with rebel forces using maiming and sexual violence as a central strategy for intimidation of civilians. Fighting commenced in March 1991 and was declared officially ended in 2002, with failed attempts at peace processes in 1991, 1996, and 1999. Not only did several international actors become involved, but there were also regional implications for the conflict, since Liberia played a key role in prolonging the fighting.

This chapter examines the historical underpinnings to the conflict, the sources of human rights violations, and the social and political cleavages that led to such widespread abuses. Chapter 12 presents the legal and institutional responses to the conflict, including the creation of the Special Court for Sierra Leone and the Truth and Reconciliation Commission.

Box 6.1 **Key facts: Sierra Leone**

Geography
Location: West coast of Africa, sharing borders with Guinea and Liberia
Area: 72,325 km²
Natural resources: Diamonds, titanium ore, bauxite, iron ore, gold, chromite

People
Population: 5.1 million
Ethnic groups: Mende 30%, Temne 30%, Creole (Krio) 10%, other ethnic groups including the Limba 30%
Religions: Islam 60%, Christian 10%, indigenous beliefs 30%
Languages: English (official), Temne (north), Mende (south), Krio (English-based Creole)
Literacy: 35.1% (male 46.9%, female 24.4%) age 15 and older can read and write English, Mende, Temne, or Arabic

Government
Country name: Republic of Sierra Leone
Government type: Constitutional democratic republic
Capital: Freetown
Administrative territorial divisions: Three provinces: eastern, northern, southern; and the western area
Independence: April 27, 1961

Economy
Gross domestic product: US$5.452 billion, per capita US$900

Source: Central Intelligence Agency, *World Factbook*, Sierra Leone country profile, https://www.cia.gov/library/publications/the-world-factbook/geos/sl.html (last accessed December 2008).

Background to the conflict

Postcolonial turmoil

Sierra Leone gained independence from Britain in 1961 and subsequently entered a period of great political unrest, with attempts at democratic multiparty elections resulting in successive coups and one-party government rule. The Sierra Leone People's Party (SLPP) formed the first postcolonial government, from 1961 to 1967. The SLPP was supported primarily by the Mende, from the south of the country, while the opposition party, the All People's Congress (APC), was supported primarily by the Limba and Temne, from the north. Following the victory of the APC in the 1967 elections, the SLPP refused to concede its position. Siaka Stevens, the leader of the APC, was deposed by a military coup immediately following the elections, but was able to take his position as head of state in 1968 when another military coup was staged to support him. These events set a precedent for future undermining of democratic processes and paved the way for a pattern of military intervention and the weakening of state institutions.

Stevens neglected the apparatus of the state and relied instead on patronage networks to consolidate his power, culminating in the enactment of a new constitution that established Sierra Leone as a one-party state in 1978. During this period, Stevens ensured that the Limba and Temne were favored both in government and in the security forces, somewhat worsening ethnic relations. Under Stevens's leadership, accountability and transparency were progressively eroded, and the general public eventually became resigned to widespread corruption in government. Stevens's approach had far-reaching influence, filtering down to regional and local levels. After 19 years in power, in August 1985 Stevens stood down and handed power to General Joseph Momoh. Momoh's corrupt rule led to economic collapse, with a declaration in 1987 of a state of economic emergency. The combination of Momoh's and Stevens's leadership undermined the country's economic development following independence, with Sierra Leone consistently ranking at the bottom of the Human Development Index since the **United Nations** (UN) introduced the index in 1990.

Emergence of the Revolutionary United Front

The Revolutionary United Front (RUF), led by Foday Sankoh, initiated a rebellion in March 1991 that led to a civil war lasting over a decade. The RUF claimed to be fighting to bring down the corrupt government, espousing a populist agenda that also aimed at igniting pan-African revolution. The RUF received critical support from Liberian fighters due to Sankoh's connections with Liberian warlord Charles Taylor, who had initiated a civil war in Liberia in 1989 to overthrow Major Samuel Doe. Taylor sought to punish Sierra Leone for participating in the 1990 intervention by the Economic Community of West African States Monitoring Group (ECOMOG) against his rebellion. It was widely believed that supporting the RUF was his means of retaliation. This backing also ensured supplies of arms in addition to fighters. With this support, the initial RUF attack comprised two contingents, one entering eastern Sierra Leone and the other entering the southwest of the country. The RUF initially gained control of the eastern province of Kailahun and the region of Kono, where many diamond mines were located. The fighting would continue for the next ten years, with the war intensifying in the south and east of the country and even reaching the capital, Freetown.

Meanwhile, the impact of mismanagement and corruption by both Stevens's and Momoh's regimes paved the way for removal of Momoh by the Sierra Leone Army (SLA), driven by its own grievances. Angered by a lack of pay and medical treatment, the junior officers of the SLA staged a military uprising in April 1992. Following the coup, Momoh fled to Guinea, and Captain Valentine Strasser was elected head of the National Provisional Ruling Council (NPRC), the name taken by the military junta. Strasser had been part of the Sierra Leonean contingent of ECOMOG that fought against Taylor in Liberia, and had been subsequently dispatched in 1991 to fight the RUF. His initial promises included the defeat of the RUF, an end to corruption, and the return of the country to civilian rule.

The NPRC was unable to defeat the RUF, and also failed to successfully restructure and organize the army. The years of neglect under Stevens and Momoh had severely weakened the military, which suffered from depletion, numbering about 3,000 troops, as well as low morale. Strasser increased recruitment, resulting in the army's expansion to an official number of 17,000 troops by 1996. However, it is not possible to confirm this estimate, since there was no accounting or census system in place. Strasser's attempt to expand the army was inadequate, however, with the SLA still ill-equipped to prevent RUF advances. Moreover, due to the rushed recruitment process the caliber of soldiers was low, and the army increasingly colluded with the RUF at the expense of the civilian population.

During this period the RUF developed its practice of targeting and terrorizing the civilian population, which was to become a cornerstone of its strategy. The NPRC was able to advance against the RUF only by hiring the South Africa-based private military company Executive Outcomes (EO) in April 1995. EO succeeded in pushing back the RUF to Sierra Leone's borders and, amid this conflict, the Bintumani Conference set the dates for the presidential and legislative elections to be held the following year. The Bintumani conference was a consultative forum for the active civil society groups that were pressing for the elections, with political representatives also participating. In January 1996, Brigadier-General Julius Maada Bio ousted Strasser as head of the NPRC following Strasser's insistence that he be nominated for the presidential election. Due to the success of EO, the RUF agreed to a cease-fire in January 1996 and the presidential election was held in February and March. The election was won by SLPP candidate and former UN official Ahmad Tejan Kabbah.

Peace talks between the RUF and the government began in April 1996 and culminated in the signing of a peace agreement in November in Abidjan, Côte d'Ivoire. Negotiations over the presence of EO and foreign troops were particularly difficult. The government finally conceded that EO would leave the country, at the RUF's request. The departure of EO proved to be instrumental in changing the balance of military power, and the RUF's retreat was short-lived. The Abidjan peace process broke down, with each side accusing the other of breaching the cease-fire. A key development at this point was the arrest of Sankoh by Nigerian authorities in Lagos for illegal possession of weapons. He was placed under house arrest until July 1998 while his field commanders in Sierra Leone ensured that RUF attacks continued.

President Kabbah mobilized traditional Mende hunters known as the Kamajors to defend their communities, and these local militia formed the basis of the Civil Defense Forces (CDF), which fought against the RUF. The CDF achieved some gains in their campaign against the RUF, but their limited victories were insufficient to secure Kabbah's personal position as president. There was still concern in the SLA over lack of provisions, as well as fear over the SLA's future under a civilian government. With the security situation in the country precarious due to the departure of EO, Kabbah was overthrown in a military coup on May 25, 1997, and went into exile. Paul Koroma was declared leader of the Armed Forces Revolutionary Council (AFRC) and claimed that the AFRC's goal was to restore peace and political stability following a lack of "commitment" from President Kabbah. Following the coup, a nine-month struggle for control in Freetown led to a large-scale evacuation of the international community and foreigners, and the exile of thousands of Sierra Leoneans.

Koroma invited the RUF to join a coalition government in June 1997, and the **rule of law** completely collapsed under the AFRC/RUF junta, which was never recognized as legitimate by either the population or the international community. Eventually, after a failed attempt at negotiation in which the AFRC/RUF junta reneged on a promise to restore Kabbah to power in October 1997, ECOMOG forces (Nigerian forces acting under a regional Economic Community of West African States [ECOWAS] mandate) were dispatched to Freetown. In the same month, sanctions were imposed under a **UN Security Council resolution**, Resolution 1132, aimed at preventing the supply of petrol and arms to the country and calling on the military junta to relinquish power to the democratically elected government. The pressure of sanctions encouraged the AFRC/RUF junta to sign the Conakry Accords, in which it agreed to a process of disarmament and demobilization by the end of the year and the eventual return of Kabbah. However, the RUF failed to comply with the disarmament process outlined within the accords, continuing to bring arms into Sierra Leone from Liberia and carrying out attacks on ECOMOG troops. In response, ECOMOG began a full offensive in February 1998 and finally ousted the AFRC and forced the RUF to retreat. On March 10, Kabbah returned to Freetown as president, and the following week the UN embargo was lifted.

Box 6.2 **Key players in Sierra Leone**

Political parties
APC: All People's Congress
SLPP: Sierra Leone People's Party

Individuals
Ahmad Tejan Kabbah: SLPP candidate who won the February 1996 Presidential elections.
Paul Koroma: Leader of the AFRC, which deposed Kabbah in a military coup.
Milton Margai: Prime minister after the SLPP won the first elections since independence.
Joseph Momoh: Elected president in 1985 in a one-candidate election.
Sam Hinga Norman: Leader of the CDF. Died in 2007.
Foday Sankoh: Head of the RUF.
Siaka Stevens: Leader of the APC. Won the 1967 elections to become prime minister in 1968, and became president in 1971 after parliament declared Sierra Leone a republic.
Valentine Strasser: Head of the NPRC, the military junta that ruled following the coup against Momoh.
Charles Taylor: Liberian warlord who became president of Liberia in 1997. Supported the RUF since 1991.

Countries
Liberia: Provided support to the RUF through the actions of Charles Taylor.

Armed groups
AFRC: Armed Forces Revolutionary Council. A group of soldiers from the SLA who overthrew the government in 1999.
CDF: Civil Defense Forces. Assisted the government in fighting against the RUF.
Kamajors: Traditional Mende hunters who formed part of the CDF.
RUF: Revolutionary United Front. Started the civil war, and was invited to join the coalition government with the AFRC in 1997.

National armies
SLA: Sierra Leone Army.

International and regional missions
ECOMOG: Economic Community of West African States Monitoring Group. Majority of troops provided by Nigeria.
UNAMSIL: UN Mission in Sierra Leone. Expanded peacekeeping mission.
UNOMSIL: UN Observer Mission in Sierra Leone.

Other actors
Executive Outcomes: South African private military company hired by the NPRC to defend against the RUF.

Widespread AFRC and RUF atrocities

The RUF was nonetheless not defeated, and committed mass human rights abuses as it fled. The atrocities continued as the RUF turned to guerrilla tactics and carried out attacks on villages in the northern part of the country. Several waves of attacks were carried out by AFRC/RUF forces targeting civilians at random in order to induce absolute terror in the provinces. A systematic campaign of abuse and attack named Operation No Living Thing was initiated by the RUF in April 1998 and continued through the rest of the year. Despite the presence of ECOMOG forces in Freetown, enabling a level of security in the capital and the south of the country, atrocities continued in the northern province and the eastern province.

A factor in the continuing attacks was the trial of Foday Sankoh, following his return from house arrest in Nigeria. Although he appeared on television and called upon the RUF to stop hostilities against the civilian population, the RUF did not follow his orders, questioning whether Sankoh's statement had been coerced. Following a short trial in October 1998, Sankoh was sentenced to death after convictions on seven of nine counts of treason. However, this sentence was never carried out, as Sankoh was of greater use to the government alive during the peace process.

ECOMOG and the CDF (primarily the Kamajors) were unable to defeat the AFRC/RUF forces and prevent the violence from reaching Freetown. In January 1999 an AFRC/RUF offensive was able to break through ECOMOG defenses and capture some areas of the city, with particularly heavy attacks occurring in eastern Freetown. Civilians were specifically targeted, with killings, random amputations, and rapes widespread. Thousands of people were made homeless in Freetown and thousands more fled Sierra Leone to become refugees in neighboring countries. Although the AFRC/RUF forces were finally pushed back, the retreat was marked by the now familiar pattern of human rights abuses and abduction of thousands of civilians as fighting continued for control of towns in the northern province and the eastern province.

Peace agreements and human rights

In the context of this military standoff, under international pressure Kabbah and the RUF signed a peace agreement in Lomé in July 1999 following a cease-fire in May. Sankoh had been permitted to travel to Lomé in March to negotiate the terms of the agreement. Under Article 3 of the Lomé Agreement, the RUF would be allowed to organize itself as a political party. In addition, Article 9 (see Box 6.3) granted Sankoh and all combatants and collaborators "absolute and free pardon," and guaranteed them immunity from prosecution.

Box 6.3 The Lomé Agreement, Article 9

Pardon and amnesty

1. In order to bring lasting peace to Sierra Leone, the Government of Sierra Leone shall take appropriate legal steps to grant Corporal Foday Sankoh absolute and free pardon.
2. After the signing of the present Agreement, the Government of Sierra Leone shall also grant absolute and free pardon and reprieve to all combatants and collaborators in respect of anything done by them in pursuit of their objectives, up to the time of the signing of the present Agreement.
3. To consolidate the peace and promote the cause of national reconciliation, the Government of Sierra Leone shall ensure that no official or judicial action is taken against any member of the RUF/SL, ex-AFRC, ex-SLA or CDF in respect of anything done by them in pursuit of their objectives as members of those organisations, since March 1991, up to the time of the signing of the present Agreement. In addition, legislative and other measures necessary to guarantee immunity to former combatants, exiles and other persons, currently outside the country for reasons related to the armed conflict shall be adopted ensuring the full exercise of their civil and political rights, with a view to their reintegration within a framework of full legality.

In addition to the pardon, the agreement also, in Article 7, made Sankoh vice president of the country and board chairman of the Commission for the Management of Strategic Resources, National Reconstruction, and Development. The agreement further outlined establishment of the Commission for the Consolidation of Peace, to which Koroma was appointed chairman, and provided for creation of the Truth and Reconciliation Commission. However, the international community found the **amnesty** clause of article 9 (Box 6.3) unacceptable. The United Nations made a reservation to the agreement stating that amnesty could not cover international crimes.

The Lomé Agreement also called on the **UN Security Council** to expand the mandate of the UN Observer Mission in Sierra Leone (UNOMSIL) beyond its limited monitoring role. This provision came in part from the desire of ECOWAS, and particularly Nigeria as the primary troop contributor, to withdraw. The UN Mission in Sierra Leone (UNAMSIL) was established on October 22, 1999, by UN Security Council Resolution 1270 under Chapter VI of the **UN Charter**. UNAMSIL was a much larger **peacekeeping** mission, and its responsibilities for supporting the peace process included assisting in the disarmament, demobilization, and reintegration (DDR) of ex-combatants, monitoring the cease-fire, facilitating humanitarian assistance, and providing support to the elections.

However, despite the detailed provisions and optimism created by the Lomé Agreement, there were successive problems in implementation. RUF and AFRC forces consistently violated the cease-fire and continued to inflict human rights abuses, including sexual violence, in the north and eastern areas of the country under their control. It was clear that the RUF would negotiate only when under military pressure, and did not truly intend to cooperate. The appointment of Sankoh to the Strategic Mineral Resources Commission did not provide the RUF with any incentive to maintain peace, because he already had significant control over diamond-mining regions.

Although the Security Council resolution initially provided for 6,000 UNAMSIL personnel, a second resolution provided for an increase of this number to 11,000 in February 2000 and finally to 13,000 in May 2000. However, provision for troops in a Security Council resolution does not mean that they are immediately deployed to the field. By May 2000, only 8,700 troops had arrived. Collapse of the peace process occurred in the same month when the RUF took 500 members of UNAMSIL hostage, leading to a renewal of the conflict and intensification of human rights abuses.

UNAMSIL numbers were increased following this incident, and British troops were dispatched to calm the situation and secure the capital. In a strange turn of events, Foday Sankoh was captured in May 2000 after being recognized by a civilian and placed in British custody. This presented the government of Sierra Leone with the challenge of deciding what to do with him. It ultimately requested the creation of a **war crimes** tribunal, which was approved by the UN Security Council in Resolution 1315. As discussed in Chapter 12, the Special Court for Sierra Leone, a **hybrid tribunal**, was created by bilateral agreement between the government and the United Nations.

A cease-fire was negotiated between the government and the RUF in November 2000 in Abuja (Abuja Agreement I; see Box 6.4), with both parties agreeing to recommence the DDR program immediately. The cease-fire was initially successful, but the RUF continued to engage in human rights abuses. Fighting spread to Guinea, threatening regional stability. A second agreement was signed in May 2001 (Abuja Agreement II), urging simultaneous disarmament of CDF and RUF forces, and withdrawal of RUF combatants from the area that cross-border attacks were coming from. Notably, the agreement did not address the issue of the Lomé amnesty or future juridical accountability. However, although the DDR process was initiated immediately and did succeed in demobilizing child soldiers, fighting and human rights abuses continued through August 2001. Following completion of the disarmament and demobilization, the conflict was declared ended and the state of emergency was lifted. Sankoh and other RUF members who had been in custody were charged with a variety of crimes by the Special Court for Sierra Leone in 2003. CDF combatants were considered heroes due to their role alongside the British troops and UNAMSIL in the defeat of the AFRC/RUF forces, and due to their overall role during the entire conflict. The leader of the CDF, Samuel Hinga Norman, retained a significant following among the population.

Box 6.4 **Abuja Agreement I, selected articles**

THE GOVERNMENT OF SIERRA LEONE AND RUF,

Reaffirming their determination to establish sustainable peace, stability and security in Sierra Leone;

Also reaffirming their commitment to the Lomé Peace Agreement of 7 July 1999 as the framework for the restoration of genuine and lasting peace to the country . . .

HEREBY AGREE AS FOLLOWS:

1. To declare and observe a cease-fire and to halt hostilities with effect from Friday 10th November 2000 starting at 23:59 hours.
2. The parties agree to refrain from committing any acts or carrying out any activities that might constitute or facilitate a violation of the cease-fire.
3. They agree that the United Nations Mission in Sierra Leone shall supervise and monitor the cease-fire. The United Nations Mission in Sierra Leone shall also investigate and report on any acts of cease-fire violation.
4. Both parties agree that UNAMSIL shall have full liberty to deploy its troops and other personnel throughout Sierra Leone including the diamond producing areas in the discharge of its responsibilities.
5. The parties undertake, with a view to restoring the authority of the Government throughout the entire territory of Sierra Leone, to ensure free movement of persons and goods, unimpeded movement of humanitarian agencies, and of refugees and displaced persons.
6. The RUF commits itself to the immediate return of all weapons, ammunitions and other equipment seized by the RUF.
7. The two parties agree to recommence immediately the Disarmament, Demobilisation and Reintegration Programme.

Done at Abuja this 10th Day of November, 2000

A refugee resettlement program began, and the RUF transformed itself into a political party to prepare for elections in May 2002, during which Kabbah was reelected president with 70 percent of the vote. The DDR program was finally completed in February 2004, six years after the government of Sierra Leone had established the National Committee for Disarmament, Demobilization, and Reintegration. The Truth and Reconciliation Commission, authorized in the 1999 Lomé Agreement, began operating in July 2002, and the Special Court for Sierra Leone was established a month later. The Special Court and the relationship between it and the Truth and Reconciliation Commission are discussed in Chapter 12.

Human rights violations in Sierra Leone

Human rights violations as underlying causes of conflict

Although human rights violations such as social and economic deprivation often act as triggers to conflict, in Sierra Leone there were two further dimensions of human rights abuses that fueled the civil war. Human rights abuses were used to strengthen the RUF, which engaged in forced recruitment and abduction, particularly of child soldiers, and terrorized the civilian population into joining the hostilities. This method perpetuated the conflict and ensured that even though the RUF lacked popular support, it had a sizable membership. Further, combatants fleeing accountability for human rights violations in neighboring countries joined the RUF.

Forced recruitment of children and other forms of coercion

Beginning 1999 there was much international reporting on the plight of child soldiers in Sierra Leone's civil war. The RUF recruited a great number of children at the beginning of the war in order to increase its numbers, and this pattern continued as it gained control over further territories, even after the signing of the Lomé Agreement, which did not provide for the demobilization of children. According to UN statistics, a total of 6,845 child soldiers were demobilized following the end of the war in 2002. However, it is unlikely that this figure represents the true number of child soldiers involved in the conflict. Further, due to the length of the conflict, many who were younger than age 16 at the time of recruitment were demobilized as adults at the end of the war. The recruitment itself was a traumatic process, with children as young as 8 being abducted. Human rights groups have documented that the RUF forced the abductees to commit atrocities, often in their home villages, so they could not return. The RUF also forced them to take drugs. These child recruits then underwent military training, and both perpetrated and witnessed many atrocities against civilians.

The RUF used terror tactics to coerce many, both children and adults, into joining the front, through threats that mutilation and other abuses would be committed against family members. The overwhelming success of the RUF's terror tactics is demonstrated by the fact that only 10 percent of fighters indicated that they joined the front for political reasons. This was clearly not a situation in which human rights abuses by other actors generated rebel support. Rather, rebels themselves perpetuated a climate of fear to aid recruitment.

Regional fighters and accountability

Although many regional fighters joined the RUF due to bribery or coercion by fear, there were also fighters who had committed gross human rights abuses in their own countries and joined the conflict to flee accountability. These fighters traveled across West Africa as mercenaries, fueling conflict in Liberia, Sierra Leone, and Côte d'Ivoire. Even after peace was established in Sierra Leone, the existence of these mercenaries led to fears that many fighters would not disarm. Rather, there was speculation that they had simply gone to other countries and would return to fight if offered proper inducements.

Abuses causing resentment

Although the Temne and Limba were dominant in government and security forces under Stevens's rule, ethnic divisions were not the basis for conflict. Ethnic relations were strained, and ethnic balance in the government and army was an important consideration after the favoritism of northerners. However, the RUF did not seek support on the grounds of ethnic discrimination. Rather, it cited corruption and poor governance by Sierra Leone's leaders since independence to initially justify its actions. The country's low ranking on the UN Human Development Index, despite its mineral wealth, indicates the level of control that a narrow elite had established over power, governance, and material wealth since 1961. The social and economic deprivation caused resentment, allowing the RUF to initially gain support in its claim that the government was corrupt and needed to be brought down. The lack of free elections, coupled with deprivation and discrimination, also enabled the RUF to claim that it was fighting on behalf of the general population. However, although these abuses of rights by successive governments did take place, support for the RUF on these issues quickly disappeared once it began to target civilians. The majority of fighters were recruited through fear or greed.

Human rights violations during the conflict

While the majority of human rights violations during the civil war in Sierra Leone can be attributed to the RUF, all parties to the conflict perpetrated abuses, and systematic, indiscriminate attacks on civilians were frequent.

Sierra Leone's Truth and Reconciliation Commission classified violations into sixteen categories: amputation, forced cannibalism, abduction, forced recruitment, sexual slavery, drugging, forced labor, assault, **torture**, rape, arbitrary detention, looting and destruction of property, extortion, forced displacement, killing, and cannibalism. Although all parties did commit human rights violations, not all groups necessarily committed all categories of abuses. RUF and AFRC forces, however, committed all of these types of abuses at various points, and at varying levels of intensity, during the ten-year conflict.

Until 1997 the RUF was responsible for most of the violations through tactics developed specifically to provoke fear in civilians. As discussed, the RUF undertook forced recruitment and abduction, followed by a cruel and violent training and initiation process. Its campaign of terror throughout the countryside included deliberate mutilation and sexual violence, as well as indiscriminate brutal killings and burning and looting. The viciousness of mutilations, including against children and elderly people, was used deliberately to punish those who were unwilling to cooperate with the RUF. In addition, rape and sexual violence directed at women and girls were frequent in RUF operations, and many girls were abducted as "wives" for the rebels.

However, the SLA also carried out serious abuses. In fact, significant numbers of Sierra Leonean army soldiers colluded with the RUF rebels and were financed by "blood diamond" trade. This blurring of lines between the RUF rebels and the supposed government soldiers engendered the phenomenon known as "sobels" – soldiers by day, rebels by night. The CDF, mobilized by Kabbah against the RUF, also inducted child soldiers and executed rebels.

The scale of human rights violations increased following the AFRC coup in May 1997. Once the AFRC invited the RUF into the government, arrests, torture, and killings increased, as well as repression of the press and use of the death penalty. After the AFRC/RUF military junta was finally ousted, it rampaged through the countryside carrying out widespread rape, mutilation, and amputation under Operation No Living Thing and Operation Pay Yourself. Although these violations had been occurring for over eight years, the abuses increased and became more systematic under the AFRC/RUF junta. In January 1999 this campaign of terror finally reached Freetown, when AFRC/RUF forces broke through ECOMOG defenses.

The AFRC/RUF junta committed atrocities targeting both civilians and military forces. Reports from nongovernmental organizations detail mutilations of children and adults, with junta forces even cutting off their limbs; only a few victims managed to reach medical assistance, and no mercy was shown to children or the elderly. A large number of abductions were carried out, and rape and other forms of sexual violence were widespread. There was rampant destruction of property during the fighting, with many victims fleeing abroad. The Truth and Reconciliation Commission attributes about two-thirds of the abuses carried out from 1997 until the end of the conflict to AFRC/RUF forces.

ECOMOG forces and government troops also committed abuses throughout the conflict, and some civilians engaged in extrajudicial killings as well. Some Nigerian troops in ECOMOG have been accused of rape, looting, and heavy involvement in the diamond trade. During the attack on Freetown in January 1999, rebels and rebel collaborators were summarily executed by ECOMOG forces, members of the CDF, and the Sierra Leonean police. Reports document that the majority of executions, including of women and children, were carried out by ECOMOG. Through the duration of the conflict, government, CDF, and ECOMOG forces were known to beat noncombatants. Government and ECOMOG forces occasionally arrested and detained persons arbitrarily; prison and jail conditions were harsh, sometimes resulting in the death of detainees. In addition, the malfunctioning judicial system caused long delays in trials and consequently prolonged detention. Other abusive actions by the government included restrictions on freedom of speech and the press and harassment and detention of journalists.

After the Lomé Agreement, abuses continued in areas under RUF control, particularly sexual violence against women and girls, who were abducted and enslaved. These abuses increased when fighting broke out again in May 2000. In September the RUF attacked refugee camps in Guinea, in collaboration with Liberian forces, which resulted in Guinean security forces retaliating against the Sierra Leonean refugees. The refugees had fled the conflict only to suffer further abuses in Guinea. Despite the signing of the Abuja Agreements, abuses such as rape, murder, and abduction persisted as fighting continued between the RUF and the CDF in the east of the country from June until August 2001. The RUF was reluctant during this period to release female child combatants, as required under the second Abuja agreement.

The human rights situation improved steadily throughout 2001 until January 2002, when the conflict was declared ended after successful disarmament and demobilization. On January 18 a symbolic burning of weapons took place during an official ceremony to mark the conclusion of the disarmament process, and President Kabbah declared a formal end to the war.

Applicable law and possible subjects of legal accountability

International humanitarian law

Sierra Leone ratified the **Geneva Conventions** in 1965. It is clear that abuses committed during the civil war are in violation of at least two of the conventions. The RUF's targeting of civilians contravenes the Fourth Geneva Convention (Convention Relative to the Protection of Civilian Persons in Time of War), and its torture and killing of combatants violates the Third Geneva Convention (Convention Relative to the Treatment of Prisoners of War). The case could easily be made for violation of specific articles, such as Articles 33–34, which prohibit pillage, destruction of property, and the taking of hostages, and Articles 32 and 13, which protect civilians from murder, torture, or brutality. However, as outlined in Chapter 4, merely violating conventions does not create individual criminal accountability, which only comes from **grave breaches** of the conventions. There is a challenge in terming clear violations of the Geneva Conventions in Sierra Leone "war crimes," because formally the civil war is defined as a noninternational armed conflict.

Nonetheless, **Common Article 3** of the Geneva Conventions does apply to noninternational conflicts, and acts that it prohibits were clearly committed. Violations of this article include violence, murder, cruel treatment and torture, taking of hostages, humiliating and degrading treatment, and sentencing and execution without judgment by a regularly constituted court. While acts by all sides may have contravened Common Article 3, these are not war crimes and therefore are not automatically subject to international criminal accountability. However, the government of Sierra Leone acceded to Additional Protocols I and II of the Geneva Conventions in October 1986. The violations committed by both the government and nonstate armed rebel groups are covered under Additional Protocol II. Thus, combatants in Sierra Leone's conflict are still subject to this protocol and are bound to its standards of behavior.

Additional Protocol II includes several key provisions. Article 4 provides for fundamental guarantees, ensuring humane treatment of civilians and prohibiting murder, torture, collective punishments, hostage-taking, humiliating and degrading treatment, rape, enforced prostitution, and pillage. Particularly relevant to the conflict in Sierra Leone is the prohibition of recruitment of children younger than age 15. Article 5 provides further protection for persons whose liberty has been restricted. Article 6 articulates procedures and limitations on penal prosecutions for acts relating to armed conflict. However, these provisions do not criminalize violation of the protections they enumerate, nor commission of acts they prohibit. Thus, in internal armed conflicts neither the Geneva Conventions nor the provisions of Additional Protocol II provide for individualized criminal accountability such as would be available were the conflict international and had grave breaches been committed.

Nevertheless, there are two arguments that might be made to justify prosecuting war crimes committed in Sierra Leone under existing law. It could be argued that under customary law some acts may have constituted war crimes even though the conflict was internal. These would include intentionally directing attacks against the civilian population and child enlistment. Further, it could be argued that the actions of the President of Liberia, Charles Taylor, internationalized the conflict.

International human rights law

Torture was widespread in Sierra Leone. Even though the country did not ratify the **Torture Convention** until 2001, prohibition against torture is enshrined in international customary law as a *jus cogens* norm. **Genocide** is also clearly prosecutable under international law; however, it is unlikely that the indiscriminate attacks on the civilian population could be defined as genocide, since there is relatively little evidence of ethnic bias, or intent to target a specific group. Although there were some ethnically directed killings, particularly of ethnic groups associated with specific political groups, these appear to have been small-scale and tribal and retaliatory rather than systematic or driven by intent to wipe out an entire ethnic group.

Key points

- The civil war in Sierra Leone lasted over a decade and also included a regional dimension through the intervention of Liberia and the involvement of mercenaries.

- Civilians were systematically targeted and atrocities included the recruitment and use of child soldiers and the abduction of "wives."
- Although the Revolutionary United Front carried out the majority of abuses, all sides to the conflict were involved in human rights violations; even so, the public perceived the Civil Defense Forces as heroes for defending the government against the RUF.
- The peace process comprised a number of failed agreements, including a controversial provision granting combatants amnesty.

Discussion questions

This section will examine the possibilities for holding perpetrators accountable and problems that existed for **peacebuilding** in Sierra Leone. We will consider the range of possible negotiation and accountability options without reference to the decisions actually made. The Special Court for Sierra Leone, a **hybrid tribunal**, was ultimately established and will be dicussed in Chapter 12.

Determining accountability

There are practical problems in identifying perpetrators, further hindered by the Sierra Leonean population's complex perception of the "good" and "bad" sides of the conflict.

- What strategies would be most suitable for dealing with human rights abuses committed by the CDF (such as recruitment of child soldiers)? What about the abuses committed by ECOMOG?
- Would prosecution of an individual such as Samuel Hinga Norman, leader of the CDF (who died in 2007), pose any risks to the peace process?
- Should low-level perpetrators be held accountable, or is it more effective to concentrate on the highest in command?

Prospects for addressing violations

Selection of institutions

The selection of appropriate institutions of accountability is challenging. Peace negotiators, and both domestic and international actors, face significant challenges when considering possible modes of accountability.

- What is the capacity of the Sierra Leonean court system to prosecute RUF members?
- What is the potential impact of locating the Special Court for Sierra Leone, as established by Security Council Resolution 1315, within the country rather than in a "neutral" country?
- How should the Truth and Reconciliation Commission (as provided in the Lomé Agreement) and the Special Court for Sierra Leone function together? What challenges might result?

Balancing human rights and security

The concept of defining the "rebels" and "heroes" in a conflict is intertwined with the broader issue of security in the country. In any postconflict situation the security of the country is paramount, and prosecutions could be seen as undermining the peace process.

- Was the inclusion of amnesty essential in ensuring that combatants would actually stop fighting and demobilize, or could it have been more limited than the "absolute and free pardon" offered?
- In light of the failure of the Lomé Agreement, what might be discerned about the motivations of the RUF? What else could have been offered to the rebel forces?
- Who has the authority to represent groups during **peace negotiations**, and how should this be decided?

Dealing with the regional dimension

When considering the conflict in Sierra Leone, it is important to recognize the specific challenges posed by regional implications.

- Should Charles Taylor be immune to prosecution for acts he committed while president of Liberia?
- With the disappearance of lower-level perpetrators across borders, which other countries could the Sierra Leonean peace and accountability processes affect?
- When conflict in a region is as intertwined as it has been in West Africa, can the issues of human rights accountability or peace negotiations be dealt with on a country-by-country basis?

Group exercise

Form two groups. One group should deem international justice as the only way to achieve accountability; the other group should deem domestic justice to be more legitimate. Debate the regional implications of the conflict in Sierra Leone, as well as the wishes of the population.

Box 6.5 **Sierra Leone timeline**

1961	Sierra Leone gains independence from Britain and SLPP forms first post-colonial government.
1967	APC victorious in elections. APC leader Siaka Stevens immediately deposed by military coup.
1968	Stevens able to take his position as head of state after another military coup.

1978	New constitution establishing Sierra Leone as a one-party state.
1985	Stevens hands power to General Joseph Momoh.
1987	Declaration of economic emergency.
1991	RUF, led by Foday Sankoh, starts rebellion against government.
1992	Military coup deposes Momoh. Captain Valentine Strasser elected head of NPRC.
1995	Arrival of Executive Outcomes from South Africa to push back RUF.
1996	*January*: Military coup forces Strasser to step down. *February*: SLPP candidate Ahmad Tejan Kabbah wins presidential election. *November*: Abidjan peace agreement signed.
1997	*May*: Kabbah overthrown in coup. *May*: Paul Koroma declared leader of AFRC. *June*: AFRC invites RUF to form coalition government. *October*: UN sanctions imposed, ECOMOG forces dispatched. *October*: Conakry Accords signed.
1998	*February*: Full offensive by ECOMOG drives out AFRC/RUF; retreating rebels commit massive human rights abuses.
1999	*January*: AFRC/RUF offensive captures parts of Freetown; widespread human rights abuses ensue, with fighting and atrocities on both sides. *May*: Cease-fire. *July*: Kabbah and RUF sign peace agreement. *October*: UNAMSIL established.
2000	*May*: 500 UNAMSIL troops taken hostage. *May*: British troops arrive. *May*: Foday Sankoh captured. *November*: Cease-fire agreement.
2001	*May*: Second Abuja agreement signed; DDR process begins. *August*: Presidential and parliamentary elections postponed.
2002	*January*: Declaration of end of war. *May*: Kabbah reelected president.

Further reading

Hirsch, John, *Sierra Leone: Diamonds and the Struggle for Democracy* (Boulder: Lynne Rienner, 2001).

International Crisis Group, "Sierra Leone: The State of Security and Governance" (September 2, 2003), http://www.crisisgroup.org/library/documents/report_archive/a401113_02092003.pdf.

———, "Sierra Leone: Time for a New Military and Political Strategy" (April 11, 2001), http://www.crisisgroup.org/library/documents/report_archive/a400278_11042001.pdf.

Pugh, Michael, and Neil Cooper, with Jonathan Goodhand, *War Economies in Regional Context* (Boulder: Lynne Rienner 2004), chap. 4, "Sierra Leone in West Africa."

Reno, William, *Warlord Politics and African States* (Boulder: Lynne Rienner, 1999).

Sriram, Chandra Lekha, and Zoe Nielsen, eds., *Exploring Subregional Conflict: Opportunities for Conflict Prevention* (Boulder: Lynne Rienner, 2005), chap. 3.

Official documents and sources

Abuja Ceasefire Accord (Abuja Agreement 1), 10 November 2000, http://www.daco-sl.org/encyclopedia/8_lib/8_3/gov/PeaceAccords/Abuja.pdf.

Peace Agreement between the Government of Sierra Leone and the Revolutionary United Front of Sierra Leone (Lomé Agreement), 7 July 1999, http://www.usip.org/library/pa/sl/sierra_leone_07071999_toc.html.

The Final Report of the Truth Commission of Sierra Leone, http://trcsierraleone.org.

United Nations, *Report of the Security Council mission to Sierra Leone* (16 October 2000), UN Doc. S/2000/992.

——, Reports of the Secretary General on UNAMSIL, http://www.un.org/Depts/dpko/missions/unamsil/UnamsilR.htm.

——, Security Council Resolution 1270 (on the establishment of UNAMSIL), (22 October 1999), UN Doc. S/RES/1270.

——, Security Council Resolution 1315 (on the establishment of a special court), (14 August 2000), UN Doc. S/RES/1315.

United Nations Mission in Sierra Leone (UNAMSIL), http://www.un.org/Depts/dpko/missions/unamsil/index.html.

United Nations Observer Mission in Sierra Leone (UNOMSIL), http://www.un.org/Depts/DPKO/Missions/unomsil/Unomsil.htm.

7 The Democratic Republic of Congo

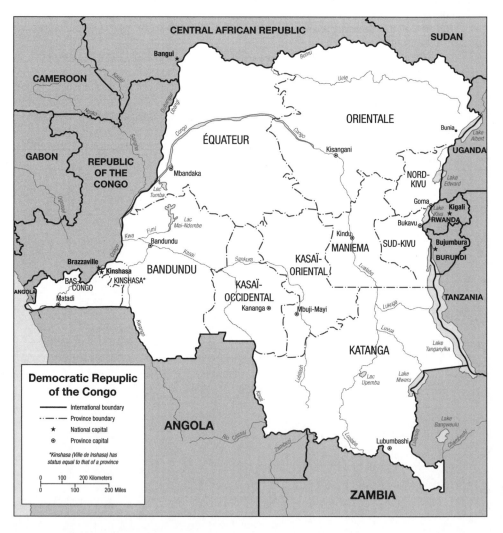

Map 7.1 Democratic Republic of Congo

Source: Adapted from the PCL Map Collection, University of Texas Libraries, the University of Texas at Austin, http://www.lib.utexas.edu/maps/africa/congo_demrep_pol98.jpg.

Overview

The conflict in the Democratic Republic of Congo (DRC), which began in 1996, has been among the bloodiest in recent history. It is also a particularly complex one, comprising several African countries, numerous rebel armed groups, and the pursuit of important economic interests by every party involved, including powerful multinational corporations. Local and regional conflicts did not end after the peace agreements of 2002, and violence still continues in parts of the country, particularly in the east. This chapter examines the historical background of the conflict, human rights violations as both causes and consequences, the **international humanitarian law** and **international human rights law** applicable to the abuses committed, and prospects for accountability. Chapter 13 analyzes in greater depth the international legal processes and institutions designed to address the atrocities committed in the DRC, in particular the prosecutorial activity by the **International Criminal Court** (ICC) in relation to the crimes committed in the Ituri region.

Box 7.1 **Key facts: the Democratic Republic of Congo**

Geography

Location: Central Africa, bordered by the Republic of Congo to the northwest; Central African Republic and Sudan to the north; Uganda, Rwanda, Burundi, and Tanzania to the east; Zambia and Angola to the south

Area: Total area 2,345,410 km², land area 2,267,600 km², water area: 77,810 km²

Natural resources: Cobalt, copper, niobium, tantalum, petroleum, industrial and gem diamonds, gold, silver, zinc, manganese, tin, uranium, coal, hydropower, timber

People

Population: 65,751,512

Ethnic groups: Over 200 African ethnic groups, the majority of which are Bantu; the four largest tribes (composing 45% of the population): Mongo, Luba, and Kongo (all Bantu), and Mangbtu-Azande (Hamitic)

Religions: Roman Catholic 50%, Protestant 20%, Kimbanguist 10%, Muslim 10%, other (including syncretic sects and indigenous beliefs) 10%

Languages: French (official), Lingala (trade), Kingwana (dialect of Kiswahili or Swahili), Kikongo, Tshiluba; more than 400 Sudanese and Bantu dialects spoken

Literacy: 65.5% (male 76.2%, female 55.1%) age 15 and older can read and write French, Lingala, Kingwana, or Tshiluba

Government

Country name: Democratic Republic of Congo (formerly: Congo Free State, Belgian Congo, Zaire)

Government type: Republic

Capital: Kinshasa

Administrative territorial divisions: One city: Kinshasa, formerly Leopoldville; ten provinces: Bandundu, Bas-Congo, Equateur, Kasaï-Occidental, Kasaï-Oriental, Katanga (capital: Lubumbashi), Maniema, Nord Kivu (capital: Goma), Orientale (capital: Kisangani; includes the Ituri region, whose capital is Bunia; and Haut-Uele, whose capital is Isiro), and Sud-Kivu (capital: Bakavu); according to

---

the constitution adopted in December 2005, these administrative divisions will be subdivided into twenty-six new provinces by 2009
Independence: June 30, 1960 (from Belgium)

Economy
Gross domestic product: US$19.03 billion, per capita US$300; real growth rate 7% (2007)
Unemployment rate: Not available

Source: Central Intelligence Agency, *World Factbook*, Democratic Republic of Congo country profile, https://www.cia.gov/library/publications/the-world-factbook/geos/cg.html (last accessed December 2008).

Background to the conflict

From colonial times to post-Cold War

The recent history of the DRC has been affected by the exploitation, trade, and plundering of its vast resource wealth, and has strong roots in the dynamics established during colonial rule. From 1885 to its independence on June 30, 1960, the DRC was under Belgian rule and known as the Congo. During this period the main interest of the administrating authorities lay in the exploitation of natural resources, and the period was characterized by dismantling of the social and political cohesion of indigenous groups and the lack of interest by colonial rulers in establishing a viable political unit in the country.

Anticolonial, nationalist sentiment in the Congo emerged in the mid-1950s and led to the formation of several political parties that channeled claims for independence. In May 1960 a parliamentary election took place and in June, Belgium was forced to accept the independence of the Congo. Patrice Lumumba became Congo's first prime minister. Shortly after the formation of the government a secessionist movement broke out in Katanga province, backed by Belgian mining interests. In October 1961, Lumumba, dismissed by his allies in government, was arrested, handed over to his enemies, and killed.

Western support allowed Colonel Joseph Mobutu to come to power, following a military coup on November 24, 1965. He changed his name to Mobutu Sese Seko Kuku Ngbendu Wa Banga ("the all-powerful warrior who goes from conquest to conquest leaving fire in his wake"), and that of the country to Zaire. His regime was among the most corrupt and dictatorial in the history of the sub-Saharan region. He drove the country to economic disaster through the so-called Zairenization program, nationalizing foreign-owned commercial and industrial assets and distributing them to patrimonial clients. Zaire became a center for corruption and the theft and smuggling of natural resources.

After the end of the Cold War in 1989, Western nations, particularly the United States, Belgium, and France, distanced themselves from Mobutu and terminated most economic aid. In 1996, President Mobutu's regime, weakened within and backed by few external supporters, was confronted by a rebellion by the Alliance of Democratic Forces for the Liberation of Congo-Zaire (Alliance des Forces Démocratiques pour la Libération du Congo-Zaïre [ADFL]) under the leadership of Laurent Kabila and backed by neighboring Uganda and Rwanda. The latter backed Kabila as part of its attempt to defeat Hutu rebels who had fled to the DRC after the 1994 **genocide** in Rwanda. Mobutu was ousted in May 1997 in what is known as the First Congo War. He fled to Rabat, Morocco, where some months later he died. Kabila took power and renamed the country the Democratic Republic of Congo.

However, Rwanda and Uganda were only temporarily allies to the DRC. In August 1998, war broke out again and Rwandan troops, backing Congolese Tutsi rebels, invaded eastern Congo, initiating what was termed the Second Congo War. Rwanda justified its activities by invoking its own genocide, claiming it necessary to eliminate bases of Hutu extremists on Congolese territory. Uganda, similarly, claimed that Kabila's regime had failed to stop incursions of Hutu extremists into its territory, and occupied the Ituri region for four years. These countries not only intervened directly, but also backed domestic Congolese rebel forces. Rwanda supported the Rally for Congolese Democracy (Rassemblement Congolais pour la Démocratie [RCD]), while Uganda supported the Movement for the Liberation of the Congo (Mouvement de Libération du Congo [MLC]).

Africa's world war

Following the invasion of Rwandan and Ugandan troops, Kabila called on Zimbabwe, Angola, and Namibia for help. Each country's motives for intervening in the war were different, but all had an interest in securing access to Congolese resources. In this bloody five-year conflict an estimated 3–3.5 million people died, and gross atrocities were perpetrated against the civilian population. Some organizations estimate that the actual number of deaths was closer to 5 million. Most of the victims died from war-related diseases, lack of medical assistance, and starvation. To a greater or lesser degree, apart from the government of the DRC the following African countries intervened in the conflict: Rwanda, Uganda, Burundi, Zimbabwe, Angola, Namibia, Chad, and Sudan. This involvement led the conflict to become known as "Africa's world war." A multiplicity of rebel forces were also involved (see Box 7.2). Resources proved to be important fuel to the conflict in the DRC, which for this reason is often largely depicted as one of greed. However, the conflict was also driven by grievances, or at least the mobilization of fears and grievances. This is most notable in the justifications offered by Rwanda and Uganda for their interventions in the DRC.

Box 7.2 Key Players in the Democratic Republic of Congo

Individuals

Joseph Kabila: Son of Laurent. Took power after his father was assassinated.
Laurent Kabila: Ousted Mobutu; backed by both Rwanda and Uganda.
Laurent Nkunda: Leader of the CNDP in North Kivu.
Mobutu Sese Seko: Dictator. Ruled the country from 1965 to 1997.

Countries

Angola, Burundi, Chad, Namibia, Rwanda, Sudan, Uganda, Zimbabwe.

Armed groups

AFDL: Alliance des Forces Démocratiques pour la Libération du Congo-Zaïre. Rebel movement that brought Laurent Kabila to power, backed by Uganda and Rwanda.
APC: Armée du Peuple Congolais, or Armée Populaire Congolaise. Armed wing of the RCD-K-ML, led by Mbusa Nyamwisi.

CNDP: Congrès National pour la Défense du Peuple. Split faction of the RCD, operating in North Kivu under Laurent Nkunda.

FLC: Merger of the MLC, RCD-ML, and RCD-N, formed under Ugandan tutelage in November 2000 and headed by the MLC's Jean-Pierre Bemba. Collapsed in August 2001.

FNI: Front des Nationalistes et Intégrationnistes. Lendu group.

Mai-Mai: Local militia recruited along tribal lines in eastern Congo. Supported Kabila during the war.

MLC: Mouvement de Libération du Congo. Formed in 1998 with extensive Ugandan backing, headquartered in the northern DRC's Equateur province, and led by Jean-Pierre Bemba.

NALU: National Army for the Liberation of Uganda. Ugandan rebel group now largely wiped out.

RCD: Rassemblement Congolais pour la Démocratie. Rwandan-backed rebel group led by Azarias Ruberwa.

RCD-Goma: Faction of the RCD.

RCD-Kisangani: Party formed by Wamba dia Wamba when he was ousted from the original RCD in May 1999. Became the RCD-ML in September 1999.

RCD-K-ML: Kisangani faction of the RCD-ML, led by Mbusa Nyamwisi, controling areas in North Kivu and Ituri. Allied with Mayi-Mayi and Kinshasa. Also the party of Jean-Baptiste Tibasima.

RCD-ML: Rassemblement Congolais pour la Démocratie–Mouvement de Libération. Formed in September 1999 by Wamba dia Wamba after he and Ugandan forces were ousted from Kisangani by Rwanda.

RCD-N: Rassemblement Congolais pour la Démocratie–National. Formed during the splintering of the RCD-ML in mid-2000, led by Roger Lumbala. Originally based in Bafwasende. Now allied with the MLC.

UPC: Union des Patriotes Congolais. Hema-dominated group. Came to prominence after taking control of Bunia in August 2002. Sometimes referred to as UPC-FRP (Front for Reconciliation and Peace).

National armies

FAC: Congolese Armed Forces. Created by Laurent Kabila in 1997, led by Joseph Kabila. Integrated into the FARDC in 2004.

FARDC: Armed Forces of the Democratic Republic of Congo. New, integrated Congolese national army established in 2004, comprising the former FAC and the rebel groups that integrated during the peace process.

FAZ: Zairian Armed Forces. Zaire's national army, led by Mobutu.

RPA/APR: Rwandan Patriotic Army/Armée Patriotique Rwandaise. The national army of Rwanda.

UPDF: Ugandan People's Defense Forces. Uganda's national army, led by Brigadier James Kazini.

International missions

Artemis: French-led EU mission in Ituri in 2003.

MONUC: UN Organization Mission in the Democratic Republic of Congo. Peacekeeping mission first deployed in 2000.

During the conflict the country was split into three areas, each effectively controlled by a distinct group. The government controlled the capital and most of central, southern, and western Congo; the MLC, the rebel group backed by Uganda, controlled northern areas in Equateur province; and the RCD, reliant on Rwanda, controlled Maniema province, most of the Kivus, and parts of Orientale, Kasaï Oriental, and Katanga provinces.

The **United Nations**, the Organization of African Unity (OAU) (now the **African Union** [AU]), and the **South African Development Community** (SADC) all sought to support and facilitate negotiations to end the conflict. The key state parties involved, namely Rwanda, Uganda, Zimbabwe, Angola, and Namibia, in addition to the DRC itself, and later joined by **nonstate actors**, signed a cease-fire at Lusaka in July 1999. The accord called for the withdrawal of all foreign forces from the DRC and the deployment of UN **peacekeeping** forces to monitor its implementation.

The **UN Security Council** established the United Nations Organization Mission in the Democratic Republic of Congo (MONUC) in 2000. The Security Council, attentive to the role of natural resources in the war, established a panel of experts in June 2000 to address the illegal exploitation of the Congo's natural resources. In a landmark report in October 2002 the panel highlighted the role of Uganda, Rwanda, and a host of multinational corporations in the looting of the Congo's natural resources and the perpetuation of the war.

Despite the 1999 Lusaka Accord and the deployment of MONUC, violence continued, and in January 2001 Laurent Kabila was assassinated. His son, Joseph Kabila, took power, becoming president and commander of the armed forces. Joseph Kabila's government enjoyed a warm welcome from Western and African countries, and was offered economic aid by the European Union (EU) and the International Monetary Fund (IMF). **Peace negotiations** were then revived.

The Inter-Congolese Dialogue and the transitional government

On April 19, 2002, the parties to the conflict met in Sun City, South Africa, to resume the process that had begun in 1999 in Lusaka. The peace process was developed through a series of small agreements, known as the Inter-Congolese Dialogue, that led to the adoption of an inclusive peace agreement on December 17, 2002: the Pretoria Accord, also known as the Global and All-Inclusive Agreement. This accord was signed by the eight parties to the peace talks: the former DRC government, the MLC, the RCD, the political opposition, civil society, the Mai-Mai, the RCD-ML, and the RCD-National. In separate agreements signed in July and September 2002, Rwanda and Uganda respectively agreed to withdraw their forces from the territory of the DRC if Interahamwe members and Hutu extremists in the Congo were apprehended, disarmed, and repatriated. It was also agreed that the withdrawal of Ugandan troops from the Ituri region would be followed by the creation of the Ituri Pacification Committee, comprising a group of local parties, which would assume control over administrative and security arrangements in the region.

The peace agreements included the creation of a transitional government to rule in the run-up to the elections, in which President Joseph Kabila would share power with four vice presidents: one from each of the two main rebel movements, one from the government, and one from the political opposition. On June 30, 2003, Joseph Kabila announced the formation of a government of national unity, with the government controlling the interior and finance ministries, the Rwandan-backed RCD controlling the economy and defense ministries, and the Ugandan-backed MLC controlling the budget and foreign affairs ministries. A civilian assumed control of the mining ministry.

The peace agreements also foresaw the integration of rebel groups into the new national army, the Armed Forces of the Democratic Republic of Congo (Forces Armées du République Démocratique du Congo [FARDC]). Kabila's army, the Congolese Armed Forces (Forces Armées Congolaises [FAC]), integrated into the new FARDC. The RCD was given important roles in the land forces and in the defense ministry, and the MLC was given more marginal roles in the naval forces but important commands in financial matters. However, some RCD units later mutinied in North and South Kivu. Most of the Kivu Mai-Mai militias, allied to Kabila during the war, were also given positions in the army and government. However, they split into several groups once in power, and many of the field commanders have since been marginalized. The Ituri militia and the Mai-Mai of northern Katanga did not sign the peace agreement and have since integrated into the army in smaller numbers following deals between the transitional government and various commanders. Most of the RCD-N troops have spontaneously demobilized and joined the new national army, and parts of the RCD-ML have also integrated or demobilized. The integration of the army has been slow and not fully effective, and there are claims that its position is precarious, posing security risks.

The transitional government held a successful constitutional referendum on December 18, 2005, and elections for the presidency, National Assembly, and provincial assemblies took place in 2006. The National Assembly was installed in September 2006, while Kabila, who had been elected president, was inaugurated in December. Antonie Ginzega, head of the Unified Lumumbist Party (Parti Lumumbiste Unifié), was appointed prime minister. In early 2007, the provincial assemblies were constituted. Kabila's Alliance of the Presidential Majority (Alliance de la Majorité Présidentielle [AMP]) won the majority of seats in the National Assembly and in eight of the eleven provincial assemblies.

Western countries generally supported President Kabila, and the peace process received significant international support, particularly through the International Committee to Accompany the Transition, based in Kinshasa, which comprised ambassadors from the United States, France, the United Kingdom, Belgium, South Africa, China, Angola, Canada, Russia, the European Union, and the African Union, and was chaired by the **Special Representative of the Secretary-General** (SRSG) for the DRC. However, this interest was perhaps not completely altruistic. Some of the Western nations that supported the process also sought to secure control over strategic reserves of copper, cobalt, and other minerals. Some were also interested in restricting China's future access to these resources.

Continuation of violence in Ituri and the Kivus

Despite the peace accords of 2002, the violence continued in several parts of the country, including Ituri, the Kivus, and Katanga, although it did not prevent that process, nor the formation of the transitional government. However, while these conflicts were at times depicted as marginal confrontations between local groups and warlords, they had brutal consequences for civilians, who suffered severe human rights violations as patterns of abuse that emerged during the nationwide conflict continued. The region of Ituri in the northeast of the country was particularly badly affected.

Ituri was occupied by Ugandan forces for four years, during which ethnic strife was exacerbated by Uganda's alternating support for two ethnic groups, the Lendu and the Hema. As part of the peace accords, Uganda agreed to withdraw its forces in September 2002 and started to do so in late April 2003, leaving a significant security vacuum in the region. The long-simmering conflicts over land and mineral wealth, as well as the ethnic rivalries, led to widespread violence and massacres during 2002 and 2003, which not even UN troops were able to stop. The armed groups that participated in the conflict developed on the basis of ethnic loyalties. The two main ones were the Union of Congolese Patriots (Union des Patriotes Congolais [UPC]), formed predominantly by northern Hemas, and the Nationalist and Integrationist Front (Front des Nationalistes et Intégrationnistes [FNI]), comprising mainly Lendus. Each group was militarily and politically supported at various points in time by the governments of the DRC, Uganda, Rwanda.

On May 5, 2003, firefights broke out between armed Lendu and Hema groups in several areas of Bunia, the capital of the Ituri region, targeting MONUC and other UN offices and provoking panic among residents. Both groups sought control of the town in anticipation of the complete withdrawal of Ugandan forces. Following this outbreak, the French led an emergency mission, Artemis, which under EU authority was deployed to the province in July 2003. Artemis managed to contain the situation, which allowed a more robust UN mission to return. It was not until mid-2004, however, that militia groups in Ituri signed an agreement with the government to disarm and participate in the transitional process. After intense work from MONUC, the militias started demobilizing; in April 2007 the FNI, the last militia to begin disarmament, started handing over its weapons.

Violence also continued in the Kivus and in Katanga after the peace negotiations. Some dissident members of the former Rwandan-backed RCD rebel movement, which had not been integrated into new national army, briefly occupied Bukavu (South Kivu) on the Rwandan border in June 2004. Their pretext was to save local Congolese Tutsis. The violence, which targeted civilians, resulted in 20,000–30,000 people fleeing to refugee camps in Rwanda and Burundi. Following the summary execution of 160 Congolese Tutsi refugees in one of these camps, the UN-operated camp of Gatumba (near Bujumbura, inside Burundi), Rwanda and Burundi threatened intervention in the DRC, either directly or through proxies. Also, in August 2004, following the Gatumba refugee camp massacre, the RCD leadership withdrew from the transition process. It was reported in May 2005 that Rwandan Hutu rebels based in eastern Congo were responsible for hundreds of summary executions, rapes, beatings, and hostage-taking of Congolese civilians in the territory of Walungu (South Kivu). Fighting continued and in August 2008 intensified greatly, especially in North Kivu. General Laurent Nkunda, who had integrated the national army in 2003, left his position and retreated to North Kivu. Backed by Rwanda, Nkunda led a faction of the RCD-Goma, transformed into the National Congress for the Defense of the People (Congrès National pour la Défense du Peuple [CNDP]), in its fighting with ethnic Hutu Rwandans in the area, the Congolese government, and the government-backed Mai-Mai militias. More than a million people fled North Kivu, and international organizations have reported widespread gross human rights abuses. These abuses prompted calls for enlargement of MONUC, which is to be supplied with an extra 3,000 troops and whose mandate is to be expanded to allow containment of the humanitarian disaster unfolding in the eastern DRC. Between August and November 2008 over 300,000 people fled the region. Also, as of December 2008, news reports claim that Angolan and Zimbabwean troops are entering the region, risking the creation of a new international conflict.

Terms of peace and attempts at accountability

As discussed, the new government was installed before the peace process was completed and before local violence was completely contained. The peace accords contained power-sharing provisions, including many of the main parties to the conflict within the government as well as a unified national army, in the hopes of stabilizing the state. Integration of rebel forces with the national army proved a challenge, as explained, but power-sharing was maintained, in large part due to significant support by the international community.

The Inter-Congolese Dialogue did address the importance of prosecuting human rights abusers, passing resolutions on the creation of both an international criminal tribunal and a **truth commission**. However, its discussion of these mechanisms provoked tension, and the formal peace accords do not mention them, or other accountability mechanisms, though they have not tried to prevent accountability through amnesties and pardons.

Following a resolution adopted on December 20, 2002, by the Inter-Congolese Dialogue, the transitional government passed a law on June 30, 2003, establishing a truth and reconciliation commission. Lack of sufficient consultation and an apparent politicization of the process of commissioner appointments have been cause for concern. Equally, a national human rights observatory and an anticorruption commission were tainted by their inclusion of known human rights abusers as members.

Another resolution adopted during the Inter-Congolese Dialogue allowed the transitional government to request the UN Security Council to establish an international criminal court for the DRC, modeled on the **International Criminal Tribunal for Rwanda** (ICTR) and the **International Criminal Tribunal for the Former Yugoslavia** (ICTY). President Kabila also raised the topic of a tribunal in an address to the **UN General Assembly** in 2003, but no further steps were taken. The lack of support by the UN itself toward these options for accountability has now effectively ruled them out.

During the pacification of the Ituri region there were some attempts to address the causes of the conflict and the human rights violations it generated. These included the Ituri Pacification Committee, created by the Luanda Accords of September 2002. These accords also established a human rights committee, but it functioned purely to educate the populace.

However, as is discussed in Chapter 13, significant strides have been made in addressing crimes committed in the DRC with the referral of the situation in Ituri to the International Criminal Court. Nonetheless, the Court will not be able to consider many of the atrocities committed in the DRC, as the majority predate the 2002 entry into force of the ICC's Rome Statute, with some dating back to 1960.

Thus, the terms of peace have not excluded the possibility of accountability, but no specific criminal procedures have been established within the country through the peace process.

Human rights violations in the DRC

Human rights violations as underlying causes of conflict

It is clear that demand for the DRC's resources constitute one of the primary causes of the conflict. Many actors, including foreign countries, nonstate armed groups, and multinational corporations, have sought to exploit the country's vast resources, including gold, oil, timber, and coltan, which have been a source of competition and violence. In Ituri and Haut Uele districts, gold mines have been the site of significant conflict and human rights abuses, driven in part by plunder by forces from neighboring Uganda. In 2005, **Human Rights Watch** claimed that more than 60,000 people had died due to direct violence in the northeastern region of the Congo. Human rights abuses connected with the exploitation of gold, particularly from 1998 to 2003, when Ugandan soldiers controlled the area, included coerced labor, beatings, and arbitrary arrest of resistant gold-miners, and several massacres of civilian populations in the area. Irresponsible mining practices caused the death of over a hundred people following the collapse of the Gorumbwa mine. The Ugandan army is also alleged to have plundered a ton of Congolese gold, valued at over US$9 million.

However, the conflict in the DRC has been driven not only by the demand for resources, but also by human rights abuses and grievances. Abuses have fomented the conflict in at least two ways, through domestic grievances and through transborder intervention.

Domestic grievances

Though demands for access to resources and political power have driven the conflict in the DRC, the impact of real and perceived slights in a country with some 200 distinct ethnic groups has also been an important factor. The violence in Ituri, for example, has been perpetuated by tensions between the Hema and Lendu populations in the region. These tensions have significant roots in colonial favoritism, in claims over land and fishing rights, and in the perceptions of discrimination held by each group. The 2002–4 conflict in the region developed out of a local land dispute between the Hema and Lendu ethnic groups in 1999, and was exacerbated by the intervention and occupation of the area by Uganda. The armed groups who participated in the conflict represented the ethic divide and originated as ethnic self-help organizations.

Transborder intervention by neighboring countries

Defense of human rights, particularly protection of kin populations across borders and defense against attacks on their own populations, has served as a pretext for both Rwanda and Uganda to intervene and even occupy parts of DRC territory. Rwanda's interventions have been driven by its desire to defeat Rwandan Hutu rebels and protect Tutsis following the genocide in 1994. Its participation in the conflict in the Kivus – where some 12,000 fully armed members of the Democratic Forces for the Liberation of Rwanda (Forces Démocratiques de Libération du Rwanda [FDLR]) remain active – and particularly its backing of the RCD in the Bukavu occupation, has had an important impact on the conflict and therefore on the perpetrated human rights abuses. When Uganda intervened in and occupied Ituri province in 1999, it argued that it was seeking to protect itself from incursions by the Lord's Resistance Army, a Ugandan rebel group that was operating within the eastern DRC. While Uganda has occasionally cited protection of vulnerable populations as a rationale for its intervention, it has also profited considerably, exporting diamonds and gold from the DRC worth millions of dollars. Rwanda has also hoped to similarly exploit resources, although it has been less successful. While both countries have cited human rights concerns as justifications for their incursions, their armed forces, as well as the armed groups to which they offered support, have committed grave atrocities.

Human rights violations emerging from and transforming the conflict

The scale of human suffering that has resulted from the war in the DRC is vast. As mentioned, casualties could number more than the officially estimated 3–3.5 million deaths, reaching up to 5 million, and the atrocities have been horrendous. The violence continues despite the peace agreements, so these figures will certainly rise further. According to the 2007 report of the independent expert of the UN Human Rights Council, abuses have included summary and extrajudicial killings, forced disappearances, **torture**, and arbitrary detention. Other reports have focused on sexual violence against women and girls, the situation of street children (*shegues*), and use of child soldiers by nearly all parties to the conflict. Some human rights organizations have reported instances of cannibalism.

Much of the violence has been ethnically targeted, even as it has been justified on the grounds of protecting another ethnicity. Ethnic conflicts have in several instances become intertwined with the struggle over natural resources. This is particularly true in the region of Ituri, where the fight over control of the gold mines has rendered the conflict particularly violent, with grave consequences for the civilian population. For example, the fight over the Mongbwalu gold-mining area between Hema and Lendu armed groups in 2002 and 2003 led to the slaughter of 2,000 civilians, as well as rape, torture, and arbitrary detentions. It resulted also in the internal displacement of tens of thousands of civilians who were forced to flee their homes after their possessions had been looted or destroyed. An estimated 50,000–60,000 civilians have died in Ituri since 1999, with more than half a million civilians forced to flee the region with no possibility to return. The armed groups have also prevented delivery of humanitarian assistance to other groups considered enemies.

Given the scale and nature of the human rights violations committed during the conflict, particularly in Ituri, it might be argued that they have transformed organized chaos into genocide, given the ethnically targeted nature of the violence. The self-help organizations for both the Hema and the Lendu, which had developed first to provide basic services in the absence of state support, became propagators of hate. The International Crisis Group, a nongovernmental organization, describes the transformation of the conflict as a "progression . . . from land-based communal violence, to land-related operations of ethnic cleansing, to repeated acts of genocide by both Hema and Lendu" ("Maintaining Momentum in the Congo: The Ituri Problem," 2005). Even if it is debatable whether any of the acts have constituted genocide, it is clear that **crimes against humanity** and violations of international humanitarian law and international human rights law have been committed.

In the eastern DRC, human rights violations have also been widespread. Since Laurent Nkunda's rebels launched their attacks in the summer of 2008, over 300,000 people have been displaced. When the rebels advanced on Goma, the Congolese army responded by looting the town and raping and killing civilians. On November 4, 2008, a massacre of suspected Mai-Mai supporters in Kiwanja was reported, first by the pro-government Mai-Mai militia and then by Nkunda's rebels.

Applicable law and possible subjects of legal accountability

In analyzing the applicable law to determine who might be held accountable for breaches, the distinction between international and noninternational armed conflict becomes salient, potentially affecting whether certain acts by armed groups can be characterized as **war crimes** even if they are clear violations of international humanitarian law.

The DRC conflict is particularly complex, as many governments have been militarily involved through use of their own armed forces or their support of armed groups, alongside the involvement of many other rebel groups. Where states have been directly involved or have used proxies who engaged in abuses, the states themselves may be liable, according to the principles of state responsibility. Further, individuals might be held criminally liable. Chapter 13 addresses in greater detail the cases that have actually been brought.

State responsibility: the DRC versus Uganda and Rwanda

On June 23, 1999, the DRC brought a case against Uganda before the **International Court of Justice** (ICJ) for the latter's activities on DRC territory, particularly its acts of armed aggression, use of force, violation of the principles of peaceful settlement of disputes and noninterference, and violation of obligations under international humanitarian and human rights law.

In its decision of December 19, 2005, the Court found that Uganda, by engaging in military activities against the DRC on the latter's territory, by occupying Ituri, and by providing military, logistic, economic, and financial support to irregular forces operating on DRC territory, had violated the principle of nonuse of force in international relations and the principle of nonintervention. It found that Uganda's armed forces had engaged in killing, torture, and other inhumane treatment of the Congolese civilian population, and had destroyed villages and civilian buildings. Further, it found that Uganda had failed to distinguish between civilian and military targets and to protect the civilian population in fighting with other combatants, had trained child soldiers, had incited ethnic conflict, and had failed to take measures to end the conflict. It also found that Uganda, as an occupying power, had failed to take measures to ensure respect for human rights and international humanitarian law in Ituri district, and had therefore violated its obligations under international humanitarian law and international human rights law. Finally, the Court found that Ugandan armed forces had engaged in looting, plundering, and exploitation of Congolese natural resources, and that Uganda, while occupying Ituri, had failed to comply with its obligations as an occupying power to prevent such acts. Therefore, the Court found that Uganda had violated obligations to the DRC under international law and owed it reparations.

Box 7.3 **The Democratic Republic of Congo's case against Uganda, International Court of Justice hearing of April 27, 2005**

"The Congo requests the Court to adjudge and declare:

1. That the Republic of Uganda, by engaging in military and paramilitary activities against the Democratic Republic of the Congo . . . has violated the following principles of conventional and customary law:

    –   the principle of non-use of force in international relations, including the prohibition of aggression;
    –   the obligation to settle international disputes exclusively by peaceful means so as to ensure that international peace and security, as well as justice, are not placed in jeopardy;
    –   respect for the sovereignty of States and the rights of peoples to self-determination, and hence to choose their own political and economic system freely and without outside interference;
    –   the principle of non-intervention in matters within the domestic jurisdiction of States, including refraining from extending any assistance to the parties to a civil war operating on the territory of another State.

2. That the Republic of Uganda, by committing acts of violence against nationals of the Democratic Republic of the Congo . . . has violated the following principles of conventional and customary law:

    –   the principle of conventional and customary law imposing an obligation to respect, and ensure respect for, fundamental human rights, including in times of armed conflict, in accordance with international humanitarian law;
    –   the principle of conventional and customary law imposing an obligation, at all times, to make a distinction in an armed conflict between civilian and military objectives;
    –   the right of Congolese nationals to enjoy the most basic rights, both civil and political, as well as economic, social and cultural.

3. That the Republic of Uganda, by engaging in the illegal exploitation of Congolese natural resources . . . has violated the following principles of conventional and customary law:

    –   the applicable rules of international humanitarian law;
    –   respect for the sovereignty of States, including over their natural resources;
    –   the duty to promote the realization of the principle of equality of peoples and of their right of self-determination, and consequently to refrain from exposing peoples to foreign subjugation, domination or exploitation;
    –   the principle of non-interference in matters within the domestic jurisdiction of States, including economic matters."

Source: http://www.icj-cij.org.

In a similar case filed by the DRC against Rwanda on the same date, June 23, 1999, the ICJ found in its judgment of February 3, 2006 that it had no jurisdiction to hear the case. However, the increase in violence in the eastern DRC since the summer of 2008 has drawn renewed attention to – and new evidence for – Rwanda's role in perpetrating human rights violations in the DRC through its backing of General Nkunda's CNDP. In Spain a case has been brought (see Box 7.4) exercising **universal jurisdiction** to address human rights abuses committed in the region, including the killings of nine Spanish nationals, missionaries, and aid workers. In February 2008 a Spanish judge issued an arrest warrant against 40 members of the Rwandan Patriotic Army accused of committing international crimes in Rwanda that also spilled over into DRC territory. Among those who have been prosecuted by the Spanish courts is General Karake Karenzi, deputy commander of the UN-AU Hybrid Mission in Darfur (UNAMID) at the time of the indictment. The Spanish courts have also considered the responsibility of Paul Kagame, president of Rwanda, but have found him immune to prosecution as a sitting head of state.

Box 7.4 **The cases against the Rwandan Patriotic Army in Spain**

Juzgado Central de Instrucción N.4 Audiencia Nacional

Case Reference Number: "Sumario 3/2008-D". Order of indictment. 6-February-2008.

(official translation)

"III. LEGAL ARGUMENTS

"FIRST

"The criminal conducts as described above could constitute the following offences established in the current Penal Code:

A) Offence of Genocide . . .

B) Offences against humanity . . .

C) Offences against persons and property protected in the case of armed conflict . . .

D) Common Provisions . . .

E) Belonging to a Terrorist Organisation . . .

F) Terrorists Acts . . .

"THIRD

". . . there is reasonable evidence that the persons with the most responsibility for the military political organisation **FRONT PATRIOTIQUE RWANDAIS (FPR)– ARMÉE PATRIOTIQUE RWANDAISE (APR)**, among whom the persons indicted in this case have unfolded a whole range of criminal methodology in their operations firstly carried out from outside of Rwanda, from Uganda and later from Rwanda and in its territory. They seized power by force by means of strategic terrorist attacks and open war operations, and took absolute control off the structure of the State, generating from then on a real terror regime.

"This terror regime was generated not only from the dictatorial structure of the State itself but, above all, from a complex hierarchical parallel structure which was put in charge of perpetrating heinous criminal acts against the population both national and foreign, which were previously selected for ethnical and/or political reasons. Their criminal plan, for alleged security reasons, culminated in the invasion and conquest in two phases of the immense Democratic Republic of Congo, with the support of their political-military groups or allies created for this purpose. An indeterminate number of persons were exterminated through these two phases of hostilities at the hand of a systematic, organised and strongly hierarchical structure.

"According to some sources, the number of persons exterminated during the periods to which these case refers to, could be four million people, approximately, a figure that includes Rwandan refugees belonging to the Hutu ethnic group, as well as the civilian population of the Congo, mainly Congolese Hutus.

"Furthermore, pillage and large scale looting was carried out centred above all in valuable natural resources such as timber and high valued and strategic minerals. The criminal network created for the exploitation and pillage of these riches enables them to maintain a powerful position and geostrategic domination of the zone, as well as to finance their wars, enriching both individuals and the group, and to continue and extend their criminal plan for extermination and domination."

International humanitarian and human rights law

The DRC ratified the **Geneva Conventions** in 1961 and its two additional protocols in 1982 and 2002, respectively. The first issue to resolve in trying to identify the international humanitarian law that is applicable to the conflict in the DRC is whether the conflict should be considered internal or international, as it presents characteristics of both. At the beginning of the conflict the UN Special Rapporteur on the Situation of Human Rights in the DRC, Roberto Garretón, considered that, notwithstanding the internationalization of the conflict, it still remained an internal one. However, following the ICJ's judgment that Uganda bore responsibility for many breaches of international humanitarian law, it is arguable that the conflict should be categorized as international.

If the conflict is to be treated as noninternational, only one provision of the Geneva Conventions is applicable. **Common Article 3** prohibits a host of activities by all parties to a conflict, and the rapes, massacres, mutilations, and cannibalism perpetrated during the DRC conflict clearly violate this article. This means that the various rebel groups and the government of the DRC violated Common Article 3. Such violations are not automatically war crimes, as they cannot be termed "**grave breaches**" under the Geneva Conventions; these can be committed only in the context of an international armed conflict. While Additional Protocol II further regulates the conduct of internal armed conflict, and the DRC is a state party, as discussed in Chapter 4, traditional international humanitarian law does not define violations in such internal conflicts as grave breaches or war crimes.

However, if the conflict is characterized as international, both Uganda and Rwanda may be responsible not only for the acts of their own militaries, but also for the acts of the armed groups they supported, if their degree of control over such groups was significant. The International Court of Justice found in the 1986 case *Nicaragua v. US: Case Concerning Military and Paramilitary Activities In and Against Nicaragua* that a foreign state is responsible for the conduct of a faction in a civil war if the faction is a de facto agent of that state or is ordered to commit crimes.

Ugandan forces that directly engaged in the types of abuses detailed here may have committed grave breaches of the Geneva Conventions and violated the protections enumerated in Additional Protocol II. Further, Uganda was an occupying power in Ituri province for four years. This means that it had an obligation under the Fourth Geneva Convention to protect and respect the rights of the civilian population under its authority. As the ICJ found in its judgment, Uganda failed to uphold its protection obligations, and its close collaboration with the UPC and Hema militias may implicate it directly in their crimes. If this is the case, then the grave breaches provisions would be fulfilled. Rwanda, though it cannot be characterized as an occupying power like Uganda, may be responsible for the acts of the UPC, given its collaboration with and support of that armed group. If Rwanda's intervention also allows the conflict to be classed as international, many of its acts might rise to the level of grave breaches. Further, Rwanda, like Uganda, may be responsible for the acts of the militias that were under its control.

As highlighted previously, the devolvement of the conflict in the eastern DRC into ethnic violence and deliberate targeting of civilian populations according to their membership in specific ethnic groups could arguably be considered genocide. As we have seen (Box 7.4), the Spanish courts have considered that some of the acts perpetrated in the eastern DRC amounted to genocide, crimes against humanity, war crimes, and terrorist offenses.

Finally, all the factions in the DRC conflict have been responsible for activities that amount to human rights violations, including the killing of civilians during conflict, as well as intentional massacres of civilians, and the use of summary execution, torture, and forced labor for gold mining by the UPC and several other groups. All armed groups have engaged in rape and other forms of sexual violence. Cannibalism is said to have been carried out by several armed groups as well. All groups have utilized child soldiers, frequently through forcible recruitment. Additional Protocol II of the Geneva Conventions, and the Convention on the Rights of the Child, ban recruitment of persons under the age of 15.

Key points

- The conflict in the Democratic Republic of Congo is particularly complex, as is assignment of responsibility for crimes, given multiple armed groups and support provided to them by a number of neighboring states.
- Exploitation and access to the country's natural resources have partly driven the conflict; multinational corporations may bear some responsibility for human rights abuses.
- Some acts committed during the conflict might be characterized as ethnic cleansing or genocide.
- Despite a number of peace agreements and the presence of a United Nations (UN) mission, violence continues in the east, leading to the risk of a new interstate war in the region.

Discussion questions

This section provides discussion guidance related to the possibilities for negotiation and accountability without reference to the decisions that were ultimately made. Part II studies the actual institutional responses that have been made, particularly via the International Criminal Court.

Determining accountability

The conflict in the DRC is complex, involving many actors. As we have seen, an important issue in determining who can be held accountable is whether conflict can be characterized as internal or international. It is also helpful to consider the role of multinational corporations in aggravating and perpetuating the conflict, and whether they too, in addition to Uganda and Rwanda, can be held accountable for complicity in human rights violations.

- Why did the International Court of Justice take a different stand in the case against Uganda compared to the case against Rwanda?
- Can the abuses carried out in the DRC, particularly in the Ituri region, be considered to fall within the definition of genocide? If so, what criminal responses do these abuses merit?
- To what extent are multinational corporations responsible for some of the human rights abuses perpetrated in the DRC? To answer this question, study the UN's *Report of the Panel of Experts on the Illegal Exploitation of Natural Resources and Other Forms of Wealth in the Democratic Republic of Congo* (see "Official Documents and Sources" at the end of this chapter).

Prospects for addressing violations

The fragile state of peace implementation imposes limitations on accountability. In examining the possibilities for addressing violations as part of the broader **peacebuilding** process, it is important to understand the complexities of the situation in the DRC. Any strategy concerning justice and reconciliation must build upon comprehensive analysis of the situation and the interests and motivations of all the key actors involved. The domestic judicial system in the DRC did not function particularly well prior to the conflict, as it was seriously corrupt and weak, and remains severely damaged still. Further prosecutions of violations pertaining to armed conflict fall under the jurisdiction of military rather than civilian courts, which leads to doubt that the military tribunals will provide accountability for human rights violations, particularly considering that the peace process included the integration of rebel groups into the national army. As we have seen, there have been several attempts to bring claims for accountability before foreign courts using the principle of universal jurisdiction. A Belgian court issued an arrest warrant for the foreign minister of the DRC, accusing him of incitement to genocide, and there is an ongoing case in Spanish courts. The DRC has strongly resisted these attempts at justice, and has retaliated by bringing a case before the ICJ against Belgium. The ICJ has ruled that Belgium failed to recognize the foreign immunity of the DRC minister.

- Does domestic accountability in a court outside the DRC seem feasible? For which perpetrators?
- Would a **hybrid tribunal** be a viable solution in this case? Why? Would the resources needed to establish a hybrid tribunal be better used for other purposes, such as rebuilding the judicial system?
- How beneficial would it be to establish a truth and reconciliation commission for the DRC? Can a politicized truth commission function as a viable instrument for domestic accountability?

Achieving stability

As we have seen, violence has not stopped in several areas of the DRC. Mistrust and fear engendered by the ethnically targeted abuses and attacks in the Ituri region and in the eastern DRC make conflict resolution much more difficult. Even if there is low risk of renewed war involving the whole country, which external powers would likely prevent, it is important to consider that increased corruption, continuation of local violence, **impunity**, and economic stagnation may lead the new government to collapse.

- How could the continued violence in Ituri and the Kivus impact the stability of the country as a whole?
- Could externally imposed accountability processes, such as those before the ICC and the Spanish courts, impact in the stability of the country?

Group exercise

The DRC's transitional government, in discussions in May 2004 designed to engage the armed groups in Ituri, made the following statement: "There will not be a peace without justice, but the government will firstly privilege the restoration of peace and security before justice starts." Form two groups. One group should argue the advantages of this strategy and the other should argue its disadvantages.

Box 7.5 **Democratic Republic of Congo timeline**

Colonial rule	**1908**	Established as a Belgian colony.
Independence	**1960**	June 30: Independence.
Mobutu's dictatorial regime	**1965**	November 24: Mobutu's military coup.
First Congo War	**1996**	Laurent Kabila's rebellion (supported by Rwanda and Uganda).
	1997	Mobutu deposed and dies in Morocco.
Second Congo War	**1998**	August: Insurrection backed by Rwanda and Uganda.
	1998–9	Uganda occupies the Ituri region.
	1999	July: Cease-fire; Lusaka Accord signed.
	2000	MONUC established.
	2001	January: Laurent Kabila assassinated. Joseph Kabila named head of state.
Inter-Congolese Dialogue	**2002**	April 19: Peace talks in Sun City.
		July: Peace accord signed.
		October: Withdrawal of Rwandan forces occupying eastern Congo negotiated.
		September: Luanda Accords signed.
		December 17: Pretoria Accord signed by all remaining warring parties, ending fighting and establishing government of national unity.
Transitional government	**2003**	Uganda begins withdrawing troops from Ituri region.
		May: Confrontation between the Lendu and Hena. Firefights break out in Bunia (Ituri).
		June: EU emergency mission in Ituri.
		July: Government of national unity confirmed.
	2004	Militia groups in Ituri sign agreement with government to disarm and participate in transitional process.

		June: Dissidents from RCD occupy Bakavu (Sud-Kivu). Massacre in Tutsi refugee camps in Rwanda and Burundi, which threaten to intervene.
	2005	December: Constitutional referendum.
Elected government	**2006**	Elections for presidency, National Assembly, and provincial legislatures.
		September: National Assembly installed.
		December: Joseph Kabila inaugurated president. Vital Kamerhe appointed president of National Assembly.
	2007	January: Provincial assemblies constituted; governors and national senators elected.

Further reading

Human Rights Watch, "The Curse of Gold: Democratic Republic of Congo" (2005), http://www.hrw.org/doc/?t=africa_pub&c=congo.

International Centre for Transitional Justice (Federico Borello), "A First Few Steps: The Long Road to a Just and Democratic Peace in the Democratic Republic of Congo" (October 2004), http://www.ictj.org/downloads/ictj.drc.eng.pdf.

International Crisis Group, "Congo: Consolidating the Peace," *Africa Report* no. 128 (July 5, 2007), http://www.crisisgroup.org/library/documents/africa/central_africa/128_congo_consol.idating_the_peace_web.pdf.

——, "Maintaining Momentum in the Congo: The Ituri Problem" (August 2005), http://www.crisis group.org/library/documents/africa/central_africa/084_maintaining_momentum_in_the_congo_the_ituri_problem.pdf.

Juma, Laurence, "The War in Congo: Transnational Conflict Networks and the Failure of Internationalism," *Gonzaga Journal of International Law* 10 (2006): 97–163.

Nest, Michael, with François Grignon and Eminzet F. Kinsangani, *The Democratic Republic of Congo: Economic Dimensions of War and Peace* (Boulder: Lynne Rienner, 2006).

Turner, Thomas, *The Congo Wars: Conflict, Myth, and Reality* (New York: Zed Books, 2007).

Official documents and sources

International Court of Justice, *Case of Armed Activities in the Territory of the Congo (Democratic Republic of Congo v. Uganda)* (December 19, 2005).

United Nations, *Report of the Panel of Experts on the Illegal Exploitation of Natural Resources and Other Forms of Wealth of the Democratic Republic of the Congo* (April 12, 2001), UN Doc. A/2001/357.

——, *Report of the Independent Expert on the Situation of Human Rights in the Democratic Republic of the Congo, Titinga Frédéric Pacéré* (February 21, 2007), UN Doc. A/HRC/4/7.

——, *Report on the Situation of Human Rights in the Democratic Republic of the Congo* (February 8, 1999), UN Doc. E/CN.4/1999/31.

8   Sudan

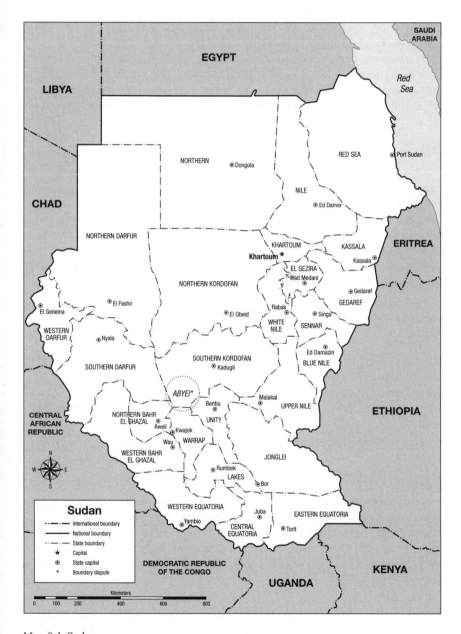

Map 8.1 Sudan

Source: Adapted from UN map no. 3707 Rev. 10 April 2007.

Overview

After decades of conflict the war between the Sudanese government and the Sudanese People's Liberation Movement/Army (SPLM/A) came to an end in 2005 with the signing of the Comprehensive Peace Agreement, which allows for some degree of autonomy for the south of the country, as well as for SPLM/A inclusion in both governance and security structures, but does not provide for accountability mechanisms. However, the situation remains fragile. Further, conflict has continued to rage in Western Darfur, threatening to undermine the peace agreements that have been developed and transform the conflict into potential **genocide**, and the **UN Security Council** has referred the situation to the **International Criminal Court** (ICC), as discussed in Chapter 13. There is an attempt at peace without justice in the south, and an attempt at justice without peace in Darfur. This chapter examines the background to the conflict, the human rights violations committed by all parties, and the applicable **international humanitarian law** and **international human rights law**.

Box 8.1 **Key facts: Sudan**

Geography

Location: Northern Africa, bordering the Red Sea, between Egypt and Eritrea

Area: Total area 2,505,810 km², land area 2,376,000 km², water area 129,810 km²

Terrain: Generally flat, featureless plain; mountains in the far south, northeast, and west; desert dominates the north

Natural resources: Petroleum; small reserves of iron ore, copper, chromium ore, zinc, tungsten, mica, silver, gold; hydropower

People

Population: 40,218,456

Ethnic groups: Black 52%, Arab 39%, Beja 6%, foreigners 2%, other 1%

Religions: Sunni Muslim 70% (in the north), Christian 5% (mostly in the south and Khartoum), indigenous beliefs 25%

Languages: Arabic (official), English (official), Nubian, Ta Bedawie, diverse dialects of Nilotic, Nilo-Hamitic, Sudanic languages (note: program of "Arabization" in process)

Literacy: 61.1% (male 71.8%, female 50.5%) age 15 and older can read and write (2003)

Government

Country name: Republic of the Sudan (local name: Jumhuriyat as-Sudan)

Government type: Government of national unity; the National Congress Party (NCP) and Sudan People's Liberation Movement (SPLM) formed a power-sharing government under the 2005 Comprehensive Peace Agreement; the NCP, which came to power by military coup in 1989, is the majority partner; the agreement stipulates national elections in 2009

Capital: Khartoum

Administrative territorial divisions: 25 states (*wilayat*, singular *wilayah*): A'ali an Nil (Upper Nile), Al Bahr al Ahmar (Red Sea), Al Buhayrat (Lakes), Al Jazirah (El

Gezira), Al Khartum (Khartoum), Al Qadarif (Gedaref), Al Wahdah (Unity), An Nil al Abyad (White Nile), An Nil al Azraq (Blue Nile), Ash Shamaliyah (Northern), Bahr al Jabal (Bahr al Jabal), Gharb al Istiwa'iyah (Western Equatoria), Gharb Bahr al Ghazal (Western Bahr al Ghazal), Gharb Darfur (Western Darfur), Janub Darfur (Southern Darfur), Janub Kurdufan (Southern Kordofan), Junqali (Jonglei), Kassala (Kassala), Nahr an Nil (Nile), Shamal Bahr al Ghazal (Northern Bahr al Ghazal), Shamal Darfur (Northern Darfur), Shamal Kurdufan (Northern Kordofan), Sharq al Istiwa'iyah (Eastern Equatoria), Sinnar (Sinnar), Warab (Warab)

Independence: January 2, 1956 (from Egypt and the United Kingdom)

Economy

Gross domestic product: US$80.98 billion, per capita US$1,900 (2007)
Unemployment rate: 18.7% (2002)

Source: Central Intelligence Agency, *World Factbook*, Sudan country profile, https://www.cia.gov/library/publications/the-world-factbook/geos/su.html (last accessed December 2008).

Background to the conflict

The conflict in the south

The north–south conflict in Sudan occurred in two phases: from independence until 1972, and again from 1983 until 2005. We focus here on the more recent conflict, although the underlying causes of both were substantially the same.

Many of the contemporary grievances in the conflict are directly related to the colonial administration of the territory that is now Sudan. Beginning in 1821, Sudan was under Ottoman-Egyptian rule, and later was subject to the Anglo-Egyptian condominium administration. The colonial powers helped to reinforce the distinctions between the cultural and religious identities between the peoples of the north and the south. During the Anglo-Egyptian rule the population in the northern two-thirds of the country, who had intermarried with Arab migrants, were under Arabic and Islamic influence, and those in the southern portion of the country, populated by animists and Christians, were regarded as African. This administration also promoted a disparate economic and social development, in which the north was considerably more advanced and gave rise to an elite who controlled government following decolonization. The government sought to force the Islamization of the country, including in the south. Discriminatory treatment, which continued into independence, fostered insecurity and resentment in the south. A mutiny in 1955 led to a 17-year war between the government and the Southern Sudanese Liberation Movement (SSLM), also known as Anya Nya. The conflict ended with the 1972 Addis Ababa Agreement, which granted political and economic autonomy to the south and established the conditions for resource and power-sharing between the regions.

It would be simplistic to understand this conflict exclusively as a religious and racial conflict between the Arab Muslims of the north and the Christian blacks of the south. The conflict was complicated by the development of oil exploitation in the south, following discoveries at the beginning of the 1970s. The concession for exploitation was granted to the Chevron Corporation in 1975. In 1980, President Jaafar Nimeiri began to change the administrative provincial borders so that the north could control oil resources. In 1983 he recentralized political and economic power, rescinded the autonomy of the south, and transferred its financial powers to the central government, abrogating the Addis Ababa Agreement. He also officially transformed Sudan into an Islamic state, declaring Arabic the official language (it had been English in the south), and imposed *sharia* law within the whole country, even though one-third of the population was non-Muslim. Southern resistance was mobilized through the SPLM/A, led by Colonel John Garang, and the war resumed.

From 1989 onward, several attempts to achieve peace were unsuccessful, with the revocation of *sharia* law as one of the main points of disagreement. By 1989 the SPLA controlled most of the south and was putting considerable military pressure on the government. In that year, Brigadier-General Omar Hassan Ahmad al-Bashir, supported by the National Islamic Front (NIF), seized power in a coup d'état and established an authoritarian government, which intensified the war. Also, the SPLA split when some among its military command questioned Garang's leadership, resulting in the creation of the SPLA-United – later the Southern Sudan Independence Movement – under the command of Riek Machar. Internal fighting within the south had devastating repercussions for both the Bor Dinka and Nuer ethnic groups.

Peace negotiations and agreements

Several peace negotiation attempts between the government, the SPLA, and the Southern Sudan Independence Movement failed. In 1993, the Inter-Governmental Authority on Development (IGAD), an African subregional organization, began facilitating the peace process, under the leadership of Kenya's president. International pressure escalated, promoted by the United States in part because of its global "war on terror" and including the imposition of UN sanctions, until the first peace agreement, the Machakos Protocol, was signed in July 2002.

The Machakos Protocol provided the basic framework for peace, including the right of the south to hold a referendum on independence after an interim period of six years, freedom of religion, and guarantees that *sharia* law would not be imposed in the south. The protocol also established the Assessment and Evaluation Commission to monitor implementation of accords during the interim period. The commission comprised equal membership from the SPLA and the government, as well as representation from the IGAD subcommittee on Sudan and from four observer states: Italy, Norway, the United Kingdom, and the United States.

Subsequent agreements, including a framework agreement in 2003 and several others in 2004, established an internationally monitored cease-fire, deployment of the UN Mission in Sudan (UNMIS), and security arrangements for the interim period, which included the formation of integrated as well as separate armed units, wealth- and power-sharing provisions, and provisions for the resolution of related regional conflicts, including those in Southern Kordofan/Nuba Mountains and Blue Nile States, and the Abyei conflict. The power-sharing provisions allowed the national government to protect the sovereignty and people of the whole country, while the government of Southern Sudan would exercise authority in relation to people in the south. The executive was to comprise a president and two vice presidents, with John Garang to be first vice president as well as president of the government of Southern Sudan, with Juba as the capital.

On January 10, 2005, in Nairobi, the government of Sudan and the SPLA signed the Comprehensive Peace Agreement. This agreement, like its predecessors, established no mechanisms for accountability for the human rights violations committed during the conflict.

Six months after signature of the Comprehensive Peace Agreement and shortly after his inauguration, Garang was killed in a helicopter accident, sparking riots in the capital of Sudan, Khartoum; many southerners suspected that the crash was no accident. The riots caused over a hundred deaths as well as fears that the growing civil unrest would derail the peace process. The peace process has been fragile since, involving significant clashes, and in October 2007 the SPLA temporarily suspended participation in the government of national unity. The overwhelming international attention on Darfur may have also come at the expense of the broader quest for peace in the whole country.

Regional dimensions

The conflict in Sudan has significant regional dimensions. Some neighbors, such as Kenya, Uganda, Ethiopia, and Eritrea, have been positively engaged in supporting negotiations in Sudan through the IGAD process.

However, regional dynamics have also fomented conflict. Until 1991, Ethiopia provided support to the SPLA because, among other things, it suspected that the Sudanese government was fostering Islamist movements in Ethiopia and Eritrea. Uganda has also provided support to the SPLA, as part of its strategy to fight the Lord's Resistance Army, which operates in Uganda along the border with Sudan, as well as in Southern Sudan.

In 2005, Chad declared war on Sudan, after the Chadian rebel group Rally for Democracy and Liberty launched an attack on the Chadian town of Adre, located near the Sudanese border and within the Darfur region, killing about a hundred people. Chad accused the Sudanese government of supporting the rebel group and its attacks, and claimed that Sudanese militias were responsible for their daily incursions into Chad to steal cattle, killing civilians and burning villages along the way. On May 3, 2007, both countries signed a peace agreement in Saudi Arabia.

Sudanese refugees have fled to neighboring countries, particularly Eritrea, Chad, Ethiopia, Uganda, and the Central African Republic (see Box 8.1).

The conflict in Darfur

Even as the north–south conflict drew to a close, violence raged elsewhere in the country. Reports of massacres and potentially genocidal attacks in Western Darfur began to emerge in early 2003. According to human rights advocates, the government of Sudan is responsible for ethnic cleansing and **crimes against humanity** in Darfur, one of the world's poorest and most inaccessible regions, on Sudan's western border with Chad. This region comprises 250,000 square kilometers, has an estimated population of 6 million persons, and is home to several sedentary and nomadic tribal groups, some predominantly agricultural, some mainly cattle herders. All of the tribes practice Islam, and Arabic is widely spoken. This conflict has historical roots but escalated in February 2003 when two rebel groups, the Sudan Liberation Army/Movement and the Justice and Equality Movement, drawn from members of the Fur, Masalit, and Zaghawa ethnic groups, initiated attacks against the government, demanding an end to economic marginalization and seeking a power-sharing deal. They also demanded government action against abuses they had suffered from rival groups, mainly

Arab pastoralists driven onto African farmlands by drought and desertification – and who had a nomadic tradition of armed militias.

The government responded to this armed and political threat by targeting the civilian populations from which the rebels were drawn, with the fighting reaching its peak in 2002–3. The government called on local tribes to assist fighting against the rebels in order to supplement its lack of military presence in the region, much of which was devoted to the conflict in the south. This ethnic manipulation by the government sought to exploit existing tensions between different tribes. It was mostly Arab nomadic tribes without a traditional homeland who responded to the call, forming the "Janjaweed" militias with support, arms, training, and organization provided by the government. The term was traditionally used in the region to refer to armed bandits or outlaws on horses or camels. The government has effectively shielded these militias from any accountability process.

The Sudanese government and the Arab Janjaweed militias have committed numerous attacks on civilians of the African Fur, Masalit, and Zaghawa ethnic groups. Together, they are responsible for killing thousands of civilians, raping women, and destroying villages, food stocks, and other supplies essential for survival. The abuses have virtually emptied rural areas that were previously populated by Masalit and Fur farmers. By the end of 2008, more than 2 million people had been displaced and nearly 2 million others were in need of humanitarian aid, according to UN reports. The region's people have been driven into camps and settlements in Darfur, where they live at the very edge of survival, subject to Janjaweed abuses, or have fled to neighboring countries, often Chad.

In August 2003 the first meeting between representatives of the rebel groups and the government was convened to seek a solution to the conflict. The host was President Idriss Deby of Chad. In November the government, the SLA, and the JEM signed two protocols, one on improvement of the humanitarian situation and the second on enhancement of the security situation in Darfur. In October 2004 an African Union mission, the AU Mission in Sudan (AMIS), was authorized to monitor the cease-fire between the parties and to help establish a secure route for refugees and **internally displaced persons**. The cease-fire was ineffective; AMIS was unable to protect civilians and stop the violence, and the humanitarian situation continued to worsen.

The Darfur Peace Agreement, between the government and the main faction of the SLA, was signed in May 2005, but another faction of the SLA and the JEM refused to participate, undermining the process. The Janjaweed militias were not party to the negotiations, nor did they sign the agreement; instead, the government promised to control and disarm them. The agreement established the so-called Darfur–Darfur Dialogue and Consultation to address the challenges of restoring peace and overcoming the divisions between communities. The agreement also contained provisions on wealth- and power-sharing. However, the agreement did not address some of the core issues at the heart of the conflict, among them land tenure and the powers and structure of local government, which were left to the Darfur–Darfur Dialogue and Consultation process. Nor was accountability addressed in the agreement, although on March 31, 2005, almost contemporaneously with the negotiations, the UN Security Council passed Resolution 1593 to refer the situation in Darfur to the ICC (see Chapter 13).

After much pressure the Sudanese government agreed to the establishment of a joint **United Nations–African Union** force, the UN–AU Hybrid Mission in Darfur (UNAMID), which was authorized in July 2007 by Security Council Resolution 1769 and began deploying troops in December. If fully deployed, this mission would be the largest in UN history. The first months of the mission proved difficult; there were staff shortages, and seven peacekeepers were killed in an attack on July 9, 2008. A new joint UN–AU mediator, Djbrill Bassole, former foreign minister of Burkina Faso, was appointed in June 2008.

Nonetheless, at the end of 2007 and beginning of 2008, the humanitarian crisis worsened and violence increased as some groups splintered and confrontations multiplied. The government launched major aerial bombardments and ground attacks in Western Darfur in February 2008. In turn, JEM rebels assaulted Khartoum in May, leaving at least 200 dead. This was a milestone in the Darfur conflict, the first military strike on the capital in 30 years.

Camps for internally displaced persons have become increasingly violent, with residents being manipulated by all sides while the government tries to force them to return to unsafe areas. The conditions for humanitarian organizations have become much more difficult, and some have withdrawn for security reasons. The personnel and assets of these organizations have also been targeted for attacks.

Box 8.2 **Key players in Sudan**

Individuals
Omar Hassan Ahmad al-Bashir: President of Sudan
John Garang: Late leader of the SPLA

Government
NIF: National Islamic Front. Dominates the National Congress Party, the party in government.
NCP: National Congress Party. The party in government, comprising a coalition of parties including the Southern National Congress, an important representative of Southern Sudan.

Armed groups
Janjaweed: Government-supported militia (based in Darfur)
JEM: Justice and Equality Movement (based in Darfur)
SPLM/A: Sudanese People's Liberation Movement/Army
SLM/A: Sudanese Liberation Movement/Army (based in Darfur)

Regional organizations
AU: African Union
IGAD: Inter-Governmental Authority on Development

International missions
AMIS: AU Mission in Sudan (deployed in Darfur)
UNAMID: UN-AU Hybrid Mission in Darfur
UNMIS: UN Mission in Sudan

Human rights violations in Sudan

Certain human rights abuses have been important factors in both the conflict in the south and the conflict in Darfur. In particular, exclusion and marginalization in language policy, access to resources, and violations of freedom of religion significantly motivated the attempts by the SPLA to either secede from the country or defeat the Khartoum government. Similar concerns also prompted the rebel movements in Darfur. The conflicts themselves, however, sparked far greater violations of human rights – by all sides, although the government does appear to bear particular responsibility.

Human rights violations as underlying causes of conflict

As we have seen, several causes underpin the conflict in Sudan, including religion, access to resources, race, and geographic distinctions. Each is contentious, and their impact on the conflict and motivation have changed over time. Further, they are interrelated, as geographic distinctions are clearly linked to racial and religious divides, whether artificial or real.

Among the apparent human rights causes of the conflict are real and perceived discrimination, and attempts to impose religion and constrain freedom of religion. So too are demands for self-rule, enshrined in part for the first time in the 1972 Addis Ababa Agreement. This autonomy worked relatively well, at least until the discovery of oil and the northern government's attempt to control it spurred old resentments. Demands over governance, self-determination claims, and access to resources also underpin the conflict.

Elitism and discrimination based on race and ethnicity

Southern resentment and at least some of the impetus for armed conflict have been rooted in historical and contemporary inequities, with the south largely excluded from access to power and wealth.

Colonial rulers exploited the racial distinction between north and south. Even if racial distinctions between Arabs in the north and black Africans in the south may have been artificial and constructed, they were embedded and reinforced through colonialism and had long-term effects on the perceptions of both groups. The Anglo-Egyptian administration encouraged separate development of the two groups, giving preference to the economic and political development of the Arab elites of the north and generally denying education, especially Arabic language skills, and development to black Africans of the south. Under colonial rule, slave trade of southerners by northern Sudanese was encouraged. Slavery has continued to the modern day, disproportionately targeting members from the non-Muslim Dinka ethnic group, and has also been common during the conflict, particularly as part of the government's strategy to depopulate parts of southern Sudan.

After independence, discriminatory policies continued. The race issue should not be over-emphasized, but understood as part of a dynamic interaction between race, religion, and geography, and within the context of elite dominance of a few tribes in the north, who also dominated other northerners. Not only has the north been traditionally disproportionately represented in state institutions of the country as a whole, but also even within the north, three Arab tribes, the Shaigiyya, the Jaalyee and the Dongollawis, have dominated key institutions. For example, the head of the state security forces has always been a member of one of these three tribes, and the National Council for the Distribution of Resources, formed for oil exploration and exploitation, is dominated by Arab elites of the north, even though most of the oil is located in the south.

In Darfur, the conflict is mainly related to ethnicity rather than religion, as all involved are generally Muslim. Fighting is linked to control over land and livestock.

In both conflicts the government has sought to stoke preexisting ethnic tensions, such as those between the Nuer and the Dinka in the area around the Upper Nile oilfield, and those between the Zaghawa, Fur, and Masalit tribes and Arab nomads.

Restrictions on freedom of religion and Islamization

Islamists of the National Islamic Front have dominated the current government since it came to power, while the SPLA has remained mainly secular and pushed for a clear division between religion and state. The attempts by the north to impose *sharia* law in the south are often signaled as the cause of the second civil war. It was clearly and explicitly an aim of the government of Khartoum to Islamize parts of the country that were home to non-Muslims, and to promote its own version of Islam to those who were already Muslim, to the extent that this could constitute a self-proclaimed jihad. International organizations and religious groups have accused the government of persecuting Christian churches and believers, and of punishing apostasy or conversion by Muslims to other religions with death. However, while freedom of religion has been a demand in the conflict, the war actually began before the imposition of *sharia* law, with disbandment of the provincial Juba assembly and alteration of provincial borders to allow for northern control of oil resources.

Human rights violations emerging from and transforming the conflict

The consequences of the conflict in the south have been catastrophic. An estimated 2 million people have lost their lives, and the conflict has generated an estimated 4 million internally displaced persons out of a total national population of 38 million. In addition to the many civilian deaths resulting from the conflict, severe human rights abuses have been committed. The government's forces and their associates have conducted the great majority of these abuses, but the SPLA has also been responsible for killing and injuring civilians.

In Darfur the death toll is strongly disputed, with the UN estimating a minimum of 200,000 killed, a number contested as being both too low, according to nongovernmental organizations (NGOs), and too high, according to the government. Some NGOs argue that 400,000 have died during the five years of conflict. Over 2 million people have been displaced in a worsening humanitarian situation in the region. All parties to the conflict have committed human rights violations, but the tactics of the government and the Janjaweed militias it sponsors have been particularly cruel.

The serious violations of human rights and humanitarian law have themselves further fueled resentment and conflict. Security forces and associated militias have carried out extrajudicial killings and disappearances, and regularly beat, harass, arbitrarily arrest, and detain, incommunicado, opponents and suspected opponents of the government; there have been reports of **torture** as well. Both security forces and associated militias have beaten refugees, raped women abducted during raids, and harassed and detained internally displaced persons, acting with complete **impunity**. The government has also manipulated humanitarian aid in some areas and prevented the delivery of food, using famine as a weapon in the war. Antigovernment insurgent groups, too, have committed numerous serious abuses. The particularly cruel and bloody tactics used in attacking civilians in Darfur have attracted international outrage, with some arguing that a genocide is under way.

Violations in the south and access to resources

As discussed, the discovery of oil in the south of Sudan in the 1970s helped reignite the conflict. Sudan's oilfields are mainly located in the boundary between north and south, with the largest deposits located in the southern region of the Upper Nile, which the government has aggressively exploited since the 1989 coup. The government has continued its operations even in areas that were abandoned by the major oil companies due to security concerns when the civil war erupted. For example, Chevron abandoned oil exploitation in 1984 after a number of its expatriate employees were kidnapped and killed. However, other companies were prepared to build the infrastructure for oil development, including Chinese and Malaysian companies, and the Canadian company Talisman Energy. Talisman Energy withdrew in 2003 following allegations of its complicity in serious human rights abuses. It now faces a lawsuit in the United States for such allegations, as is discussed in greater detail later in this chapter and in Chapter 11.

Government tactics have included coordinated attacks on civilian settlements involving aerial bombardment and raids by helicopter gunships, followed by ground attacks in which government forces and militias burn villages and crops, loot livestock, and kill and abduct civilians. Oil companies such as Talisman Energy have been accused of providing launching areas for these attacks.

Clashes over agricultural lands and livestock led to further abuses during the north–south conflict. Since the mid-1980s, successive governments have supported armed groups that raid villages and abduct people to be sold as slaves to commercial farms and children to act as "domestic helpers." The SPLA has also been accused of abducting people for the slave trade. The government denies that slavery is practiced, and there are serious disagreements about the extent of it. NGOs estimate that between 5,000 and 200,000 people have been abducted as slaves since the mid-1980s. Those enslaved often live in appalling conditions. They are denied access to their families and cultural background and identity, and are even forced to adopt Islam. Some are sexually abused as well. Attempts to escape are harshly punished, including by death.

Abuses in Darfur transforming the conflict

Despite the peace process, the conflict, abuses, and humanitarian crisis have continued in Darfur, with wide-scale destruction of villages throughout the three states of Darfur resulting in deaths of civilians and massive displacement of the population.

In 2004 the Security Council asked the **UN Secretary-General** to commission a report on the situation of Darfur. The International Commission of Inquiry, instituted by the UN Secretary-General, issued its report on January 15, 2005. The commission established that Janjaweed attacks, with government support and with direct government involvement in some cases, include massacres, summary executions of civilians (including women and children), burnings of towns and villages, and the forcible depopulation of wide swathes of land long inhabited by the Fur, Masalit, and Zaghawa. The Janjaweed militias, although Muslim like the African groups they attack, have destroyed mosques, killed Muslim religious leaders, and desecrated Qurans belonging to their enemies.

The atrocities in Darfur have transformed the internal conflict into ethnic cleansing and perhaps even genocide. The International Commission of Inquiry established that persecution and "ethnic cleansing" have taken place, but did not term the abuses "genocide." It is clear from the facts of the situation that African tribes have been targeted. The rebel groups allege that the government and the Janjaweed have committed genocide by specifically targeting people from African tribes, specifically the Fur, Masaalit, Zaghaba, Birgit, Aranga, Jebel, and Tama. Rebel groups allege that extensive rapes have been committed by the government and the Janjaweed forces, targeting only women from African tribes. They accuse the government and the Janjaweed of abducting women and children and systematically looting property, including livestock, cash, and utensils. Conversely, the government insists that the conflict has no ethnic dimension, but instead is related to historical intertribal conflict. The government maintains that it is protecting civilians in the area. It justifies attacks as counterinsurgency responses, accusing the SLA and JEM of most of the atrocities committed in Darfur and of the displacement and destruction. The government admits that its forces follow rebels into villages where the latter hide, but claims that destruction of villages is caused by the subsequent fighting and that casualties are the consequence of civilians being caught in the crossfire.

Although there is less information on the violations committed by the rebel groups in Darfur, the SLA (particularly the SLA faction led by Minni Minawi) and the JEM are also guilty of abuses, including killings, beatings, rape, robbery, destruction of property, forced conscription, restricting freedom of movement of populations under their control, kidnapping, restricting access of relief workers and supplies, killing NGO workers, as well as targeting AU **peacekeeping** personnel.

Applicable law and possible subjects of legal accountability

The north–south conflict

The widespread abuses that took place in the conflict in the south – disappearances, rapes, and massacres – are clearly violations of human rights law and humanitarian law. Sudan is party to the four **Geneva Conventions**, which it ratified in 1957, and to their two additional protocols, ratified in 2006. This conflict, despite its regional repercussions, is an internal one. Therefore, **Common Article 3** of the Geneva Conventions applies, as does Additional Protocol II. This would mean that the violations committed during the conflict do not amount to **grave breaches** of the Geneva Conventions, excepting, perhaps, the violations committed in the context of the Sudan–Chad confrontation between 2005 and 2007. However, they can be considered crimes against humanity, as the violations have involved systematic and widespread attacks against civilians.

Government-related militias have allegedly engaged in slave raiding and trading. The Slavery Convention, which entered into force on March 9, 1927, established that state parties are obligated to prevent and suppress the slave trade, and to bring about the complete abolition of slavery in all its forms, in the territories under their jurisdiction. Sudan ratified this convention in 1957; regardless, the prohibition on slavery has achieved the status of a *jus cogens* norm.

During the north–south conflict there were also numerous violations for which the state might be responsible, such as its failure to protect human rights under its jurisdiction.

Militias and rebel groups have also been responsible for violations of human rights and violations of international humanitarian law. Companies involved in the exploitation of natural resources in Sudan may also have culpability if they participated in the abuses. As discussed, the Chevron Corporation withdrew in 1984, but Talisman Energy, one of the companies that took over the concession, currently faces a civil suit in the United States under the **Alien Tort Claims Act** (see Chapter 11) brought forward by the Presbyterian Church of Sudan (see Box 8.3).

Box 8.3 *Presbyterian Church of Sudan v. Talisman Energy*

In 2001 in the United States, a number of Sudanese individuals and the Presbyterian Church of Sudan brought a claim against the Canadian company Talisman Energy under the Alien Tort Claims Act. The plaintiffs alleged that the company had been complicit in the Sudanese government's human rights abuses against non-Muslim Sudanese living in the area of Talisman's oil concession in southern Sudan. From 1998 to 2002, Talisman owned a 25 percent share of an oil pipeline project in the area. The plaintiffs argued that the acts committed by the government, to which the company was complicit, amounted to genocide. They claimed that these acts were part of an armed campaign of ethnic cleansing against the non-Muslim Sudanese that included massive civilian displacement, extrajudicial killing of civilians, torture, rape, and the burning of villages, churches, and crops. The primary allegation involved the use of Talisman's facilities as a base for government bombing missions. On September 12, 2006, the District Court of the Southern District of New York granted Talisman's motion to dismiss the case. In February 2007 the plaintiffs appealed this dismissal to the US Court of Appeals for the Second Circuit.

The lawsuit attracted international attention, and the Canadian government even intervened, urging the Second Circuit not to hear the case on the basis of lack of jurisdiction, and warning that such a move would "create friction in Canada–U.S. relations."

Partly due to the security situation in the area but also due to adverse public relations, Talisman withdrew from Sudan in 2006. Talisman strongly denies any participation in human rights abuses, maintaining that it did not know that government troops were using its facilities for bombing missions, and that it successfully demanded a halt to these operations as soon as it learned of them in the fall of 1999. The company praises itself for its support to human rights in general and for several community programs in the country in particular.

Abuses in Darfur: genocide?

Most of the types of human rights violations committed during the north–south conflict have also been committed in Darfur. The attacks that have taken place appear to target civilians, not rebels, offering a clear case for crimes against humanity. However, it is less clear whether the attacks in Darfur also meet the definition of genocide – that is, whether attacks by the government and the Janjaweed militias demonstrate an intent to destroy a group in whole or in part.

Some advocacy groups, and the United States, have characterized the abuses as genocide. The Special Envoy of the United States to Darfur, Andrew Natsios, expressed this view before the Foreign Relations Committee of the US Senate (see Box 8.4).

The International Commission of Inquiry concluded that both the government of Sudan and the Janjaweed militias were responsible for serious violations of international human rights law and international humanitarian law, amounting to crimes against humanity. However, it asserted that there was no evidence of an intent to destroy a group, in whole or in part. Therefore, the acts committed in Darfur could not be considered genocide (see Box 8.5).

Box 8.4 **Genocide in Darfur? The US position**

Darfur: A "Plan B" to Stop Genocide?
Andrew S. Natsios, President's Special Envoy to Sudan
Testimony Before the Senate Foreign Relations Committee
Washington, DC
April 11, 2007

"As Prepared
"Thank you, Mr. Chairman and Members of the Committee. I appreciate the oppor-tunity to be here with you today to discuss how the United States (U.S.), together with the United Nations (UN) and our international partners, is addressing the crisis in Darfur.

"A great deal has happened since I last gave testimony – some of it frustrating, some of it hopeful – but what has not changed is the Administration's firm commitment to ending the violence and responding to the immeasurable suffering of the people of Darfur. The only U.S. interest in Darfur is a peaceful end to the crisis. . . . While we have a relationship with the Sudanese government on counter-terrorism issues, this relationship has not prevented us from elevating humanitarian and human rights concerns to a pre-eminent position in our policy toward Sudan. As a country and as a government we are appalled by the atrocities that have occurred in Darfur including those in 2003 and 2004 when some of the worst violence occurred, and the United States has made solving conflict in this region a priority.

"This is the third war in Darfur in just over twenty years, but it is by far the most destructive in terms of lives lost and people displaced. The current war is not a 'simple' conflict between Arab and African tribes, but a much more complex dispute fueled by drought and desertification, disputes over land rights, competition between nomadic herders and farmers, and longstanding marginalization of Darfur by the Government in Khartoum. The Sudanese government's disastrous decision to arm, direct, and pay Northern Arab tribes, now called the Janjaweed, as their proxies in the war against Darfur's rebels led to genocide and resulted in the deaths of hundreds of thousands of innocent civilians and the destruction of their villages and livelihoods." [emphasis added]

Source: http://www.state.gov/p/af/rls/rm/82941.htm.

Box 8.5 **Genocide in Darfur? Conclusions of the International Commission of Inquiry**

Extract from *Report of the International Commission of Inquiry on Darfur to the United Nations Secretary-General*, January 25, 2005, paras. 507–22:

"507. *General*. There is no doubt that some of the objective elements of genocide materialized in Darfur. . . . The Commission has collected substantial and reliable material which tends to show the occurrence of systematic killing of civilians belonging to particular tribes, of large-scale causing of serious bodily or mental harm to members of the population belonging to certain tribes, and of massive and deliberate infliction on those tribes of conditions of life bringing about their physical destruction in whole or in part (for example by systematically destroying their villages and crops, by expelling them from their homes, and by looting their cattle). However, two other constitutive elements of genocide require a more in depth analysis, namely whether (a) the target groups amount to one of the group protected by international law, and if so (b) whether the crimes were committed with a genocidal intent. . . .

"518. *Conclusions*. . . . the Commission concludes that the Government of Sudan has not pursued a policy of genocide. Arguably, two elements of genocide might be deduced from the gross violations of human rights perpetrated by Government forces and the militias under their control. These two elements are: first, the *actus reus* consisting of killing, or causing serious bodily or mental harm, or deliberately inflicting conditions of life likely to bring about physical destruction; and, second, on the basis of a subjective standard, the existence of a protected group being targeted by the authors of criminal conduct. Recent developments have led to the perception and self-perception of members of African tribes and members of Arab tribes as making up two distinct ethnic groups. However, one crucial element appears to be missing, at least as far as the central Government authorities are concerned: genocidal intent. Generally speaking the policy of attacking, killing and forcibly displacing members of some tribes does not evince a specific intent to annihilate, in whole or in part, a group distinguished on racial, ethnic, national or religious grounds. Rather, it would seem that those who planned and organized attacks on villages pursued the intent to drive the victims from their homes, primarily for purposes of counter-insurgency warfare."

Following the Security Council's referral of the Darfur situation to the ICC, the Court is now in a position to determine whether the campaign of violence undertaken by the Sudanese government and the Janjaweed militias constitutes genocide, as discussed in Chapter 13, and may reach a decision different than that of the International Commission of Inquiry.

According to the Sudanese government, the attacks are carried out by the Janjaweed militias and are therefore not attributable to it (or that its involvement, where acknowledged, is for counterinsurgency purposes). The government claims that it is actually trying to restrain these militias, and that what is taking place is "tribal warfare." In June 2005 the Sudanese government established a tribunal, the Special Criminal Court on Events in Darfur, purportedly to try individuals guilty of abuses. However, this appears to have been an attempt to prevent international trials. None of the first cases tried by the new tribunal concerned major crimes associated with the conflict. No mid- or high-level government officials or militia leaders were suspended from duty, investigated, or prosecuted for serious crimes in Darfur. The government also tried to prevent international trials by establishing "tribal" or "traditional" justice courts for Darfur, which also have not conducted significant proceedings.

The government's denial of cooperation with the Janjaweed is not convincing, as documented in a 2003 report authored by **Human Rights Watch**. This report documents joint attacks, often with air support from the Sudanese military. According to the report, although the Janjaweed always outnumber regular soldiers, during attacks the government forces usually arrive first and leave last. In the words of one displaced villager, "They [the soldiers] see everything" that the Janjaweed are doing. "They come with them, they fight with them and they leave with them." However, the government asserts that it has acted only for counterinsurgency purposes, and the International Commission of Inquiry, as shown in Box 8.5, seems to accept this claim.

Key points

- There are two main conflicts in Sudan: the north–south conflict between the government of Sudan and the Sudanese People's Liberation Movement/Army (SPLM/A), and the conflict in the Darfur region between the government of Sudan and the Sudan Liberation Movement/Army (SLM/A) and the Justice and Equality Movement (JEM), but also involving the Janjaweed militia.
- Widespread atrocities have been carried out in both conflicts by all parties, with systematic targeting of civilians by the Janjaweed in Darfur.
- There is no consensus in the international community as to whether the events in Darfur can be considered genocide.
- The north–south conflict did not result in accountability mechanisms, while the Darfur situation is under consideration by the International Criminal Court.
- Two international peacekeeping missions are present in the country, including a joint mission undertaken by the United Nations (UN) and the African Union.

Discussion questions

Determining accountability

As we have seen, all parties to the conflict in Sudan – the government, the militias, and the rebel groups – have been responsible for atrocities. We must now consider the extent to which the actions of the Janjaweed militias may be attributed to the government, and the potential role of foreign corporations in aggravating the conflict.

- According to the International Commission of Inquiry, the actions in Darfur do not constitute genocide. What does this mean in terms of individual responsibility for those involved?
- Could the actions of the Janjaweed militias be attributed to the state? If so, what difference would this make in identifying specific acts as international crimes?
- Could officials of Talisman Energy be prosecuted for violations of international law?

Prospects for addressing violations

The government of Sudan has no evident interest in pursuing extensive accountability, which could implicate its high-level officials. To date, no proceedings, either outside or inside Sudan, have been initiated to address abuses committed during the north–south civil war, excepting the case concerning Talisman Energy. However, a great deal more attention has been paid to the violence and abuses being committed in Darfur, including the case before the ICC, which has triggered vigorous opposition from the government. But as we have seen, there have been few Darfur-related domestic trials.

- How does the absence of accountability provisions in the Comprehensive Peace Agreement affect the possibility of prosecutions for violations committed during the north–south conflict?
- Given the nature and behavior of the Sudanese government to date, do you think that domestic trials could provide accountability for the human rights violations?

Achieving stability

The peace agreement between the government of Sudan and the SPLA remains fragile, and there are fears that it could collapse. Despite the signing of the Darfur Peace Agreement in 2005, the conflict and human rights violations have continued.

- What are the main risks of a return to conflict in the south?
- Would investigations and prosecutions by the International Criminal Court help, or jeopardize, the chances for achieving peace in the region and ending human rights abuses?

Group exercise

Form two groups. Gather evidence from reports by international and state bodies on the human rights abuses committed in Darfur. One group should argue for treating the acts in Darfur as genocide, and the other group should argue against. Both groups should discuss the legal repercussions that such a designation would have.

Box 8.6 **Sudan timeline**

1899–1955	Sudan under joint British-Egyptian rule.
1956	Independence.
1958	Military coup against the civilian government elected earlier in the year.
1962	Civil war begins in the south, led by the Anya Nya movement (SSLM).
1964	"October Revolution" overthrows the government; new national government established.
1969	New military coup, the "May Revolution," led by Jafar Numeiri.
1972	Addis Ababa Agreement between the government and the Anya Nya movement; the south becomes a self-governing region.

1978	Oil discovered in Bentiu in the south.
1983	Civil war breaks out again in the south, involving government forces and the SPLM, led by John Garang. President Numeiri declares the introduction of *sharia* law.
1985	Numeiri deposed by a group of officers; Transitional Military Council established to rule the country.
1986	Coalition government formed after general elections, led by Sadiq al-Mahdi as prime minister.
1989	National Salvation Revolution takes over in military coup.
1993	Omar al-Bashir appointed president; Revolution Command Council dissolved.
1999	President Bashir dissolves National Assembly and declares a state of emergency.
	Sudan begins to export oil.
2000	Bashir reelected president for further five years.
2001	Islamist leader Hassan al-Turabi's party, the Popular National Congress (PNC), signs a memorandum of understanding with the SPLA; al-Turabi arrested the next day, with more arrests of PNC members in following months. Government accepts a Libyan–Egyptian initiative to end the civil war after the failure of peace talks between President Bashir and SPLM leader John Garang in Nairobi.
2002	*July*: The government and SPLA sign the first peace agreement: the Machakos Protocol.
2003	*February*: Rebels in Western Darfur rise up against the government. *January*: The army moves to quell a rebel uprising in Western Darfur; hundreds of thousands of refugees flee to neighboring Chad. *May*: Government and southern rebels agree on power-sharing protocols as part of a peace deal to end the north–south conflict.
2005	*January*: Government and southern rebels sign a peace agreement that includes a permanent cease-fire and accords on wealth- and power-sharing. *March*: The UN Security Council votes to refer those accused of war crimes in Darfur to International Criminal Court. *June*: The government and the exiled opposition group National Democratic Alliance (NDA) sign a reconciliation deal allowing NDA into power-sharing administration. President Bashir frees the Islamist leader Hassan al-Turabi, detained since March 2004 over an alleged coup plot. *July 9*: Former SPLM leader John Garang sworn in as first vice president; a constitution giving significant autonomy to the south is signed.

August 1: Vice president and former rebel leader John Garang killed in a plane crash and succeeded by Salva Kiir; Garang's death sparks deadly clashes in the capital between southern Sudanese and northern Arabs.
September: A power-sharing government formed in Khartoum.
October: An autonomous government formed in the south, in line with the January 2005 peace deal; the administration is dominated by former rebels.

2006   *May*: The Khartoum government and the main rebel faction in Darfur, the SLM, sign a peace accord, but fighting continues.
November: The African Union extends the mandate of its peacekeeping force in Darfur for six months.

2007   *April*: Sudan says it will accept partial UN troop deployment to reinforce AU peacekeepers in Darfur, but not a full 20,000-strong force.
May: The International Criminal Court issues arrest warrants for both a minister and a Janjaweed militia leader suspected of committing war crimes in Darfur.
July: The UN Security Council approves a resolution authorizing UNAMID.
October: The SPLM temporarily suspends participation in the national unity government, accusing Khartoum of failing to honor the 2005 peace deal.
December: The SPLM resumes participation in the national unity government.

2008   *January*: The UN takes over the Darfur peace force; the Sudanese government bombs rebel positions in Western Darfur, preventing access by aid workers.
March: The Presidents of Sudan and Chad sign an accord aimed at halting five years of hostilities between their countries.
May: The southern defense minister, Dominic Dim Deng, is killed in a plane crash in the south; tension increases between Sudan and Chad, resulting in severed diplomatic relations; intense fighting breaks out between northern and southern Sudanese forces in the disputed oil-rich town of Abyei.
June: President Bashir and the southern leader, Salva Kiir, agree to seek international arbitration to resolve the dispute over Abyei.
July: The International Criminal Court's top prosecutor calls for the arrest of President Bashir for genocide, crimes against humanity, and war crimes committed in Darfur, representing the first ever request to the ICC for the arrest of a sitting head of state; Sudan rejects the indictment.
November: President Bashir announces an immediate cease-fire in Darfur, but the region's two main rebel groups reject the move, saying they will fight until the government agrees to share power and wealth in the region.

Further reading

Abass, Ademola, "Proving State Responsibility for Genocide: The ICJ in *Bosnia v. Serbia* and the International Commission of Inquiry for Darfur," *Fordham International Law Journal* 31, no. 4 (2008): 871–910.

——, "The United Nations, the African Union, and the Darfur Crisis: Of Apology and Utopia," *Netherlands International Law Review* 54, no. 3 (2007): 415–40.

Human Rights Watch, "Sudan, Oil, and Human Rights" (2003), http://www.hrw.org/reports/2003/sudan1103/sudanprint.pdf.

Idris, Amir, *Conflict and Politics of Identity in Sudan* (London: Palgrave Macmillan, 2005).

International Crisis Group, "Darfur's New Security Reality" (2007), http://www.crisisgroup.org/library/documents/africa/horn_of_africa/134_darfur_s_new_security_reality.pdf.

——, "God, Oil, and Country: Changing the Logic of War in Sudan" (2002), http://www.crisisgroup.org/library/documents/report_archive/a400534_28012002.pdf.

——, "The Khartoum–SPLM Agreement: Sudan's Uncertain Peace" (July 25, 2005), http://www.crisisgroup.org/library/documents/africa/horn_of_africa/096_the_khartoum_splm_agreement_sudan_uncertain_peace.pdf.

Iyob, Ruth, and Gilbert M. Khadiagala, *Sudan: The Elusive Quest for Peace* (Boulder: Lynne Rienner, 2006).

Johnson, Douglas, *The Root Causes of Sudan's Civil Wars* (Oxford: James Currey, 2003).

Sriram, Chandra, *Peace as Governance* (London: Palgrave, 2008), chap. 4.

Official documents and sources

United Nations, *Report of the International Commission of Inquiry on Darfur to the United Nations Secretary-General* (January 25, 2005), http://www.icc-cpi.int/library/cases/report_to_un_on_darfur.pdf.

——, Office of the UN Deputy Special Representative of the UN Secretary-General for Sudan, *Darfur Humanitarian Profile* no. 29 (October 1, 2007), http://www.unsudanig.org/docs/hnp%2029_narrative_1%20october%202007.pdf.

9   The "global war on terror"

Carmen Draghici

Overview

The case studies discussed in preceding chapters illustrate traditional types of conflicts that may entail violations of **international human rights** and **humanitarian law**. However, it is useful to include in our overview of contemporary conflict situations that affect human rights an account of what is commonly referred to as the "global war on terror." This chapter discusses the tension between the struggle to guarantee human security and the infringement of human rights stemming from antiterrorist action, whether military or not. Counterterrorism tends to impair fundamental human rights, such as the right to life, personal liberty, humane treatment, fair trial, privacy, and freedom of expression. This is caused by the emergency legislation and investigative practices adopted by governments, even in democratic countries, in order to respond to the terrorist threat, by unlawful conduct during military operations motivated by self-defense against terrorism, as well as by certain multilateral counter-terrorism strategies, particularly those undertaken through the **UN Security Council**.

The war on terror as a new type of conflict

The association of antiterrorism with the concept of war has emerged in the aftermath of the catastrophic events of September 11, 2001, when coordinated suicide attacks upon the United States by Islamist terrorists affiliated with the Al-Qaida network resulted in the deaths of nearly 3,000 victims. The Al-Qaida terrorists hijacked four commercial passenger airliners and deliberately crashed two of them into the twin towers of the World Trade Center in New York, causing huge civilian casualties, while a third airliner was crashed into the Pentagon. The terrorist leader considered to be responsible for the attacks was Osama bin Laden, a key player in the alliance between the Al-Qaida network and the Taliban regime, the Islamic fundamentalist movement in power in Afghanistan since 1996. The refusal of the Taliban to extradite bin Laden led to the US attack on Afghanistan starting on October 7, 2001. In a **UN Security Council resolution**, Resolution 1378 of November 14, 2001, the United Nations also condemned the Taliban for allowing Afghanistan to be used as a base for the export of terrorism by Al-Qaida and for providing safe haven to bin Laden, and expressed support for international efforts to root out terrorism. The invasion of Afghanistan in the fall of 2001 signaled the beginning of the war on terror – a war in which terrorists have been apprehended in different countries and denied their rights as prisoners of war. In the meantime, civil liberties have also been curtailed domestically, as a means to prevent further attacks.

Launched by the US government, the campaign against terrorism has been joined by the whole international community, and undoubtedly bears resemblance to a conflict situation.

Nonetheless, for the most part this campaign falls short of war. The accurate distinction between a state of war in a strict legal sense and war as a metaphor in political discourse determines the extent of states' obligations under international human rights law, and the applicability of international humanitarian law. As discussed in Chapter 4, international humanitarian law is a set of norms applying in the case of armed conflict that protect civilians and parties who no longer participate actively in the hostilities (prisoners, wounded combatants). Where antiterrorism involves proper military operations, international humanitarian law is applicable, alongside core norms of international human rights law. It is important to stress in this regard that international human rights law, while potentially limited due to the possibility of some derogation in situations of public emergency and armed conflict, does not cease to apply. Conversely, when the war on terror does not amount to an armed conflict, all human rights norms continue to be fully applicable, though states may temporarily suspend the application of specific provisions of human rights treaties in order to face terrorist emergencies.

Although most people associate terrorism with the indiscriminate killing of innocent civilians, suspected terrorists are also potential victims of human rights abuses. Moreover, the rights of the citizenry at large are also at stake, as preventive antiterrorism measures tend to encroach upon their rights and liberties. As this chapter discusses, the necessity to strike a proper balance between security interests and individual rights in the global war on terror is not always duly considered.

The "Bush Doctrine"

The concept of "war on terror" is one of the pillars of the so-called Bush Doctrine, which encapsulates the US approach to international affairs since the attacks of September 11, 2001. Its most significant expression is found in *The National Security Strategy of the United States* of September 2002 (see Box 9.1), a policy document published by the White House in the aftermath of Al-Qaida's attacks.

Box 9.1 The National Security Strategy of the United States

"The United States of America is fighting a war against terrorists of global reach. The enemy is not a single political regime or person or religion or ideology. The enemy is terrorism – premeditated, politically motivated violence perpetrated against innocents. . . . The struggle against global terrorism is different from any other war in our history. It will be fought on many fronts against a particularly elusive enemy over an extended period of time. . . . While the United States will constantly strive to enlist the support of the international community, we will not hesitate to act alone, if necessary, to exercise our right of self-defense by acting preemptively against such terrorists, to prevent them from doing harm against our people and our country."

Source: White House, *The National Security Strategy of the United States* (September 2002), chap. 3, "Strengthen Alliances to Defeat Global Terrorism and Work to Prevent Attacks Against Us and Our Friends," at http://www.whitehouse.gov/nsc/nss.pdf.

In light of the Bush Doctrine, the war on terror can be described as an atypical conflict characterized by three elements of novelty: asymmetric warfare, self-defense doctrine applied against **nonstate actors**, and attempts to legitimize "preventive war."

Asymmetric warfare

The exact legal significance to be attached to the war on terror is highly controversial. Conventionally, war is waged between states, or between government and insurgents, or between rival factions. Al-Qaida and, more generally, terrorist networks cannot be engaged in an international armed conflict so long as their actions cannot be attributed to a state. On the other hand, such terrorist cells cannot qualify as well-identified parties to an internal conflict, for, unlike rebel groups or insurgents, they do not have a responsible command structure and control over a specific territory. Their international, variably cohesive membership compounds the difficulty of classifying terrorist networks as parties to an internal conflict as defined in Chapter 4. Their lack of distinctive characteristics required by international humanitarian law, and their sporadic attacks, are further obstacles to such a classification.

However, an international conflict did exist with the initiation on October 7, 2001, of military operations against Afghanistan, including an aerial bombing campaign, led by a US–UK coalition whose declared purpose was to capture Osama bin Laden, defeat Al-Qaida, and remove the Taliban regime, which had provided support and safe harbor to the terrorist group. In fact, the Bush Doctrine extended the concept of "enemy" to states harboring or supporting terrorists, and indeed under international law the conduct of armed groups acting under the overall control of a government may be imputed to that government.

Since the removal from power of the Taliban and the creation of a new Afghan regime led by President Hamid Karzai, sworn in on June 19, 2002, the engagement of US and allied forces in Afghanistan no longer amounts to an international conflict. Rather, if the ongoing military confrontation between pro-government and opposition forces is an internal conflict, US support to the Afghan government arguably makes the United States party to an internal conflict.

Thus, with the exception of those situations in which terrorist acts can be considered as conduct of a state, the term "war" is misleading. While it is true that they commit offenses of significant gravity, terrorists are essentially criminals, and not combatants. Thus, the more appropriate legal framework for antiterrorism is *law enforcement*, even though this occasionally implies *extraterritorial* law enforcement mechanisms (when operations, such as the seizure of suspects, take place on the territory of other states). Consequently, international human rights law rather than international humanitarian law is the applicable human rights standard governing counterterrorism. In fact, for the most part, unlike conventional war, which involves military confrontation, the war on terrorism, understood in a nontechnical sense, involves police and intelligence operations, economic sanctions, and criminal justice.

Self-defense doctrine applied against nonstate actors

The Bush Doctrine introduced a new legal approach to terrorism, with the US administration characterizing the attacks of September 11 as an act of war rather than a criminal act. An important consequence of this qualification was that the war on terror was theoretically grounded on the inherent right to self-defense provided for by general customary law and enshrined in Article 51 of the **UN Charter** (see Box 9.2).

Box 9.2 **The UN Charter, Article 51**

> "Nothing in the present Charter shall impair the inherent right of individual or collective self-defence if an armed attack occurs against a Member of the United Nations, until the Security Council has taken measures necessary to maintain international peace and security. . . ."

At the same time, the preamble of Security Council Resolution 1368, adopted on September 12, 2001, also speaks about self-defense against terrorist acts, even though the operative paragraphs emphasize police and judicial cooperation. The resolution has generated doctrinal confusion, as it appears to contradict the reference to self-defense in the UN Charter, which only concerns interstate relations. Indeed, even though Article 51 does not further qualify the "armed attack" to explicitly attribute it to a state, the July 9, 2004, advisory opinion of the **International Court of Justice** (ICJ) on the legal consequences of constructing a wall in occupied Palestinian territory interprets it in this way (see Box 9.3).

Box 9.3 **Self-defense in the UN Charter: opinion of the International Court of Justice**

> "Article 51 of the Charter thus recognizes the existence of an inherent right of self-defence in the case of armed attack by one State against another State. However, Israel does not claim that the attacks against it are imputable to a foreign State. . . . Consequently, the Court concludes that Article 51 of the Charter has no relevance in this case" (para. 139).
>
> *Source*: International Court of Justice, "Legal Consequences of the Construction of a Wall in the Occupied Palestinian Territory" (July 9, 2004), http://www.icj-cij.org/docket/files/131/1671.pdf.

Some commentators, however, emphasize that state practice is favorable to a broader interpretation of the notion of self-defense. In the context of the Israeli attack in Lebanon in the summer of 2006, states' criticism did not address the right of Israel to react to incursions by Hezbollah from Lebanese territory, but rather the proportionality of those reactions.

Even if the concept of self-defense in international law is expanded to include defense against attacks by nonstate actors, its relevance in the context of terrorism remains controversial. In fact, self-defense may be exercised in response to actions by belligerent groups of foreign nationals (e.g. armed bands organizing raids into a state) if they are openly supported by the government of the national/territorial state, or if that state proves unable (or unwilling) to effectively remove the danger despite the appeal of the targeted state. The 2006 conflict in Lebanon was such a situation. But this is not the case in the war on terror, unless a specific state is sponsoring terrorism. Therefore, the language of self-defense may be inappropriate.

However, in the aftermath of the attacks of September 11, the United States and its main ally, the United Kingdom, reported to the Security Council, invoking Article 51. In this context, the shelter and support provided by the Afghan regime might justify attributing to it the attacks by Al-Qaida, and the use of self-defense doctrine. However, the generalized self-defense rationale for the fight against terrorists is not sufficiently grounded in international law. Some argue that it is rather an effect of US unilateralism, for it is invoked to rationalize the use of force outside the collective security system.

Attempts to legitimize "preventive" war

There is increasing agreement that the inherent right to self-defense is not strictly limited to situations in which an armed attack is already occurring or has occurred. Action in self-defense can also be legitimately taken in the face of imminent peril of an armed attack. However, the Bush Doctrine further stretches the *preemptive* defense theory, asserting the legitimacy of *preventive* war. Preemptive war is a reaction to an arguably imminent and specific threat, though falling short of the "ongoing armed attack" criterion for self-defense under international law. Preventive war, on the other hand, is a strategy aimed at anticipating merely potential threats. The phrasing of relevant US documents does not make a clear distinction between these terms, and they are used rather interchangeably. Legal scholars, however, underline the importance of the technical distinction: the lawfulness of preemptive war is disputable, but it may be found justified, whereas preventive war, referring to speculative threats, cannot be deemed lawful under the UN Charter and existing customary rules. The war on Iraq launched by a US-led multinational coalition on March 20, 2003, illustrates a self-proclaimed right to preventive war by the United States.

Terrorism as threat to international peace

Another effect of the 2001 attacks against the United States was a radical shift in the **United Nations'** (UN) approach to terrorism. While prior to that date the Security Council had addressed terrorism sporadically, in relation to specific crises, beginning with Resolution 1368 (2001) the Security Council has since treated acts of terrorism in general as a threat to peace and security, irrespective of their geopolitical context.

Resolution 1368 condemned the September 11 attacks and considered that such acts, "like any act of international terrorism," represent a threat to international peace and security. The preamble of the resolution expressed the Council's determination "to combat by all means threats to international peace and security caused by terrorist acts" and recognized "the inherent right of individual or collective self-defence in accordance with the Charter."

The emergence of a new, general, and abstract threat to international peace and security – the phenomenon of terrorism as such, rather than particular episodes of terrorist violence – was bolstered by Resolution 1373 of September 28, 2001. This resolution, adopted by the Security Council under Chapter VII, went far beyond being a specific response to Al-Qaida's attacks against the United States. In fact, it established new rules of international law, prompted by, but not tightly connected to, the September 11 events, requiring states to criminalize certain behavior and adopt specific antiterrorist measures. Resolution 1373 was viewed by some as a coercive ratification of parts of the Convention for the Suppression of the Financing of Terrorism, adopted on December 9, 1999, and not yet in force at that time.

The UN Security Council's new leading role in international action against terrorism was further demonstrated by Resolution 1377 (2001), which contained a "declaration on the global effort to combat terrorism." The resolution emphasized that acts of terrorism constitute one of the most serious threats to international peace and security, and urged states to fully implement Resolution 1373. Many subsequent resolutions pointed in the same direction, and it could be argued that the post-September 11 activism of the UN Security Council "internationalized" the global antiterror strategy of the United States.

The problems of defining terrorism

International counterterrorism law is elaborated in several conventions addressing prevention and suppression of specific acts of terrorism (see Box 9.4). However, attempts to adopt one comprehensive convention centered on a well-defined notion of terrorism, such as the ad hoc committee established by the **UN General Assembly** in 1996, have failed.

Box 9.4 Terrorism conventions

Convention on Offenses and Certain Other Acts Committed On Board Aircraft (1963)

Convention for the Suppression of Unlawful Seizure of Aircraft (1970)

Convention for the Suppression of Unlawful Acts Against the Safety of Civil Aviation (1971)

Convention on the Prevention and Punishment of Crimes Against Internationally Protected Persons (1973)

Convention on the Physical Protection of Nuclear Material (1979)

International Convention Against the Taking of Hostages (1979)

Protocol for the Suppression of Unlawful Acts of Violence at Airports Serving International Civil Aviation (1988)

Convention for the Suppression of Unlawful Acts Against the Safety of Maritime Navigation (1988)

Protocol for the Suppression of Unlawful Acts Against the Safety of Fixed Platforms Located on the Continental Shelf (1988)

Convention on the Marking of Plastic Explosives for the Purpose of Identification (1991)

International Convention for the Suppression of Terrorist Bombing (1997)

International Convention for the Suppression of the Financing of Terrorism (1999)

International Convention for the Suppression of Acts of Nuclear Terrorism (2005)

For the text of the conventions and their state of ratification, see http://untreaty. un.org/english/terrorism.asp.

The UN Security Council has repeatedly called for states to take action against terrorism, without detailing the notion of terrorist acts. The absence of a universally accepted definition of terrorism encourages states to adopt a definition at their convenience, for instance in order to oppress political adversaries by labeling them as terrorists. Moreover, states have often misused the momentum of UN calls for antiterrorist action to adopt disproportionate emergency legislation, and legislation restricting human rights.

Treaty-based human rights monitoring bodies have deplored the manipulative invocation of Resolution 1373 by countries with poor human rights records. The UN Counterterrorism Committee's June 2008 report to the Security Council on assessing the implementation of Resolution 1373 raised concerns about human rights violations, including restrictions on individual rights such as the right to a fair trial, freedom from torture, freedom of expression, and right to privacy.

Some guidance on the definition of terrorist behavior was provided by Resolution 1566 (2004), which asserted that

> criminal acts, including against civilians, committed with the intent to cause death or serious bodily injury, or taking of hostages, with the purpose to provoke a state of terror in the general public or in a group of persons or particular persons, intimidate a population or compel a government or an international organization to do or to abstain from doing any act, which constitute offences within the scope of and as defined in the international conventions and protocols relating to terrorism, are under no circumstances justifiable by considerations of a political, philosophical, ideological, racial, ethnic, religious or other similar nature.
>
> (para. 3)

This definition emphasizes the intent of terrorist acts (intimidating a population or compelling a government to act in a certain manner), and refers to international conventions on terrorism, but is not sufficient to identify actions that can be legitimately criminalized.

Applicable law

Post-September 11 counterterrorism encompasses measures adopted by states against foreign citizens and beyond national boundaries (for instance, arrest or detention abroad). The measures developed in the context of the global war on terror have restricted and derogated the enjoyment of certain human rights, and the rights of suspected terrorists have often been infringed by Western states on foreign territory, where these states can more easily bypass standards they are bound to observe under the scrutiny of domestic public opinion. It is essential, therefore, to emphasize the broad applicability of international human rights law, two aspects in particular.

The first is the irrelevance of nationality for the enjoyment of human rights. States are bound to respect the human rights of all individuals within their jurisdiction (i.e. over whom they exercise authority), and not only the rights of their own citizens. For instance, a German citizen held in US police custody has exactly the same rights to humane treatment or judicial protection as a US citizen.

The second is the extraterritoriality of human rights law. A state must observe human rights norms not only on its own territory, but wherever it exercises authority over an individual. Thus, while the United States and its allies were occupying powers in parts of Afghanistan and Iraq, they were bound not only by humanitarian law and customary human rights standards, but also by treaty-based human rights provisions.

Restrictions under human rights law

The **European Convention on Human Rights** (ECHR) (Article 1) and the American Convention on Human Rights (ACHR) (Article 1) explicitly require states to secure the rights and freedoms recognized therein to all persons within their jurisdiction. The UN Human Rights Committee has also interpreted the International Covenant on Civil and Political Rights (ICCPR) in a similar way, even if the UN covenant does not contain such explicit provision.

Nevertheless, human rights law allows some restrictions to accommodate security concerns. In the general human rights treaties the articulation of rights is accompanied by "safeguard clauses" designed to respond to security demands in situations falling short of emergencies (see Box 9.5). Such safeguard clauses appear in articles securing freedom of movement, freedom of religion, freedom of expression, and freedom of assembly.

Box 9.5 Sample text of a safeguard clause: the International Covenant on Civil and Political Rights, Article 21

"The right of peaceful assembly shall be recognized. *No restrictions may be placed on the exercise of this right other than those imposed in conformity with the law and which are necessary in a democratic society in the interests of national security or public safety, public order (ordre public), the protection of public health or morals or the protection of the rights and freedoms of others.*" [safeguard clause in italics]

The restrictions must satisfy certain criteria, however. They must be provided for by the law, and pursue one of the legitimate aims envisaged by the treaty (rights of others, public order, national security, etc.). As international case law indicates, in order to be deemed necessary they must be strictly required by, and proportionate to, the achievement of the aim pursued. Further, the right to life, personal liberty and security, humane treatment, and the majority of due process guarantees are not among the rights that can be restricted.

Derogations in situations of public emergency

General human rights treaties allow for the temporary suspension of the exercise of one or several rights (also referred to as *derogation*) in situations of public emergency that threaten "the life of the nation" (ICCPR, Article 4; ECHR, Article 15) or "the independence or security of a State Party" (ACHR, Article 27).

Derogations should take place only in exceptional circumstances where the need to suspend a right is compelling, and the measures must be adopted only to the extent, and for no longer than, strictly necessary. Quasi-permanent states of emergency are impermissible, as are derogations in areas not related to the emergency. Moreover, in any event, derogation measures must be adopted in a manner consistent with the principle of nondiscrimination. States cannot use the power to derogate unilaterally; rather, it must be subject to the supervision of treaty-based monitoring bodies.

There are, however, some rights that states are bound to enforce in any situation, called *nonderogable rights*. The list of nonderogable rights differs slightly from one treaty to another, but many of these rights do coincide, such as the right to protection against arbitrary deprivation of life, slavery, punishment without law, torture, and inhuman or degrading treatment. These rights are also protected by *peremptory norms* of international law, or *jus cogens* ("compelling law") – that is, norms accepted by the international community of states as reflecting its highest values, and from which no derogation is therefore permitted under any circumstance.

Substantive rights

Arbitrary deprivation of life

Under treaty-based human rights law, states have two types of obligations: not only are they bound to "respect" (i.e. not interfere with) fundamental rights and liberties (*negative* obligations), but they are also expected to "ensure" or "secure" such rights (i.e. actively enforce them, and defend them against violations by third parties) (*positive* obligations).

NEGATIVE OBLIGATIONS

The obligation to refrain from impairing the fundamental right to life means that states bear responsibility for the use of lethal force during antiterrorist operations. Such operations must aim at all times at preserving the life of individuals suspected of terrorism. In the fight against terrorism, the use of force employed must be absolutely necessary in order to prevent an attack or effect lawful arrest, and operations must be carefully planned and carried out in such a way as to minimize incidental loss of innocent civilian life. Furthermore, if death or injury occurs when a suspected or convicted terrorist is in state custody, there is a strong presumption of state responsibility. In such cases the burden of proof is on state authorities, who are expected to provide a satisfactory explanation for the cause of the individual's death.

When the war on terror takes the form of an armed conflict proper, and terrorists can be considered lawful military targets, international humanitarian law does not prohibit deprivation of life. However, the extrajudicial killing of suspected terrorists in circumstances falling short of war constitutes arbitrary deprivation of life, and violates human rights law.

POSITIVE OBLIGATIONS

While states normally do not incur responsibility for wrongful acts of private persons, positive human rights obligations require that states exercise due diligence in preventing such acts. This entails, however, only reasonable precautions against possible attacks. On the other hand, states must carry out effective investigations into unlawful killings, such as those arising from terrorist acts, in order to bring perpetrators to justice. In fact, according to the case law of the **European Court of Human Rights**, a violation of the right to life may also result from ineffective investigation, or a lack of investigation, into acts of private violence. Inaction amounts to a procedural violation of the obligations connected to the right to life, as opposed to the substantive violations that occur when the unlawful acts have been actually committed by state agents. The state is considered responsible for both substantive and procedural violations when the authorities fail to investigate an illegitimate use of lethal force by state agents.

Arbitrary deprivation of liberty

Preventive detention of terror suspects can be for longer than that of ordinary criminal suspects, as human rights monitoring bodies have recognized. However, the deprivation of liberty cannot be arbitrary, and there must be certain procedural safeguards. Detention without charge or access to a judge for persons suspected of participating in terrorist activities is, for the European Court, a violation of Article 5 of the ECHR, which secures the right to liberty. Moreover, according to the UN Human Rights Committee's "General Comment no. 29," the norm prohibiting the arbitrary prolonged deprivation of liberty has evolved into a peremptory norm. The multiple forms of violation of the right to personal liberty in the war on terror are illustrated more in detail later in this chapter.

Torture as an interrogation technique

The prohibition of torture and inhuman or degrading treatment (see Box 9.6) is a non-derogable provision of general human rights treaties (ICCPR, Article 7; ECHR, Article 3; ACHR, Article 5.2), which allow for no exception under any circumstances. It is also barred by the **Torture Convention** and two regional conventions, the Inter-American Convention to Prevent and Punish Torture (1985) and the European Convention for the Prevention of Torture and Inhuman or Degrading Treatment or Punishment (1987). The prohibition of torture irrespective of the presumed or proven conduct of an individual is among a few uncontroversial peremptory norms of general international law that cannot be superseded by a conflicting customary or treaty norm.

Box 9.6 Torture, inhumane treatment, and degrading treatment

The European Court of Human Rights differentiated among the concepts of torture, inhuman treatment, and degrading treatment in *Ireland v. UK* of 1978: "torture" means deliberate inhuman treatment causing very serious and cruel suffering; "inhuman treatment or punishment" means infliction of intense physical and mental suffering; "degrading treatment" is ill-treatment designed to arouse in victims feelings of fear, anguish, and inferiority capable of humiliating and debasing them and possibly breaking their physical or moral resistance.

No exceptional justifications, such as the need to obtain information to impede an imminent terrorist attack, may be used to circumvent this absolute norm. In the landmark case *Chahal v. UK* of 1996 the European Court insisted that the fight against organized crime or terrorism cannot be invoked as a justification for the ill-treatment of a detainee. Prohibited treatment includes humiliating or brutal techniques of interrogation, and prolonged detention in extreme conditions (such as solitary confinement or sensory deprivation).

The effects of the international prohibition of torture go beyond the obligation imposed on states not to resort to torture. As found in *Soering v. UK* of 1989 and in subsequent cases, expelling an individual to a country in which he or she may be subjected to torture or prohibited ill-treatment also constitutes an indirect violation of this norm. Stressing the unconditional nature of the prohibition against ill-treatment, the European Court has established that a state wishing to deport even an individual found guilty of a serious criminal offense, or constituting a threat to national security, must nevertheless make an independent assessment of the circumstances the individual would face in the country of return, as explored further later in this chapter.

Unlike with many other rights, a state must enforce the right to protection from torture even when an armed conflict is taking place on its territory. This right is articulated in **Common Article 3** of the 1949 *Geneva Conventions* (see Box 4.7).

Suppression of due process guarantees

The principles of due process of law encompass not only the right of terrorism victims to justice, but also the right of suspected terrorists to a fair trial, including an independent and impartial tribunal, presumption of innocence, the right to be informed of charges, access to independent legal advice, nonretroactivity of criminal sanctions (*nullum crimen sine lege*), and the right to be tried within a reasonable time. With reference to the latter aspect the European Court has specified that it is incumbent on states to organize their legal system in order to ensure that trials can be held within a reasonable time. The principle prohibiting the retrospective application of criminal law is among those provisions of general human rights treaties that do not allow for derogations. The UN Human Rights Committee has found violations of Article 15 of the ICCPR (nonretroactivity) in cases where an individual received a significantly more severe criminal sanction than the one specified by the law in force at the time the terrorist offense was committed.

Human rights bodies have often found that special tribunals (such as military tribunals in charge of trying civilian suspects) do not satisfy fair trial guarantees. European cases on court-martials have found the trial of civilians by military tribunals inconsistent with the ECHR, particularly where there are close structural links between the executive authorities and the military officers conducting such trials. The jurisprudence of the Human Rights Committee also suggests that tribunals comprising serving members of the armed forces do not ensure the necessary independence and impartiality guarantees.

Disproportionate interference with private life and freedom of expression and association

The right to private life, freedom of expression, and freedom of association can be limited by states in order to protect collective interests, such as public order and security. The actual need for interference with one of these rights will depend on the assessment of the states, which enjoy a wide margin of appreciation. However, interference must be strictly necessary and proportionate.

International monitoring bodies have upheld freedom of expression even in situations of turmoil and violence. This is particularly the case for political speech, considered to be a cornerstone of democratic society. States may take action against speech that incites people to violence, but the line between legitimate interference with, and unnecessary repression of, free speech is not always clear-cut.

The right to association can also be curtailed for fear of terrorist threats, and not always on lawful grounds. Restrictions on freedom of association can include the dissolution of organizations considered to promote violence and destabilization. However, the dissolution of political parties cannot be decided in the absence of specific evidence of threat or harmful action by such parties, as the European Court found in *United Communist Party v. Turkey* of 1998.

Restrictions on rights of aliens

The absolute prohibition of torture, even in cases involving terrorist acts, has a direct impact on states' duty of *nonrefoulement*: as explained previously, a person cannot be extradited or expelled to a country where there are serious grounds for fearing that the person will be subjected to ill-treatment. This principle, upheld by international case law, is explicitly stated in the Torture Convention (Article 3), in the Inter-American Convention to Prevent and Punish Torture (Article 13), and in the Charter of Fundamental Rights of the European Union (Article 19). Recently, the European Court has suggested, in *Mamatkulov v. Turkey* of 2007, that not only the risk of torture, but also the risk of a "flagrant denial of justice" (i.e. a significant violation of fair trial rights) may bar extradition. A risk in the war on terror is that in expulsion proceedings and asylum proceedings, guarantees might not be strictly observed.

Contentious issues since September 11

Spatial limitations do not allow for a broad comparative account of antiterrorism policies. We examine here US practice, which is particularly relevant for several reasons: the links between the conceptual origins of the war on terror and US advocacy, the global dimensions of alleged US abuses, the mixed – domestic and international – policy areas where human rights are at stake, and the multiple court cases available.

The erosion of civil liberties: the USA Patriot Act

The Uniting and Strengthening America by Providing Appropriate Tools Required to Intercept and Obstruct Terrorism Act – known as the USA Patriot Act – was adopted by the US Congress in the fall of 2001. It contains many controversial provisions on the expansion of police and prosecutorial powers. A key concern is the apparent inconsistency of the act with constitutionally guaranteed civil rights, as the use of "national security letters" allows the Federal Bureau of Investigation (FBI), without a court order, to require institutions and agencies (hospitals, banks, libraries, businesses, car rental agencies, phone companies, Internet providers, etc.) to reveal the personal records of their customers. The introduction of home searches with delayed notification to affected individuals may also involve an infringement of the right to privacy. Further, many have been critical of the creation of a fingerprint identification system for the recognition of foreign nationals before issuance of visas to them, or before permitting them entry to or exit from the United States.

One of the most contentious provisions of the USA Patriot Act involves indefinite detention without charge of foreigners suspected of connections to terrorism or representing a threat to national security. The act provides for mandatory detention until removal from the United States of an alien certified by the Attorney General as a suspected terrorist or a threat to national security. A person may be held up to seven days without charges, after which removal proceedings or charges must be instituted, or the person must be released. However, after removal proceedings have been initiated, a nonnational whose removal is "unlikely in the reasonable foreseeable future" may be detained indefinitely if the Attorney General considers that his or her release will "threaten the national security of the United States or the safety of the community or any person." This provision may apply, with adverse consequences, to stateless individuals, and to individuals who cannot be removed because their country of origin will not accept them or who cannot be deported because they would face torture if returned to their country. **Amnesty International** has argued that US practice is inconsistent with international procedural guarantees aimed at protecting people from arbitrary or wrongful deprivation of liberty.

Treatment of suspected terrorists

Status of "enemy combatants" and "unlawful combatants"

INDEFINITE ARREST WITHOUT CHARGE OF US CITIZENS

The George W. Bush administration classified hundreds of foreigners and some US citizens as "enemy combatants," a notion covering members or affiliates of Taliban or Al-Qaida forces engaged in, or supporting, hostilities against the United States or its allies. This qualification allows the US authorities to hold individuals without access to counsel and without charges or trial for the duration of the war on terror, which actually means for an indefinite duration. However, if the war on terror is construed as an armed conflict, the legal status of any person under detention should correspond to one of the categories recognized by international humanitarian law, either injured combatants, prisoners of war, or civilians under occupation, each category being entitled to the protection afforded by the relevant Geneva Convention.

The extensive use of this designation by the US administration creates a broad exception to the guarantees of criminal justice, as anyone can be seized, far from any recognizable battlefield, and detained indefinitely upon unverified allegations by US or other governments. As the famous *Padilla* case shows (see Box 9.7), when applied to US nationals the "enemy combatant" designation can arbitrarily limit their constitutional rights.

Box 9.7 The *Padilla* case

A well-known example of arrest and detention of US citizens as "enemy combatants" is that of José Padilla. Padilla was born in Brooklyn, New York, in 1970, and grew up in Chicago from the age of 5. He converted to Islam after a tumultuous adolescence that saw him involved in street-gang activity, resulting in an extensive criminal record for gun and assault charges. In May 2002, on his return home from overseas traveling to Egypt, Saudi Arabia, Afghanistan, Pakistan, and Iraq, he was arrested on suspicion of planning to build and explode a radioactive "dirty bomb" in the United States. Initially arrested on a material witness warrant, he was shortly afterward declared an enemy combatant by a memorandum issued by President Bush, and transferred from the Department of Justice to the custody of the Department of Defense, which detained him without formal charges at a military naval prison in Charleston, South Carolina. The transfer occurred without any notice whatsoever to his attorney or to his family. According to the memorandum, Padilla had engaged in hostile and warlike acts, was closely associated with Al-Qaida, with which the United States was "at war," and represented a grave danger to US security.

Overruling the December 2002 decision of the district court that Padilla's attorney petitioned for a writ of *habeas corpus*, the Second Circuit Court of Appeals found in its December 2003 decision (*Padilla v. Rumsfeld*) that the president of the United

States did not have the constitutional authority to detain US citizens on US soil outside a zone of combat, insofar as the power to curb civil liberties in times of crises (such as the suspension of the right to *habeas corpus*) lay with the Congress, and that Padilla should be released from military custody and tried by a civilian court. His case was moved to a civilian court, and in 2008 he was eventually sentenced to 17 years and 4 months in prison for criminal conspiracy – paradoxically, a different crime than the one originally alleged for his arrest and detention.

US courts have challenged the legitimacy of detention without trial of US "enemy combatants" as an exercise of the president's war powers. In the June 2004 *Hamdi v. Rumsfeld* decision (see Box 9.8) the US Supreme Court established that members or supporters of hostile forces in Afghanistan could be lawfully detained as "enemy combatants," a category whose recognition was loosely based on international humanitarian law; however, citizen-detainees were still entitled to their constitutional right to be informed of the factual basis for detention and contest it before an independent decisionmaker. The *Hamdi* case is somewhat analogous to the *Padilla* case, although the suspect was initially seized in Afghanistan (therefore on a battlefield) by the Northern Alliance, a group opposed to the Taliban and allied with the US-led coalition. The Court relied on international humanitarian law when it established that detention may not last longer than active hostilities, and emphasized that indefinite detention for interrogation purposes is not allowed. The Court rejected the government's claim that an "enemy combatant" had no right to a hearing in order to challenge this status. Taking into consideration the risk that Hamdi might be erroneously deprived of liberty, the plurality of the Court stressed that "a citizen 'shall not be deprived of life, liberty, or property, without due process of law,' pursuant to the Fifth Amendment to the US Constitution; not even a decision of the President has the authority to supersede that provision." However, the plurality opinion allowed a rebuttable presumption in favor of the government's evidence in the proceedings, and accepted the use of a military tribunal rather than a court hearing. The *Hamdi* ruling left unclear the status of "enemy combatants" held prisoners in the broader "war on terror" outside the Afghanistan context.

Box 9.8 *Hamdi v. Rumsfeld* (US Supreme Court, June 28, 2004)

"Striking the proper constitutional balance here is of great importance to the nation during this period of on-going combat. But it is equally vital that our calculus not give short shrift to the values that this country holds dear or to the privilege that is American citizenship. It is during our most challenging and uncertain moments that our nation's commitment to due process is most severely tested; and it is in those times that we must preserve our commitment at home to the principles for which we fight abroad. . . .

"In sum, while the full protections that accompany challenges to detentions in other settings may prove unworkable and inappropriate in the enemy-combatant setting, the threats to military operations posed by a basic system of independent review are not so weighty as to trump a citizen's core rights to challenge meaningfully the Government's case and to be heard by an impartial adjudicator."

It has been suggested that the resort to "enemy combatant" classifications actually concealed a desire by the executive branch to avoid judicial oversight, and its reaction to the *Hamdi* decision seemed to confirm it. Instead of allowing Hamdi to challenge his detention in court, the US administration surprisingly decided that he no longer represented a threat to national security. He was flown to Saudi Arabia after he renounced his US citizenship, as a condition for his release.

GUANTÁNAMO BAY DETAINEES AND THE "NO LAW" ZONE

The restrictive, and largely disputed, interpretation of the 1949 Geneva Conventions by the US administration placed the individuals captured in the "war on terror" and detained at Guantánamo Bay – allegedly Taliban and Al-Qaida members – in what was described as a "legal black hole." In a memorandum of February 7, 2002, President Bush denied the status of prisoner of war (the protection afforded by the Third Geneva Convention) to both categories: to Al-Qaida members because Al-Qaida was not a contracting party to the Geneva Conventions, and to the Taliban insofar as it unilaterally classified its fighters as *unlawful combatants*.

The Bush administration's analysis does not appear consistent with international humanitarian norms. Since an international conflict between the United States and Taliban-led Afghanistan was in progress at that time, Taliban soldiers did qualify as prisoners of war under Article 4(a)(1) of the Third Geneva Convention on the treatment of prisoners of war, in their capacity as "members of the armed forces of a party to the conflict." Also, many of the Guantánamo Bay detainees were captured outside zones of armed conflict, and many alleged that they had been erroneously arrested. According to the Geneva provisions, persons suspected of having committed a belligerent act must be treated as prisoners of war until a "competent tribunal" clarifies their status (Article 5). US authorities did not comply with the requirement in this provision when they refused to bring the inmates before a tribunal, and subjected them to long-term arbitrary detention. Also, former Afghan soldiers of the Taliban army were not repatriated once "active hostilities" ended (in June 2002, after the installation of the US-friendly Karzai government), despite the explicit provision of the Third Geneva Convention requiring it (Article 118). Granting prisoner of war status to Taliban soldiers would not have prevented US authorities from interrogating or prosecuting them for terrorist acts or **war crimes**, nor would it have impeded detention without charge for the limited duration of the military conflict.

Conversely, Al-Qaida members did not belong to the regular forces, nor to paramilitary forces (militia and volunteers corps) having a responsible chain of command, wearing a distinctive sign, carrying arms openly, and conducting operations in accordance with the laws and customs of war (requirements of Article 4[a][2] of the Third Geneva Convention). They could therefore be considered *unlawful* or *unprivileged combatants* – that is, civilian belligerents not allowed to conduct hostilities, and therefore not protected from prosecution for engaging in the armed conflict, nor eligible for prisoner of war status in the event of capture. However, Al-Qaida members not aligned with the Taliban are protected by Article 5 of the Fourth Geneva Convention, which specifies that civilians suspected of activity hostile to the security of the territorial state or occupying power are entitled to the same treatment as civilian noncombatants, and may forfeit the right of communication only if absolute military security so requires; the convention specifically stresses that they cannot be deprived of fair trial rights.

The practice of indefinite detention without charge of terrorist suspects in the "no law" zone of Guantánamo, for the alleged purpose of assessing evidence against them, was criticized by the US Supreme Court. In the *Rasul v. Bush* decision of June 29, 2004 (see Box 9.9), the Court ruled that foreign detainees at Guantánamo Bay had the right to challenge the lawfulness of their detention through petition for a writ of *habeas corpus* (a judicial mandate ordering that a person under detention be brought to court so that it may be determined whether or not he or she is lawfully imprisoned, and whether or not he or she should be released from custody). After the Supreme Court's decision in *Rasul*, the US administration established the Combatant Status Review Tribunals, panels composed of three military officers with a mandate to review the factual information for the enemy combatant classification of Guantánamo inmates. The July 2004 memorandum establishing these military tribunals allowed for the detainees to be present at the proceedings, but did not confer the right to counsel, access to classified evidence, or access to sources of allegations against them. These special military tribunals have subsequently been challenged in domestic courts.

Box 9.9 *Rasul v. Bush* (US Supreme Court, June 28, 2004)

"Consistent with the historic purpose of the habeas corpus writ, this Court has recognized the federal courts' power to review applications for habeas relief in a wide variety of cases involving Executive detention, in wartime as well as in times of peace. The question now before us is whether the habeas statute confers a right to judicial review of the legality of Executive detention of aliens in a territory over which the United States exercises plenary and exclusive jurisdiction, but not "ultimate sovereignty."

"Respondents' primary submission is that the answer to the jurisdictional question is controlled by our decision in Eisentrager v. Forrestal. . . . Petitioners in these cases differ from the Eisentrager detainees in important respects: They are not nationals of countries at war with the United States, and they deny that they have engaged in or plotted acts of aggression against the United States; they have never been afforded access to any tribunal, much less charged with and convicted of wrongdoing; and for more than two years they have been imprisoned in territory over which the United States exercises exclusive jurisdiction and control. Not only are petitioners differently situated from the Eisentrager detainees, but the Court in Eisentrager made quite clear that all six of the facts critical to its disposition were relevant only to the question of the prisoners' constitutional entitlement to habeas corpus. The Court had far less to say on the question of the petitioners' statutory entitlement to habeas review."

Military commissions and trials for non-US terrorism suspects

Military commissions designed to try aliens charged with terrorism were first established pursuant to President Bush's military order of November 13, 2001 ("Detention, Treatment, and Trial of Certain Noncitizens in the War Against Terrorism"). The operation of these commissions is primarily regulated by Military Commission Order no. 1, issued by the US Department of Defense on March 21, 2002, which set forth the guidelines on membership, procedures, admissibility of evidence, procedural safeguards for defendants, and review.

The military commissions have been widely criticized for failing to meet basic fair trial guarantees. They allow the use of coerced evidence and hearsay, and place restrictions on the ability of military and civilian legal counsel to present an effective defense. Further, unlike US courts-martial, against whose decisions individuals can appeal to the US Court of Appeal for the Armed Forces (a civilian court outside the control of the executive), and ultimately to the US Supreme Court, the commissions' regulations permit appeal only to another military panel, whose members answer to the US president. There is an obvious risk of undue political influence, and the commissions do not satisfy the minimum requirement of an impartial and regularly constituted court respecting the generally recognized principles of regular judicial procedure, prescribed by Article 75 of Additional Protocol I to the 1949 Geneva Conventions. The United States never ratified the additional protocols, but this provision is nevertheless binding insofar as it is declaratory of customary law. Moreover, according to Article 102 of the Third Geneva Convention, detainees entitled to be considered as prisoners of war cannot be validly sentenced unless the sentence has been pronounced by the same courts according to the same procedure as in the case of members of the armed forces of the detaining power; the clear double standard created by the establishment of these "special" commissions is not consistent with this provision. In *Hamdan v. Rumsfeld* (2006) the US Supreme Court held that the Bush administration did not have authority to establish particular military commissions to try Guantánamo Bay detainees without congressional authorization, insofar as their structure and procedures violated both the US Uniform Code of Military Justice and the four Geneva Conventions.

The Military Commissions Act of 2006, adopted in response to the *Hamdan* decision, retained many aspects of the Bush administration's counterterrorism policy, such as the president's authority to classify individuals as unlawful enemy combatants, to deny them the protections of both the US Uniform Code of Military Justice and the Geneva Conventions, and to deny the jurisdiction of federal courts to review claims of wrongful detention or abuses brought by the inmates.

In the *Boumediene v. Bush* decision of June 12, 2008, the US Supreme Court found that the Detainee Treatment Act of 2005 and the Military Commissions Act of 2006 fail to provide appropriate *habeas corpus* protection, and it recognized the right of Guantánamo prisoners to challenge their detention in civilian courts. The majority decision found that the constitutionally guaranteed right of *habeas corpus* review does apply to persons held at the naval base of Guantánamo, and to persons designated as enemy combatants. According to the Court, if Congress intends to suspend the right, an adequate substitute must be offered to prisoners, providing them with an effective opportunity to demonstrate that their detention is due to an erroneous application or interpretation of relevant law; the reviewing decisionmaker must have the ability to redress errors, to assess the sufficiency of the evidence relied on by the executive, and to consider any relevant exonerating evidence.

Extraordinary renditions, secret detention facilities, and torturous interrogation

The US administration has often resorted to so-called *extraordinary renditions*, effectively outsourcing the interrogation of suspected terrorists to foreign countries that may engage in torture. The practice involves the secret seizure of persons from US or foreign soil and transfer to overseas detention facilities outside ordinary legal avenues (deportation, extradition). The individuals concerned do not have an opportunity to contest their detention; they are held incommunicado, subjected to ill-treatment, and sometimes executed. Secret US detention facilities abroad, beyond the reach of the law or international independent scrutiny, are the location of multiple violations, such as arbitrary deprivation of liberty, subjection to torture, cruel, inhuman, or degrading treatment, suppression of procedural safeguards, and even arbitrary deprivation of life. Suspects are held for extended periods of detention without access to legal counsel, review of the grounds for detention, or supervision by the International Red Cross or other organizations monitoring respect for human rights.

The use of torture in the war on terror became notorious after the publicity surrounding the revelation of abuses on prisoners in the Abu Ghraib prison in Iraq in 2004. "Stress and duress" interrogation techniques have apparently been used in Afghanistan at the US air force base in Bagram (north of Kabul). Detailed press accounts indicate the use of techniques such as prolonged hooding, standing while handcuffed to the ceiling, sleep deprivation, and confinement in painful positions. While falling short of torture, these techniques amount to cruel, inhuman, and degrading treatment prohibited by a peremptory norm of international law, as discussed previously.

Global dimensions of counterterrorism

UN and EU financial sanctions against alleged terrorists

The UN Security Council has increasingly used its power to resort to nonmilitary sanctions, conferred by Article 42 of the UN Charter, to impose measures against specific individuals rather than states. After the events of September 11, financial sanctions were aimed at the Al-Qaida network and its supporters, with no reference to the attacks on the United States or to the Afghan regime (Resolution 1390 [2002]). This broad and indeterminate objective may lead to the inclusion of innocent individuals on the proscription list. This list is drawn up by the Sanctions Committee of the Security Council on the basis of information and requests from member states, using often unverifiable intelligence information. Until recently a designated individual could be removed from the list only if the state of nationality or residence was willing to seek cancellation through bilateral consultations with the designating state or addressing the Sanctions Committee. The possibility of direct individual requests for delisting addressed to the Sanctions Committee has been subsequently provided for by Resolution 1730 (2006). However, the process for seeking the removal of a name from the list still depends on the willingness of the states represented on the committee to reexamine the case, and continues to be based on political negotiation rather than on independent third-party control.

The mechanism arguably entrenches upon the right to a fair trial, the right to peaceful enjoyment of property, and the right to an effective remedy. Individual claims have begun to be filed with national and regional courts for human rights violations. Until recently the case law of European Community courts on EU legislation that incorporates UN proscription lists has not offered significant judicial protection of suspects' rights in the face of Security Council counterterrorism measures (the *Yusuf and Al-Barakaat* and *Kadi* decisions of September 2005; the *Ayadi* and *Hassan* decisions of July 2006). The Court of First Instance stated that UN Charter obligations, and consequently the Security Council's binding resolutions, prevail over any other international obligations. According to the Court, such resolutions, but also the EC legislation adopted in order to give effect to the former, cannot be submitted to the judicial review of the EC jurisdictional bodies, with the extremely limited and unlikely exception of *jus cogens* violations.

However, the *Kadi* appeal judgment issued by the Court of Justice of the European Communities on September 3, 2008, introduced a major shift. The Court stated that the

EC must ensure the consistency of any piece of legislation – including EC acts implementing Security Council decisions – with the fundamental principles of EC law, which comprise the respect for individual rights and liberties. The Court emphasized that this was particularly important in the absence of effective UN remedies, as the reexamination procedure open to blacklisted individuals does not ensure the guarantees of judicial protection.

Obligations of states when acting under Chapter VII

The 2006 *Al-Jedda* case before the London Court of Appeal illustrates the reluctance of domestic courts to monitor the action of states when holding terrorist suspects within an operation authorized by the UN Security Council. This deference relies on Article 103 of the UN Charter, which indicates that in the event of a conflict between the obligations of member states under the Charter and their obligations under any other international agreement (such as human rights treaties), the former are to prevail. Charter obligations are given broad meaning, encompassing binding Security Council decisions, which member states agree to accept and carry out under Article 25 of the UN Charter.

Hilal Abdul-Razzaq Ali Al-Jedda, the plaintiff in the case, was a dual British and Iraqi national who had traveled to Iraq, where he had been arrested and detained by British forces on the grounds that he was suspected of membership in a terrorist group, and of terrorist activities. No evidence to support this claim was given, and no intention to press criminal charges was presented. British forces were part of a multinational force that was acting under the authority of Resolution 1546 (2004), adopted by the Security Council under Chapter VII. By that resolution the Security Council gave the multinational force "authority to take all necessary measures to contribute to the maintenance of security and stability in Iraq," and according to one of the letters annexed to the resolution, the force might undertake internment where "necessary for imperative reasons of security." During the proceedings the UK secretary of state contended that the UN Charter and Resolution 1546 imposed an obligation on the United Kingdom to detain Al-Jedda that prevailed over the latter's conflicting right under Article 5.1 of the ECHR to be promptly brought before a judge after arrest. Conversely, the plaintiff argued that the resolution at most authorized the United Kingdom to take action to detain him, but did not oblige it to do so, and thus there was no conflict within the meaning of Article 103. The London court found, however, that the "obligations" in Article 103 were not to be construed narrowly, and thus the authorized action was also to be regarded as compulsory.

In its December 2007 judgment on Al-Jedda's appeal, the House of Lords confirmed that the detention was not contrary to the right to liberty under Article 5.1 of the ECHR (and under the Human Rights Act 1998), because the application of that provision was restricted by virtue of the operation of Articles 25 and 103 of the UN Charter. Though the United Kingdom did not have the obligation to detain the plaintiff specifically, it was bound to exercise its power of detention wherever necessary for imperative reasons of security. Therefore, the United Kingdom could lawfully exercise the power to detain as authorized by the Security Council, although it had to ensure that the detainee's rights under Article 5 were not infringed to any greater extent than was inherent in such detention.

As this judicial outcome shows, when states adopt counterterrorism measures under the authorization of Chapter VII resolutions, they have almost unconstrained discretion not to enforce internationally-recognized human rights.

Key points

- The global war on terror is a peculiar type of conflict: at times it involves military operations, subject to international humanitarian law, but for the most part it consists of law enforcement action, subject to international human rights law.
- In times of war or other public emergencies, states can lawfully derogate some of their human rights obligations. In times of peace, some measure of interference with certain rights may also be permitted to accommodate security concerns. The proportionality of such restrictions should, however, always be respected.
- The war on terror has entailed arbitrary deprivations of life and liberty, the use of torture and degrading treatment against suspected terrorists, the suppression of due process guarantees, unwarranted interference with the right to private life and freedom of expression and association, as well as restrictions on the rights of aliens.
- The human rights costs of the global war on terror result from the excesses of both national policies and multilateral action, especially action by the United Nations.

Discussion questions

Balancing human rights and security is one of the major challenges of post-September 11 antiterrorism, nationally and internationally. A significant risk of the "war on terror" rhetoric is that it attempts to justify the suspension of some rights protected by international human rights law without observing the legal protection deriving from international humanitarian law, which eventually means that neither set of norms is fully acknowledged. The longer-term resort by states to derogations from human rights motivated by the war on terror reduces standards for civil rights and liberties and may have negative effects on the **rule of law**, on democratic institutions, and on the public administration of justice.

The status of terrorists and terrorist acts under international law

The correct assessment of the lawfulness of antiterrorism measures, including from the viewpoint of their consistency with human rights and humanitarian law, largely depends on the understanding of the exact legal framework of the "war on terror," and on the classification of the parties to it under international law.

- How would you qualify the September 11 terrorist attacks: individual crimes, or acts of war?
- Can a state be at war with a terrorist group or a transnational criminal organization?

The relationship between security and fundamental rights

The global war on terror has prompted the view that security and human rights are necessarily antagonistic goals, and that the former should prevail over the latter. Nearly a decade after the inauguration of post-September 11 counterterrorism, it is important to reconsider their relationship and inquire how far we are ready to compromise human rights in the pursuit of security.

* Is the curtailment of human rights indispensable to combat terrorism?
* Should harsh treatment falling short of torture be permitted in order to prevent imminent major loss of life?
* From the viewpoint of the citizenry, is the renouncement of some civil liberties desirable for increased personal security?

Applicable law

The war on terror is significantly different from traditional international and internal conflicts, which constituted the factual background for the development of current international law. The existing norms of international law might not be apt in a global fight against terrorism, or might need to be reinterpreted and adapted.

* Is international law adequately equipped to address the new challenge of international terrorism?
* Should humanitarian law apply to captured terrorists, and if so, how?

Further reading

Almquist, Jessica, "A Human Rights Critique of European Judicial Review: Counter-terrorism Sanctions," *International and Comparative Law Quarterly* 57, pt. 2 (April 2008): 303–32.

Beard, Jack M., "The Geneva Boomerang: The Military Commissions Act of 2006 and U.S. Counterterror Operations," *American Journal of International Law* 101, no. 1 (January 2007): 56–73.

Bianchi, Andrea, ed., *Enforcing International Law Norms Against Terrorism* (Oxford: Hart, 2004), esp. pp. 3–62, 83–210, 377–452, 491–534.

Duffy, Helen, *The "War on Terror" and the Framework of International Law* (Cambridge: Cambridge University Press, 2005), esp. pp. 332–78, 379–442.

Ehrenreich Brooks, Rosa, "War Everywhere: Rights, National Security Law, and the Law of Armed Conflict in the Age of Terror," *University of Pennsylvania Law Review* 153, no. 2 (December 2004): 675–761.

Marks, Susan, "Civil Liberties at the Margin: The UK Derogation and the European Court of Human Rights," *Oxford Journal of Legal Studies* 15, no. 1 (Spring 1995): 69–95.

Roth, Kenneth, "The Fight Against Terrorism: The Bush Administration's Dangerous Neglect of Human Rights," in Thomas G. Weiss, Margaret E. Crahan, and John Goering, eds., *Wars on Terrorism and Iraq: Human Rights, Unilateralism, and U.S. Foreign Policy* (New York: Routledge, 2004).

Sadat, Leila Nadya, "Shattering the Nuremberg Consensus: US Rendition Policy and International Criminal Law," *Yale Journal of International Affairs* 3, no. 1 (Winter 2008): 65–77.

Weigend, Thomas, "The Universal Terrorist: The International Community Grappling with a Definition," *Journal of International Criminal Justice* 4, no. 5 (November 2006): 912–32.

Official documents and sources

European Community case law, http://curia.europa.eu/en/content/juris/index.htm.

European Convention on Human Rights, http://www.echr.coe.int/nr/rdonlyres/d5cc24a7-dc13-4318-b457-5c9014916d7a/0/englishanglais.pdf.

European Court of Human Rights case law, http://cmiskp.echr.coe.int/tkp197/search.asp?sessionid=4993629&skin=hudoc-en.

Inter-American Convention on Human Rights, http://www.oas.org/juridico/english/treaties/b-32.html.

International Court of Justice cases, http://www.icj-cij.org/docket/index.php?p1=3.

International Covenant on Civil and Political Rights, http://www.unhchr.ch/html/menu3/b/a_ccpr.htm.

UN Security Council resolutions, http://www.un.org/docs/sc/unsc_resolutions.html.

Part III

Building peace and seeking accountability

Recent mechanisms and institutions

10 Ad hoc tribunals

The International Criminal Tribunal for the Former Yugoslavia

History and legal basis

The **International Criminal Tribunal for the Former Yugoslavia** (ICTY) was established in order to bring to trial those responsible for the atrocities committed during the conflict in the region. See Chapter 5 for a detailed analysis of the conflict in the former Republic of Yugoslavia (FRY).

A number of **United Nations** (UN) and **Security Council** actions laid the groundwork for the development of the ICTY. The first comment of the Security Council on the situation in Yugoslavia came in Resolution 713 of September 1991. This was followed by another ten resolutions through 1992 reaffirming concern about the fighting and stating that continuation of the conflict constituted a threat to international peace and security. In addition to this concern, the Security Council noted in Resolution 764 that all parties to the conflict were bound to comply with **international humanitarian law** and that those who committed **grave breaches** of the **Geneva Conventions** were individually responsible. This led to the establishment of a UN commission of experts, under Resolution 780, tasked with examining grave breaches of the Geneva Conventions and other violations of international humanitarian law committed in the FRY. The commission of experts confirmed that grave breaches and other violations of international humanitarian law, including ethnic cleansing, mass killings, **torture**, and rape, had been committed, and recommended the establishment of an ad hoc international tribunal. This led to the Security Council decision of February 1993, under Resolution 808, to establish a tribunal to address the widespread violations of international humanitarian law in the FRY.

Resolution 808 asked the **UN Secretary-General** to make recommendations on the establishment of such a tribunal. His subsequent report considered the legal basis and suggested that the tribunal be established through a **UN Security Council resolution**. Although the normal procedure would be to establish an international tribunal by treaty, drafting such a treaty and getting enough countries to ratify it would take a significant amount of time. In addition, the treaty process would also be unable to guarantee ratification from the states involved. Establishing the tribunal by decision of the Security Council under Chapter VII of the **UN Charter** was quicker and would ensure that all states were under a binding obligation to carry out the decision. The Secretary-General also noted that the Council had previously established subsidiary organs for the maintenance of peace and security, so the only difference here was that this would be a judicial organ. Although established by Security Council resolution, the tribunal would be independent of any political considerations in its operations and instead apply existing international humanitarian law.

Resolution 827 established the ICTY in May 1993 and adopted the statute of the tribunal (see Box 10.1). The ICTY website states four objectives in carrying out the purposes of this resolution:

- to bring to justice persons responsible for violations of international humanitarian law;
- to contribute to the restoration of peace by holding these persons to account;
- to bring justice to the victims;
- to deter further crimes.

Box 10.1 **Key articles from the statute of the International Criminal Tribunal for the Former Yugoslavia**

Article 1: Competence of the International Tribunal
The International Tribunal shall have the power to prosecute persons responsible for serious violations of international humanitarian law committed in the territory of the former Yugoslavia since 1991. . . .

Article 2: Grave Breaches of the Geneva Conventions of 1949
. . . shall have the power to prosecute persons committing or ordering to be committed grave breaches of the Geneva Conventions. . . .

Article 3: Violations of the Laws or Customs of War
. . . shall have the power to prosecute persons violating the laws or customs of war. . . .

Article 4: Genocide
. . . shall have the power to prosecute persons committing genocide. . . .
. . . the following acts shall be punishable:
a)   genocide
b)   conspiracy to commit genocide
c)   direct and public incitement to commit genocide
d)   attempt to commit genocide
e)   complicity in genocide

Article 5: Crimes Against Humanity
. . . shall have the power to prosecute persons responsible for the following crimes when committed in armed conflict, whether international or internal in character and directed against any civilian population. . . .

Article 7: Individual Criminal Responsibility
A person who planned, instigated, ordered, committed or otherwise aided and abetted . . . shall be individually responsible for the crime.

ICTY organs

Chambers

The Chambers consist of 16 permanent judges divided between three trial chambers and one appeals chamber. At any one time, there are a maximum of 16 *ad litem* (ad hoc) judges, who join particular trials as necessary. All judges are appointed by the **UN General Assembly** for four-year terms; the 16 permanent judges can be reelected, but the *ad litem* judges cannot. The *ad litem* judges were appointed in November 2000 in order to maximize the efficiency of the court following criticism of the time taken for trials.

Office of the Prosecutor

The Office of the Prosecutor conducts investigations and is independent of any country or organ of the ICTY. It prepares indictments and initiates prosecutions. The office is staffed by police officers, crime experts, analysts, lawyers, and trial attorneys as necessary to carry out its activities. There have been three prosecutors: Richard Goldstone, Louise Arbour, and Carla Del Ponte.

Registry

The Registry carries out the administration and judicial support services of the tribunal, including record-keeping and translation, and has responsibility for custody of defendants and protection for witnesses.

Detention Unit

The Detention Unit holds the accused until the completion of proceedings. If the accused are found guilty, the Detention Unit transfers the prisoners to appropriate states, as previously agreed with the UN, to serve their sentences.

Functioning of the ICTY

The ICTY's first session was from November 17 to 30, 1993; its first indictment was issued a year later. This delay was due to political challenges in establishing the tribunal, such as funding, appointing the chief prosecutor, and staffing the court. It took time to build the logistical and procedural infrastructure needed for the court to function, as well as to establish agreements with governments to provide assistance. As a result, the ICTY was not really a fully functioning international court until 1999. Beyond the initial organizational problems in establishing the tribunal, there has been an ongoing lack of cooperation by key governments, hindering the gathering of evidence and enforcing of arrest warrants. When states do cooperate, they have tended to want evidence kept confidential; and even if evidence is shared during early stages, it might still be blocked at trial. In the FRY there was no cooperation with the ICTY, with the Yugoslav authorities failing to arrest two key accused: Radovan Karadžić and Ratko Mladić. With the 1999 Kosovo conflict and the indictment of Slobodan Milošević, the situation worsened. The Croatian government publicly stated that it would cooperate with the ICTY, but in reality used legal arguments to obstruct the court's work. Still, in November 2000 the ICTY prosecutor acknowledged that cooperation by Croatia had improved compared to the past. The situation was better in Bosnia, where there had been some ad hoc interaction with the UN Protection Force (UNPROFOR). The situation improved with the deployment of the Implementation Force (IFOR) and the Stabilization Force (SFOR); and after the UN Transitional Administration in Eastern Slovenia (UNTAES) carried out the first arrest in June 1997 in Slovenia, SFOR troops then carried out a detention operation in July.

The ICTY has also experienced ongoing organizational and logistical difficulties. Dealing with such complex cases means that a great deal of evidence needs to be collected, as well as translated. And with public indictments, some suspects go into hiding to avoid prosecution. In response, the ICTY has shifted to using sealed indictments in order to better enable the arrest of suspects.

ICTY jurisprudence

Competence

The ICTY recognizes the principle of ***nullum crimen sine lege***, meaning that a person cannot be accused of a crime unless it was a crime under law at the time it was committed. In order to avoid accusations of applying the law retroactively, the tribunal applies principles of international humanitarian law that are customary law. This avoids the question of ratification of specific conventions. The tribunal thus goes to great lengths to justify the customary bases that it uses as its source of law, and this elaboration of customary law through its jurisprudence provides an important basis for future decisions beyond the ICTY (and ICTR). The tribunal can prosecute the following offenses that have been committed on the territory of the former Yugoslavia since 1991:

* grave breaches of the 1949 Geneva Conventions;
* violations of the laws or customs of war;
* genocide;
* crimes against humanity.

The court has the authority to try natural persons only, and as such cannot indict organizations, political parties, administrative entities, or other legal subjects. Bosnian courts are unable to prosecute cases where the ICTY has jurisdiction.

Focus

The ICTY has focused on cases of human rights abuse against civilians, with its first trials indicting lower-level perpetrators. This enabled the tribunal to operate during the ongoing conflict, and to be seen as proceeding with its mandate. The reasoning behind this strategy was that trying lower-level perpetrators would eventually lead to enough evidence to indict the higher-level perpetrators. As the work of the ICTY continued and its legitimacy grew, outside pressure increased, there was more cooperation, and higher-level perpetrators began to be indicted. This approach was consolidated in the completion strategy for the ICTY as elaborated in Security Council Resolutions 1503 and 1534. These resolutions state that the ICTY should finish its work by 2010 and that in order to achieve this, the tribunal should concentrate on the prosecution of those who bear the most responsibility and refer lower-ranking individuals to the national courts. The most famous of these high-level indictments came in May 1999, when the ICTY charged President Slobodan Milošević with **crimes**

against humanity and **war crimes** against Kosovar Albanians. He was arrested in April 2001, following his fall from power, and the trial started in February 2002. The prosecution took two years, finishing in February 2004, and the defense phase started several months later, in August, due to Milošević's ill health. Milošević represented himself, would not speak to the court-appointed defense lawyers, refused to enter a plea, and questioned the legitimacy of the court. Milošević died in March 2006, toward the end of the trial, before a verdict could be rendered. The prosecutor, Carla Del Ponte, stated at the time that Milošević's death deprived his victims of the justice they needed and deserved.

Another significant ICTY success was the capture of Radovan Karadžić on July 21, 2008, 13 years after his first indictment. He was accused of orchestrating the Srebrenica massacre, the shelling of Sarajevo, and the use of peacekeepers as human shields. He went into hiding in 1996 and assumed the life of an alternative health therapist, changing his appearance and fooling all those around him. Karadžić has decided to represent himself, denies all charges, and has complained that the proceedings are proceeding too quickly, but it is unlikely that the judge will allow him to delay the trial; he will have to comply with all deadlines set by the ICTY. Bosnian Serb commander Ratko Mladić and Croatian Serb leader Goran Hadžić are still at large and it is unclear whether the mandate of the ICTY will be extended to try them.

As of November 2008 the ICTY has concluded proceedings for 116 accused, with 43 trials ongoing and 2 indictees still at large.

ICTY landmark cases

Tadić

The first determination of individual guilt or innocence by the ICTY was the trial of Duško Tadić in May 1995. Tadić was a leading member of the Serbian Democratic Party and of a Serb paramilitary group. He was accused of taking part in ethnic cleansing against the non-Serbian population in the town of Kozarac in Bosnia-Herzegovina, where 800 civilians out of a population of 4,000 were killed and the rest were forced to leave the town. After the takeover of the area, thousands of Muslims and Croats were put into camps and severely mistreated. Tadić was indicted for crimes against humanity, grave breaches of the Geneva Conventions, and violations of the laws or customs of war, under Articles 5, 2, and 3 of the ICTY statute, respectively. This case resulted in several key developments.

JURISDICTION OF THE ICTY

The Tadić defense objected to the ICTY's assertion of jurisdiction, challenging the legality of the establishment of the tribunal, and its subject-matter jurisdiction. The tribunal determined that, as a subsidiary organ of the United Nations, it could review Security Council resolutions. Tadić had objected that the Security Council had acted outside its mandate under Article 41 of the UN Charter by creating a court, which is not one of the measures envisioned in that article. The tribunal had to consider whether the Council is limited to the measures listed in Articles 41 and 42 of the UN Charter. However, the tribunal found that the measures listed in Article 41 (see Box 10.2) are illustrative rather than comprehensive and therefore did not rule out the establishment of an international tribunal.

Box 10.2 The UN Charter, Article 41

Charter of the United Nations

CHAPTER VII

ACTION WITH RESPECT TO THREATS TO THE PEACE, BREACHES OF THE PEACE, AND ACTS OF AGGRESSION

Article 41
The Security Council may decide what measures not involving the use of armed force are to be employed to give effect to its decisions, and it may call upon the Members of the United Nations to apply such measures. These may include complete or partial interruption of economic relations and of rail, sea, air, postal, telegraphic, radio, and other means of communication, and the severance of diplomatic relations.

INTERNATIONAL VERSUS INTERNAL ARMED CONFLICT

The defense team claimed that under Articles 2 and 3 of the ICTY statute, the alleged acts needed to have taken place in an international armed conflict. The Tadić defense claimed that the alleged crimes had been committed in the context of an internal armed conflict and therefore were outside of the jurisdiction of the ICTY. The tribunal agreed, and determined that Article 2 of the statute, invoking grave breaches of the Geneva Conventions, did require the presence of an international armed conflict. The court found that after May 19, 1992, when the Yugoslav People's Army withdrew from Bosnia and Herzegovina, the FRY did not have effective control over the Bosnian Serb forces. This meant that the conflict could not be defined as international, and that the victims were not protected persons under the Geneva Conventions – and Tadić was acquitted on this count (although he was found guilty on the other counts). The appeals chamber reversed this decision by finding that the conflict was in fact international. It determined that the trial chamber had used too stringent a test, and that instead of proving effective control, the prosecution only had to prove overall control of the Bosnian Serbs by Serbia. This overall control consists of a state organizing, coordinating, or planning military actions of the military group as well as financing, training, equipping, or providing operational support, and does not need to include specific orders or planning of operations. The appeals chamber found Tadić guilty of grave breaches of the Geneva Conventions.

DEFINITION OF ARMED CONFLICT

The ICTY determined that the crimes listed under Articles 5 and 3 of its statute required the presence of conflict, but not one of a specifically international type (see Box 10.1), and so had to consider under what circumstances armed conflict could occur, for the purposes of **Common Article 3** of the Geneva Conventions, in order to try Tadić. The court determined that conflict between states or protracted armed violence between governmental authorities and organized armed groups was required. It found that international humanitarian law applies from the start of such conflict and ends at the peace settlement. It is noteworthy that the decision did not require the armed group to exercise territorial control. This alone did not solve the problem of prosecuting Tadić, since Common Article 3, unlike the grave breaches provisions of the Geneva conventions, does not specifically criminalize specific acts; it just prohibits them. So the ICTY further determined that while Common Article 3 does not explicitly refer to individual criminal liability, as the Nuremberg Tribunal had determined, the absence of specific treaty provisions does not rule out such liability.

Krstić

Radislav Krstić was the deputy commander and chief of staff of the Drina Corps within the Bosnian Serb Army, which was tasked with planning and carrying out "Krivaja 95" – the operation to attack Srebenica. The ICTY trial chamber found that Krstić had participated in plans to ethnically cleanse Srebenica of all Muslims and to kill the men of military age there. He was found guilty of murder, persecutions, and **genocide**. The latter represented an important elaboration of the definition of genocide, with the court finding that intent to destroy a part of a group within a limited geographical area can still be held as genocide. There is therefore no need to show the intent of the accused to destroy the entire group, but only a part that is a distinct entity, in this case Bosnian Muslims in Srebenica. Even though the focus of the killing was on men of fighting age, the perpetrators knew this would have an impact on the group and that, coupled with the forcible transfer of women, children, and elderly, this would result in the Bosnian Muslim population disappearing from that area.

Čelebiči

In the Čelebiči case the ICTY made important advances in attributing command responsibility. The court confirmed that superior commanders have an obligation to ensure that their subordinates do not carry out war crimes and crimes against humanity. The case concerned four individuals who worked in the Čelebiči prison camp: Zdravko Mucić, the camp commander; Hazim Delić, the camp deputy commander; Esad Landžo, a camp guard; and Zejnil Delalić, coordinator of the Bosnian Muslim and Bosnian Croat forces. It was alleged that Bosnian Muslim and Bosnian Croat forces took control of Bosnian Serb villages around the Konjic municipality in central Bosnia. Persons detained during these operations were held at the Čelebiči camp, where it was alleged that detainees were killed, tortured, sexually assaulted, and beaten. In this case, the first concerning command responsibility since the Nuremberg trials, the ICTY found that a superior can be held criminally responsible for failing to prevent crimes committed by subordinates, whether this position was held de jure or de facto, and whether the superior was a civilian holding a position of authority or a military commander. Mucić was found guilty of command responsibility for murder, torture, and ill-treatment; Delić and Landžo were not found to have had command responsibility for the offenses of others, but were still found guilty for murder, willful killings, and rape. Delalić was found not to have had command responsibility over the Čelebiči prison camp and so was acquitted of all charges.

Aleksovksi

The ICTY appeals chamber in the *Aleksovski* case widened the definition of protected persons under Article 4 of Fourth Geneva Convention. This article states:

> Persons protected by the Convention are those who, at a given moment and in any manner whatsoever, find themselves, in case of a conflict or occupation, in the hands of a Party to the conflict or Occupying Power of which they are not nationals.

Zlatko Aleksovski, a Bosnian Croat and commander of a prison facility at Kaonik, near Busovača in Bosnia-Herzegovina, was accused of committing abuses against Bosnian Muslim prisoners. It was alleged that detainees under his control were subjected to inhumane treatment such as excessive and cruel interrogation, physical and psychological harm, and forced labor, and that some detainees were used as human shields and killed. He was indicted on charges under Articles 2 and 3 of the ICTY statute. The trial chamber in 1999 first acquitted Aleksovski of inhumane treatment and willfully causing great suffering or serious injury to body or health, because the chamber did not consider the Bosnian Muslim victims to be protected persons as defined by the Fourth Geneva Convention and because the offenses did not take place during an international armed conflict. The appeals chamber overturned this verdict and considered the conflict to be international in character, as shown by the overall control test in the *Tadić* case. The appeals chamber found that the provision of protection to civilians can be widened so that a person can have protected status even if they have the same nationality as their captors. The appeals chamber stated that this understanding of Article 4 is in keeping with the spirit of the Geneva Conventions and is especially important for interethnic conflict, in which the question of nationality is not so clear-cut.

Furundžija

Anto Furundžija was the local commander of a special unit – known as "the Jokers" – of the Croatian Defense Council's military police force. He was accused of being present while a female Muslim civilian was raped and a Croatian soldier was beaten during an interrogation at the Jokers' headquarters. The ICTY trial chamber found that the ban on torture has reached the level of *jus cogens* under international law, which means that no derogation is permitted under any circumstance. The definition of torture used by the court was based on that in the **Genocide Convention**:

> the intentional infliction, by act or omission, of severe pain or suffering, whether physical or mental, for the purpose of obtaining information or a confession or of punishing, intimidating, humiliating or coercing the victim or a third person, or of discriminating on any ground against the victim or a third person. For such an act to constitute torture, one of the parties thereto must be a public official or must, at any rate, act in a non-private capacity, e.g. as a de facto organ of a State or any other authority wielding entity.

Definition of rape and sexual violence

The ICTY (and the ICTR) made great advances in the recognition of rape and sexual violence as crimes of genocide, torture, war crimes, or crimes against humanity. In the *Čelebići* case the court determined that "there can be no question that acts of rape may constitute torture under customary law." The court found that because Delić was a public official, any rapes committed by him would constitute torture, since in this circumstance rape would always involve "punishment, coercion, discrimination, or intimidation." The court also found that rape was also a crime against humanity. In the *Kunarac* (or *Foca*) case, sexual slavery too was defined as a crime against humanity. Foča and its surrounding villages were occupied by Serb military forces, and Muslim and Croatian inhabitants were detained under deplorable conditions in facilities in the area. Dragoljub Kunarac was the head of a special unit of the Serb military forces, and Radomir Kovač and Zoran Vuković were paramilitary commanders. Among other indictments, the three were charged with rape as a crime against humanity, and

Kunarac and Kovać were charged with enslavement as a crime against humanity. It was alleged that they had taken women and girls from the detention centers and held them in sexual slavery. The ICTY judgment defined enslavement, including control of sexuality, exploitation, sex, prostitution, and trafficking, as a crime against humanity. This is important because it broadened the definition of enslavement beyond an economic crime. In the Furundžija case the accused was convicted of torture even though he did not personally commit the rapes, and the ICTY expanded the definition of rape to mean

> the sexual penetration, however slight, either of the vagina or anus of the victim by the penis of the perpetrator, or any other object used by the perpetrator, or of the mouth of the victim by the penis of the perpetrator, where such penetration is effected by coercion or force or threat of force against the victim or a third person.

The trial chamber noted in the *Kvocka* case that sexual violence included sexual mutilation, forced marriage, and forced abortion, as well as the crimes listed in the Rome Statute (see Chapter 13, on the **International Criminal Court** [ICC]): rape, sexual slavery, forced prostitution, forced pregnancy, and forced sterilization.

ICTY sentencing

In determining sentencing under the ICTY statute, the trial chamber can look to the practice of the courts of the FRY, but is not obligated to follow their precedent. When the trial chamber is sentencing, it must look to the gravity of the offense and circumstances of the convicted person as well as to other mitigating and aggravating circumstances. There is no minimum sentence required and life is the maximum penalty. In practice, sentencing is at the discretion of the court, and its practices have differed from those of the ICTR. Early release can be granted depending on the law of the state where the sentence is being served, such as after two-thirds of sentence has been served.

The International Criminal Tribunal for Rwanda

History and legal basis

The ICTY paved the way for the **International Criminal Tribunal for Rwanda** (ICTR). With the events following the death of Rwandan president Juvenal Habyarimana, ethnic tensions in the country escalated, leading to a genocide in April 1994 during which 800,000 Tutsis and moderate Hutus were killed. Outraged over the slaughter, the international community demanded prosecutions. As with the establishment of the ICTY, many allege that the establishment of the ICTR was to assuage the international community's guilt from failing to act to stop the atrocities.

The establishment of the ICTR followed a pattern similar to that of the ICTY. Following the genocide, on April 30, 1994, the president of the Security Council stated that those who had participated in breaches of international humanitarian law in Rwanda were individually responsible, and requested the Secretary-General to investigate these violations. The Secretary-General's report on the situation led to Security Council Resolution 935, which established a commission of experts to examine the evidence for grave violations and possible acts of genocide. Their commission found that individuals from both sides of the Rwandan conflict had perpetrated serious breaches of international humanitarian law, that both sides had perpetrated crimes against humanity, and that Hutus had perpetrated acts of genocide. The commission recommended that those responsible for the human rights violations be brought to justice before an independent and international criminal tribunal.

The Security Council established the ICTR, under Chapter VII of the UN Charter, through Resolution 955 in November 1994. Following the experience of the ICTY, it was decided that a single resolution was sufficient. The statute of the ICTR (see Box 10.3) was adapted from that of the ICTY, and certain institutional links were made between the two international courts, such as sharing a prosecutor and the appeals chamber. There was a great deal of discussion about where to situate the court; although the Rwandan government wanted the court to be situated in its own country, suitable premises were lacking in Kigali due to damage caused by the war. Claiming that it would be too expensive to build appropriate infrastructure in Rwanda in sufficient time, as well as citing concerns over fairness and impartiality, the Secretary-General recommended that the tribunal be located in a neutral country. Nairobi, Kenya, and Arusha, Tanzania, were both considered, although Kenya was ultimately unable to offer a seat for the tribunal; Tanzania, on the other hand, could provide an international conference center. In Resolution 977 of February 1995, the Security Council decided that the ICTR would be located in Arusha.

Box 10.3 Key articles from the statute of the International Criminal Tribunal for Rwanda

---

Article 1: Competence of the International Tribunal for Rwanda
The International Tribunal for Rwanda shall have the power to prosecute persons responsible for serious violations of the international humanitarian law committed in the territory of Rwanda and Rwandan citizens responsible for such violations committed in the territory of neighbouring States between 1 January 1994 and 31 December 1994, in accordance with the provisions of the present Statute.

Article 2: Genocide
. . . shall have the power to prosecute persons committing genocide. . . .

Article 3: Crimes Against Humanity
. . . shall have the power to prosecute persons responsible for the following crimes when committed as part of a widespread or systematic attack against any civilian population on national, political, ethnic, racial or religious grounds. . . .

Article 4: Violations of Article 3 Common to the Geneva Conventions and of Additional Protocol II
. . . shall have the power to prosecute persons committing or ordering to be committed serious violations of Article 3 common to the Geneva Conventions . . . and of Additional Protocol II. . . .

Article 6: Individual Criminal Responsibility
1. A person who planned, instigated, ordered, committed or otherwise aided and abetted in the planning, preparation or execution of a crime . . . shall be individually responsible for the crime.

---

2. The official position of any accused person, whether as Head of State or Government . . . shall not relieve such person of criminal responsibility. . . .
3. The fact that any of the acts . . . was referred to by a subordinate does not relieve his or her superior of criminal responsibility if he or she knew or had reason to know that the subordinate was about to commit such acts or had done so and the superior failed to take the necessary and reasonable measures to prevent such acts.

ICTR organs

Chambers

The Chambers consist of 9 judges divided between 3 trial chambers. The appeals chamber, shared with the ICTY, is based at The Hague and comprises 7 judges. Security Council Resolution 1431 of 2002 established a pool of 18 *ad litem* judges, with 4 *ad litem* judges attached to the trial chambers. Security Council Resolution 1512 of 2003 increased the latter number of *ad litem* judges to 9. As with the ICTY, judges for the ICTR are elected by the UN General Assembly for four-year terms.

Office of the Prosecutor

The Office of the Prosecutor was initially shared with the ICTY, until September 2003. This was to ensure that both tribunals were operating under the same prosecutorial strategy. Hassan Bubaca Jallow was eventually appointed as the ICTR's prosecutor. The office has two divisions: the Prosecution Division, which collects evidence and assembles trial teams to handle cases; and the Appeals and Legal Advisory Division, which is responsible for appeals and providing advice to trial teams.

Registry

The Registry is responsible for administration and management of the tribunal, judicial and legal support services for the work of the trial chambers, and prosecution.

Witnesses and victim support

Support and protection are provided for the witnesses for both the prosecution and the defense, including physical and psychological rehabilitation, and judges may be requested to order relocation of witnesses if necessary.

Defense counsel and detention management

The detention facility has 56 cells within the Arusha complex. There are 200 lawyers available for defense counsel to ensure the accused their right to a fair trial.

Functioning of the ICTR

The first accused arrived in Arusha in May 1996, and the first trial started in January 1997. The delay between Resolution 955 and the first trial was due to a number of logistical and operational problems. Arusha is less well equipped and considered less prestigious than The Hague, which made it harder to staff the court, and the conference center in Arusha was not intended to house court facilities. Two courtrooms were operating in 1997, and a third was added in 1998. The ICTR has faced the same challenges as the ICTY: for example, the cases are complex; testimony in Kinyarawanda, the most widely spoken language in Rwanda, must be translated into English and French (the two official languages of the tribunal); and witnesses are difficult to transport and are often unavailable.

ICTR jurisprudence

Competence

The statute of the ICTR covers:

* genocide;
* crimes against humanity;
* violations of Common Article 3 and Additional Protocol II of the Geneva Conventions.

Although the statute of the ICTR draws heavily on the statute of the ICTY, there is a key difference: the conflict in Rwanda was clearly noninternational. Therefore, the ICTR statute considers only violations of humanitarian law that can be committed in both internal and armed conflict: genocide and crimes against humanity. The ICTR statute is more expansive than the ICTY statute in that the former includes international instruments, whether or not they are part of customary law, and so includes violations of Common Article 3 as well as breaches of Additional Protocol II of the Geneva Conventions. The ICTR also has a much more limited temporal jurisdiction, covering events only from January 1 to December 31, 1994.

Focus

In contrast to the ICTY, the ICTR has from the beginning targeted those bearing the greatest responsibility for the genocide. Lower-level perpetrators have been dealt with through national courts and the *gacaca* process, which uses a modified traditional mechanism of conflict resolution. The completion strategy imposed by Security Council Resolution 1503 of 2003 is the same as that for the ICTY, and confirms the emphasis on leaders of the genocide. The resolution states that the ICTR should conclude new investigations by the end of 2004, complete trial activities by end of 2008, and complete all its work by 2010. As of December 2008, 13 accused remain at large. There has been a great deal of criticism that only Hutus have been indicted, and no Tutsis.

In contrast to the lack of cooperation experienced in the former Yugoslavia, in Rwanda the government requested a tribunal. Rwanda was a member of the Security Council and participated in all discussions concerning the ICTR's establishment. However, Rwanda voted against the resolution that established the tribunal. Its concerns included the tribunal's location outside Rwanda and its limited temporal jurisdiction. There was also a difficult relationship between the Rwandan government and the joint ICTY and ICTR prosecutor, Carla Del Ponte, who, contrary to the wishes of the government, insisted on carrying out investigations into the Rwandan Patriotic Front (RPF). The RPF, a Tutsi-led rebel group, committed atrocities during the genocide but afterward became the ruling political party, leading to a conflict of interest between the government and the ICTR. It was partly due to these ongoing problems that a separate prosecutor for the ICTR was appointed to the tribunal. Despite these problems with the Rwandan government, West African countries have been more cooperative with the ICTR, with successes such as Operations NAKI and Kiwest, which resulted in the arrest of key former ministers who had sought refuge abroad.

As of December 2008 the ICTR had completed 34 cases, with 29 cases in progress, 2 case on appeal, 9 individuals awaiting trial, and 13 accused still at large.

ICTR landmark cases

Akayesu

This *Akayesu* case provided the first definition of rape in international law. Jean Paul Akayesu was a prefecture head (*bourgmestre*) who was accused of failing to prevent acts of sexual violence and ordering and instigating acts of sexual violence against Tutsi women. The ICTR observed that rape is included in its statute as an element of several crimes. It also offered a definition, for purposes of international law, of both rape and sexual violence. Article 3(g) of the ICTR statute states that rape constitutes a crime against humanity if it is committed as part of a widespread or systematic attack against a civilian population on national, political, ethnic, racial, or religious grounds. In *Akayesu* the ICTR found that the targeting of Tutsi women constituted a widespread attack due to ethnicity and so could be punishable as a crime against humanity. Another important aspect of the case was the inclusion of rape as a possible element of the *actus reus* of genocide – that is, one of the acts that constitute genocide. According to Article 2 of the ICTR statute, genocide means any of the following acts committed with intent to destroy a group: (a) killing members of the group, (b) causing serious bodily or mental harm to members of the group, (c) deliberately inflicting on the group conditions calculated to bring about its physical destruction in whole or in part, (d) imposing measures intended to prevent births within the group, and (e) forcibly transferring children of the group to another group. The ICTR found that rape and sexual violence were among the worst ways to inflict bodily and mental harm and that the rapes were carried out as part of the process of specifically targeting Tutsi women for destruction. This systematic campaign of sexual violence resulted in physical and psychological destruction of Tutsi women and as such constituted genocide.

The ICTR also interpreted the definition of genocide from the Genocide Convention, specifically in considering how to define a "protected group." The ICTR gave a fairly broad interpretation, stating that whether someone belongs to a protected national, ethic, racial, or religious group depends on whether that person is treated as belonging to a group, and whether that person considers him- or herself as belonging to a group. This concept of self-identification (subjective) or identification of others (objective) is elaborated in the *Kayishema* case.

Although the ICTR could not find that Akayesu had personally raped women, it concluded that he had aided and abetted the offenses, and as such was subject to individual criminal responsibility. Akayesu was found guilty of genocide and incitement to genocide, and of crimes against humanity, including rape. The court determined that the Rwandan conflict was of sufficiently noninternational character that Article 4 of its statute applied.

Nahimana *et al.*

Also known as the *Media* case, this was the first international trial involving the media since Julius Streicher, the publisher of a Nazi propaganda newspaper, had been convicted at Nuremberg in 1946. In December 2003 the ICTR trial chamber found Ferdinand Nahimana, Hassan Ngeze, and Jean-Bosco Barayagwiza guilty of genocide, direct and public incitement to commit genocide, and persecution and crimes against humanity, due to their broadcasts on Radio Television Libre des Mille Collines (RTLM) and articles in the Kangura news-paper throughout 1994. The appeal chamber reversed this decision and found that only the RTLM broadcasts after April 6, 1994, which specifically encouraged extermination of Tutsis, constituted incitement to commit genocide; there was lack of proof that broadcasts before that date had any causal connection. The appeals chamber also found that hate speech can be as serious as other crimes against humanity where it is accompanied by other acts of per-secution, such as violence and destruction of property. It therefore found that the broadcasts after April could be considered for persecution as a crime against humanity. The appeals chamber did not rule on whether hate speech that is not accompanied by violence constitutes persecution as a crime against humanity.

Kambanda

The *Kambanda* case, the first concerning a former head of state to be brought by either the ICTY or the ICTR, was significant in demonstrating the nonimmunity of the accused from prosecution. Jean Kambanda became prime minister of the interim government of Rwanda on April 9, 1994, after President Juvenal Habyarimana was killed in a plane crash on April 6. It was also the first case in which the accused entered a guilty plea to all counts. No agreement was made between the prosecution and defense concerning Kambanda's sentencing to life in prison. The trial chamber found that although Kambanda had cooperated, and although his guilty plea could encourage others to recognize their responsibilities, and although a guilty plea is usually considered a mitigating circumstance, this did not mean that the sentence could be reduced. The ICTR found that Kambanda's crimes were extremely grave and shocking to the human conscience, that he had committed the crimes knowingly and with premeditation, and that he had abused the trust of the Rwandan population. The court deemed that the aggravating circumstances thus negated the mitigating circumstances. The life sentence was upheld by the appeals chamber in 2000.

ICTR sentencing

The ICTR statute is similar to that of the ICTY in that it can look to general sentencing practices in Rwanda and provides no minimum sentence. The ICTR has handed down harsher sentences than the ICTY, including a number of life sentences (the ICTY has issued only term imprisonments) and much higher average sentence lengths.

Criticism of the tribunals

A major criticism of the ICTY and ICTR has been the enormous costs incurred by both courts and the lengthy time taken for trials. The ICTY began with a budget of US$276,000 in 1993, which progressively increased to US$223,169,800 for 2002–3 and to US$310,952,100 for 2008–9. Similar amounts are also allocated to the ICTR. Although the trials are complex and involve high-profile cases, some doubt that they are worth the cost in view of the relatively low numbers of indictments and sentences. When sentences do result, many of the ICTY's have been particularly short, although the ICTR has imposed longer sentences. The Security Council resolution that allowed the addition of *ad litem* judges to increase the overall number of judges did try to address the criticism of slowness. Extra trial chambers were added to both tribunals, and standby witnesses were also allowed when witnesses were unable to testify.

Although many have welcomed the ICTY and ICTR for bringing perpetrators of human rights abuses to account, some have criticized the siting of the trials, in The Hague and Arusha. This argument, raised by the Rwandan government, centers around the distance between the courts and those to whom they were meant to bring justice. As well, both tribunals have been criticized for their lack of engagement with the local populations, although they have undertaken limited outreach programs. Another criticism is that the tribunals have not built the capacity of the Yugoslav and Rwandan domestic systems, which were left shattered following the conflicts. Although both courts are mandated to assist domestically, capacity building has been neglected. It was hoped that international legal norms would penetrate into the national legal systems and that the proceedings of the tribunals would have a pedagogic effect, but demonstrable results have yet to be achieved. However, the ICTR's outreach program, under way since November 2007, has helped to train Rwanda's judicial sector in international criminal law, indictment and prosecution, advocacy, information management, and legal research. This training has been aimed at judges, the Rwandan Bar Association, court staff, and judicial and academic institutions.

Beyond criticisms based on distance and lack of capacity building, serious concerns have been raised about the jurisdictional relationship between the ICTR, based in Arusha, Tanzania, and domestic prosecutions in Rwanda, with the ICTR trying organizers and leaders while the Rwandan courts handle more ordinary cases. The ICTR and Rwanda's domestic courts have concurrent jurisdiction over crimes relating to genocide; however, there are several notable distinctions between the two. In terms of sentencing, Rwandan courts can impose the death penalty for genocide, while the ICTR cannot. The Rwandan courts also use a specialized plea-agreement system in cases of genocide, which helps to expedite them and bring out more information, though there is potential for miscarriage of justice. The ICTR has far greater resources and far fewer defendants to process, but has been slow to render sentences and has not been capable of handling the vast number of cases that the Rwandan courts are seeking to address.

One argument made by advocates for the establishment of the tribunals was that they would act as deterrents to future abuses. It was hoped that, by showing that war crimes and crimes against humanity would be prosecuted, they would dissuade combatants and leaders from carrying out such acts. However, history shows that the situation in the former Yugoslavia worsened with the 1999 Kosovo conflict, and that the ICTY did not have such a deterrent effect in this instance. Both tribunals did have an effect, though, in that those indicted were arrested and kept in detention while others were forced into hiding or had their assets frozen. It was perhaps unrealistic to believe that courts would prove a deterrent on their own, outside their role in a broader strategy.

Contributions of the tribunals

Despite the criticisms leveled at the tribunals, they have achieved much. The focus of both the ICTY and the ICTR on abuses against civilians has demonstrated a stance against conflict that specifically targets noncombatants and allowed the Yugoslav and Rwandan peoples to see that justice is being done on their behalf, although the extent of those peoples' engagement with tribunals that are located outside their countries is debatable. Despite the criticism over lengthy trials, the ICTY and ICTR are comparable to domestic courts in terms of the time and resources need to try complicated cases such as murder. As an innovative response of the international community, the tribunals were bound to experience problems, but crucial lessons have been learned that can provide a basis for the work of **hybrid tribunals** and the International Criminal Court, discussed in Chapters 12 and 13, respectively.

Advances in international humanitarian law will be the long-term legacy of the tribunals. The ICTY and ICTR have enabled international humanitarian law to be applied to domestic as well as international conflicts. The ICTY has applied its provisions creatively, and the ICTR has been able to treat violations of Common Article 3 of the Geneva Conventions as criminal. These advances have helped to address the potential datedness of international humanitarian law and its inability to cope with contemporary, largely internal, armed conflicts, and serve as precedents for future cases. As stated in the statute of the ICTR and in the jurisprudence of ICTY, violating Common Article 3 leads to individual criminal responsibility in both internal and international conflict. It is also highly significant that the ICTR, soon followed by the ICTY, indicted a head of government, setting the precedent that leaders are not immune from prosecution.

The ICTY and ICTR have been widely acknowledged for their advances in terms of gender crimes. It is now clear in international humanitarian law that rape is a crime against humanity and can also be part of genocide, torture, and war crimes – a development long overdue despite substantial advocacy within the human rights community. It is the jurisprudence of the ICTY and ICTR that provides the basis for future cases of gender crimes, whose pioneering judgments have led to the broad definitions of sexual violence in the ICC's Rome Statute.

Key points

- The International Criminal Tribunal for the Former Yugoslavia (ICTY) and the International Criminal Tribunal for Rwanda (ICTR) are international tribunals established by the UN Security Council.
- The ICTY and ICTR prosecute violations of international law during the conflict in the former Yugoslavia and the Rwandan genocide respectively.
- Both tribunals have carried out a number of landmark cases leading to important advances in international humanitarian law, particularly regarding gender-related crimes.
- Criticisms of the tribunals include the relatively low numbers of indictments when compared to the enormous costs involved, as well as the slow progression of cases.

Discussion questions

- What do the experiences of the ICTR and ICTY demonstrate about the reliance of ad hoc tribunals on political goodwill?
- What difficulties might the Office of the Prosecutor face in assembling cases for the ICTY and ICTR?

- Were the Rwandan government's reasons for wanting the ICTR to be situated in Kigali valid?
- How do the activities of the international courts affect perceptions of justice, domestically and internationally?
- What do you think has been the most important development in international humanitarian law to result from the ICTY and ICTR?

Group exercise

Form two groups to debate the value of the ICTY and ICTR.

- *Group 1*: Argue in support of the tribunals. Think about how to justify the enormous resources (time, money, personnel) they require. You may wish to consider the scale of the atrocities, the role of the international community, and important jurisprudence.
- *Group 2*: Argue that the tribunals are not worth the time or resources required. Think about the number of people who have been indicted and sentenced, the length of trials, organizational and operational difficulties, and alternative prosecution options.

Further reading

Askin, Kelly D., "Reflections on Some of the Most Significant Achievements of the ICTY," *New England Law Review* 37, no. 4 (2003): 903–14.

Cassesse, Antonio, *International Criminal Law* (Oxford: Oxford University Press, 2003).

Drumbl, Mark A., *Atrocity, Punishment, and International Law* (New York: Cambridge University Press, 2007).

Kerr, Rachel, and Eirin Mobekk, *Peace and Justice: Seeking Accountability After War* (Cambridge: Polity, 2007), chap. 2, "Ad Hoc International Criminal Tribunals: The ICTY and ICTR."

Meron, Theodor, "Reflections on the Prosecution of War Crimes by International Tribunals," *American Journal of International Law* 100, no. 3 (July 2006): 551–79.

Møse, Erik, "Main Achievements of the ICTR," *Journal of International Criminal Justice* 3, no. 4 (September 2005): 920–43.

Ratner, Steven R., and Jason S. Abrams, *Accountability for Human Rights Atrocities in International Law: Beyond the Nuremberg Legacy* (Oxford: Oxford University Press, 2001), chap 9, "The Progeny of Nuremberg: International Criminal Tribunals."

Official Documents and Sources

International Criminal Tribunal for Rwanda, http://www.ictr.org.

International Criminal Tribunal for the Former Yugoslavia, http://www.un.org/icty.

United Nations, *Interim report of the Commission of Experts established pursuant to Security Council resolution 780 (1992)*, (10 February 1993), UN Doc. S/25274.

——, *Preliminary report of the Independent Commission of Experts established in accordance with Security Council resolution 935 (1994)*, (4 October 1994), UN Doc. S/1994/1125.

——, *Report on the completion strategy of the International Criminal Tribunal for Rwanda (as at 1 May 2008)*, (12 May 2008), UN Doc. S/2008/322.

11 Enforcing human rights transnationally

Overview

Elsewhere in this book we consider accountability mechanisms in international courts, whether ad hoc, such as those for the former Yugoslavia and Rwanda (Chapter 10); hybrid, such as the Special Court for Sierra Leone (Chapter 12); or permanent, such as the **International Criminal Court** (ICC) (Chapter 13). In such situations, international law, both **international human rights law** and **international humanitarian law**, is applied by international or internationalized courts, not wholly domestic courts. However, there are also processes by which accountability is imposed transnationally. What is unusual about such processes is that they involve the application of international law in domestic courts, but not in the domestic courts of the country where the abuses or crimes actually took place. Instead, accountability may be found extraterritorially through the exercise of **universal jurisdiction**, imposing criminal accountability, or civil accountability processes in a number of states. In such situations, accountability is ultimately imposed quite far from the locus of the crime. You may already be familiar with the phenomenon of universal jurisdiction, thanks to cases brought against former Chilean dictator Augusto Pinochet Ugarte in Spain and elsewhere. You may be less familiar with another tool, that of civil accountability. It is particularly available in the United States through the use of the **Alien Tort Claims Act**. However, the United States is not the only country to have civil accountability tools for past abuses: the United Kingdom has also imposed civil accountability for human rights violations committed abroad.

This chapter discusses universal jurisdiction and civil accountability in turn, considering critical cases and debates. The debates include both legal arguments – about the scope of and limits to extraterritorial jurisdiction – and also political ones – about the appropriateness of the courts of one nation sitting in judgment over the actions of citizens and officials of another nation.

Criminal accountability through universal jurisdiction

It is important to understand that universal jurisdiction is a principle of international law, but one that has emerged in customary law over time, with little mention in international treaties or conventions, even by implication. It permits and perhaps requires prosecution of certain serious crimes in the domestic courts of any state in the world, regardless of where the crimes occurred.

Universal jurisdiction can be exercised only in response to a very limited number of crimes. These include **war crimes**, **crimes against humanity**, **genocide**, and **torture**;

slavery is sometimes included, as is piracy, for largely historical reasons. The cases brought against Pinochet in Spain, and complaints filed against Ariel Sharon in Belgium and Donald Rumsfeld in Germany, are but a few of the most famous examples of the exercise of universal jurisdiction to prosecute a defendant accused of crimes committed far from the nation and from the court seeking to try him or her. The exercise of universal jurisdiction may potentially fill gaps in accountability globally, where domestic courts are unable or unwilling to try alleged perpetrators, and where no international venue is available or where those that are lack jurisdiction. However, universal jurisdiction is controversial, precisely because it does involve the exercise of jurisdiction by one state over the citizens of another, and often over high-profile officials or former officials.

Under the principle of universal jurisdiction, then, a state is competent to judge someone alleged to have committed certain international crimes and found in its territory, or to seek the extradition of that person from the territory of another state. Unlike other bases for jurisdiction, specific contacts with the state that is seeking to assert jurisdiction are not required. The nationality of the victims and the location of any alleged crimes are not relevant. The ability to exercise such jurisdiction over international crimes enables states to fulfill treaty commitments (such as the ***aut dedere aut judicare*** principles in treaties such as the **Genocide Convention**) to try or extradite individuals suspected of certain crimes.

Universal jurisdiction and national sovereignty

It is important to recognize that the exercise of universal jurisdiction may constitute a significant infringement upon national sovereignty, and may even violate the principle of noninterference in the internal affairs of states, as enshrined in Article 2(7) of the **UN Charter**. Historically, juridical jurisdiction has been closely tied to territorial sovereignty, with states generally exercising exclusive jurisdiction over acts committed on their own territories or by their own nationals. The instances in which a state could exercise jurisdiction extraterritorially have been very limited. The exercise of extraterritorial application of jurisdiction has tended to require a nexus – some kind of connection – between the alleged act and the state that is seeking to hear a case. Universal jurisdiction is the only form of extraterritorial jurisdiction that requires no such nexus. The other generally recognized bases for extraterritorial jurisdiction, apart from universal jurisdiction, are:

- *territorial*, in that jurisdiction is based upon the location where the offense had its effects, but is in fact extraterritorial in that it is exerted over a nonnational acting outside the territory;
- *national*, based upon the nationality of the offender;
- *protective*, based upon injury to the national interest; and
- *passive personal*, based upon the nationality of the victim.

The reason why extraterritorial jurisdiction is limited is perhaps obvious: respect for sovereignty. There is a concern not to have the courts of one country sitting in judgment upon the internal activities of others, but also a concern to avoid jurisdictional conflicts – with courts of several countries considering what is essentially the same case. Infringement upon sovereign powers is not taken lightly in international law, and states emerging from conflict often defend their sovereignty as strongly as do stable states.

While universal jurisdiction is a general principle in international law, it is not one that most domestic judges are prepared to exercise. Even those who do exercise universal jurisdiction often do so cautiously, relying upon other bases such as passive personality or the nationality of the victims of crimes. Judges may also rely upon a range of domestic legislation enacted by states to incorporate international treaty obligations, and to fulfill their obligations under such treaties to enact effective domestic legislation. Such may explicitly refer to universal jurisdiction, or spell out the power of state courts to hear cases involving specific crimes, in the absence of any nexus. Some scholars have referred to the use by judges of universal jurisdiction and other bases of jurisdiction simultaneously as *universal jurisdiction plus*.

As we have seen, this exceptional jurisdiction can be exercised only in the event of exceptional crimes: war crimes, crimes against humanity, genocide, and torture, as well as slavery and piracy. It is justified on the grounds that such crimes are of concern to all humankind and all nations. It is claimed that such jurisdiction signals that certain crimes are so heinous that they both threaten the international community and are forcefully condemned by it, and that it is in the interests of justice everywhere that perpetrators be brought to account. However, such cases are politically charged, and states and individuals may vigorously resist extradition and trial, particularly where the accused are current or former state officials. As discussed later in this chapter, official immunity is often raised as a defense against such charges, although prosecutors may argue, and judges may concur, that official immunity cannot apply where the crimes alleged are international crimes such as genocide. The question of official immunity is hotly contested by potential defendants who are state officials or sitting or even former heads of state, such as Pinochet. Similarly, states may object to the exercise of universal jurisdiction by other states to prosecute their citizens, and in two cases, discussed later, they have brought cases before the **International Court of Justice** (ICJ) to prevent its exercise over their sitting or former officials.

The *Pinochet* cases

The cases against Augusto Pinochet Ugarte arise from events that took place between the coup that carried Pinochet and his junta to power in Chile on September 11, 1973, and the return of the country to democratic rule in April 1990. During that time, thousands of individuals who supported the democratically elected leader, Salvador Allende, and the return to democracy in the country, were kidnapped, detained, tortured, killed, or "disappeared," allegedly at the direction of Pinochet and his regime. The regime passed self-amnesty legislation in 1978, and Pinochet sought to insulate himself further with "senator for life" status when he stepped down from power.

Cases seeking to bring General Pinochet to justice for killings, torture, disappearances, and genocide during his rule have been filed in several countries in recent years. These include cases brought in Spain, Belgium, and the Netherlands. We focus here upon proceedings against him that were initiated in Spain and were consequently triggered in the United Kingdom by a Spanish request for his extradition. We also highlight a related civil case in Spain dealing with assets looted by Pinochet during his rule (see Box 11.2). Finally, we briefly consider proceedings within Chile not based upon universal jurisdiction, but that appear to have been inspired by the proceedings against Pinochet abroad.

Proceedings in Spain

Proceedings in Spain began with the submission of a complaint in July 1996 by the Progressive Prosecutors Union (Union Progresista de Fiscales [UPF]), a group of Spanish prosecutors, against Pinochet and others for crimes against humanity and genocide committed during his rule. The complaint was submitted in a penal chamber of the Spanish Audiencia Nacional – the court having competence over particularly serious crimes such as offenses to the crown, fraud, drug trafficking, and crimes committed outside Spanish territory, among others – and articulated the legal basis and factual allegations that formed the foundation of subsequent actions against Pinochet.

The complaint alleged, and Spanish judges claimed, that Spain had jurisdiction, through a combination of domestic and international law, to address crimes of genocide, torture, and terrorism. Under the Law on Judicial Power (see Box 11.1), Spanish courts are competent to hear cases that address these crimes even if they occur outside Spanish territory and whether they are committed by a Spaniard or a foreigner. The legislation thus empowers courts to exercise universal jurisdiction. The complaint thus claimed that under domestic law, Spain could address these crimes even if no Spanish citizen had been killed in Chile, although there were in fact Spanish victims. In addition to articulating domestic legislation as grounds for the exercise of jurisdiction to pursue these crimes, the complaint also emphasized Spanish obligations under international law.

Box 11.1 **The Spanish law that establishes universal jurisdiction**

Law on Judicial Power (1 July 1985) Spain

Article 23.4 creates Spanish judicial competence over acts committed by Spaniards or foreigners outside Spanish national territory, for the following crimes:

a)   genocide
b)   terrorism
c)   piracy and airplane hijacking
d)   counterfeiting foreign currency
e)   acts relating to prostitution
f)   traffic in illegal drugs
g)   and any other acts that Spain ought to pursue under its international treaty and convention obligations

Source: http://www.derecho.com/xml/disposiciones/trini/disposicion.xml?id_disposicion= 33022; informal translation.

The complaint had to further establish not only that there was potential jurisdiction, but also that acts committed under Pinochet's rule constituted crimes for which that jurisdiction could be exercised, under Spanish or international law. The complaint sought to undermine any potential immunity defenses to genocide and torture in several ways. First, it argued that Spanish national interests in the crimes, due to the presence of Spanish victims, would override the 1978 self-amnesty, which in any event would not have extraterritorial application. Similarly, the complaint argued that defenses of official status or superior orders are excluded under the **Torture Convention**, and that the International Covenant on Civil and Political Rights (ICCPR) indicates no immunity for persons acting in an official capacity.

The complaint thus requested judicial assistance, including provision of information, and the extradition of those responsible to Spain, under the treaty of judicial assistance and extradition between Spain and Chile. It was this aspect of the request that brought about the most notorious aspect of the case: efforts to extradite Pinochet from the United Kingdom, where he was seeking medical treatment.

Late in 1998, Judge Baltasar Garzón of Investigating Court no. 5 of the Audiencia Nacional, acting on the complaint, agreed with the complainants that Spain had jurisdiction to hear allegations of genocide and torture that took place under Pinochet's leadership. This provoked a diplomatic outcry, with the Chilean government objecting vehemently to the assertion of jurisdiction, and to the principle of universal jurisdiction generally. Chile argued that Spanish courts were not competent to judge allegations of crimes against humanity committed in any third countries, and that in any event, Pinochet would have immunity, either as a former of state or as a "senator for life." Despite these objections from Chile, in October 1998 Judge Garzón ordered that Pinochet be subjected to "provisional imprisonment," issued an international arrest warrant, and issued an extradition request to the United Kingdom. He also ordered that Pinochet's assets, and those of his accused associates, be frozen.

These orders were issued on the grounds that the alleged acts could constitute genocide, terrorism, and torture subject to universal jurisdiction. Having found that extraterritorial jurisdiction was granted by the Law on Judicial Power, the judge further reasoned that, beyond domestic law, Spain had the power to address the crime of genocide under the Genocide Convention, which was incorporated into domestic law in 1971. The proscription of genocide was further found to be a *jus cogens* norm – a customary norm of international law that cannot be derogated from, and for which the exercise of universal jurisdiction is permitted. Finally, Spain was not a party to the Torture Convention at the time that torture allegedly occurred in Chile, and thus would in principle have been barred from seeking extradition of individuals accused of acts that were not at the time criminalized in Spain. However, the decision rejected this objection, reasoning that if Spain had jurisdiction over crimes of genocide and terrorism, of which torture forms a part, then it would also have jurisdiction over crimes of torture as defined by the Torture Convention.

Critical judicial action then moved to the United Kingdom, where courts deliberated upon whether to honor the Spanish extradition request. As we shall see, Pinochet would ultimately be returned to Chile, but other proceedings against him, civil rather than criminal, continued in Spain (see Box 11.2).

Box 11.2 Civil actions in Spain

In addition to committing serious violent crimes, Pinochet and his cohorts were also alleged to have looted the Chilean state, smuggling out millions of dollars to overseas accounts. In September 2004, private individuals and the Fundación Salvador Allende filed civil and criminal claims for concealment of assets and money laundering by Pinochet. The claims were filed using the tool of *actio popularis*, which allows individuals to act, in essence, as "private prosecutors." The civil claim asked the Spanish courts to seek action by the courts of the United States and Chile to address those responsible for economic crimes by freezing their foreign assets. The complaint specifically requested that the United States be asked to embargo funds in Riggs

Bank identified as belonging to Pinochet, in the amount of €10,300,000, which the Investigative Court no. 5 of the Audiencia Nacional so ordered. While these cases were not explicitly based upon universal jurisdiction, and indeed involved civil penalties, they were related directly to the earlier criminal charges against Pinochet. Further, as with use of the Alien Tort Claims Act in the United States, discussed later in this chapter, these cases brought attention to the use of freezing and confiscating assets as an alternative form of punishment.

Extradition proceedings in the United Kingdom

On October 16, 1998, Pinochet was arrested in the United Kingdom, where he was seeking medical treatment, on the basis of Judge Garzón's international arrest warrant. Pinochet's attorneys promptly claimed privilege and immunity from arrest on grounds that he was a former head of state and that he had parliamentary immunity based on his status of "senator for life." His attorneys further argued that he had never been a subject of Spain and thus that there was no crime in Spain for which he could be extradited. Chile then intervened in the proceedings in the United Kingdom, arguing that Spain's request and any UK extradition involved an exercise of jurisdiction over Chilean subjects contrary to international law, and directly affected Chile's "rights," including its transition to democracy and its relations with the United Kingdom and Spain. Arguing that the appropriate place to judge Pinochet was in Chile, the Chilean government asserted national "sovereignty" and, like Pinochet's attorneys, immunity for Pinochet as a former head of state. The Chilean government further invoked international policy and practice supporting noninterference in the "sovereign" acts of nations.

The Law Lords in the United Kingdom – part of the House of Lords, which exercises judicial functions and acts as the highest court of appeal for most domestic issues – examined the issue. They first rejected the claim that immunity as a head or former head of state could be a bar to prosecution, finding that such immunity does not apply where certain grave international crimes such as torture and hostage-taking have been alleged, in line with the reasoning laid out by the complaint in Spain, discussed above. However, the decision was set aside on appeal because one of the Law Lords had undisclosed links with the human rights advocacy group **Amnesty International**, which had been active in condemning Pinochet and advocating his accountability.

Thus, the case was reheard before a new panel. It held that while former heads of state did enjoy immunity in the United Kingdom for acts engaged in as part of their official functions, torture could not be viewed as an official function. There were other limits, though – specifically temporal ones, as the Lords indicated that the United Kingdom could extradite Pinochet only for crimes that would have been crimes not just in Chile or Spain, but also in the United Kingdom when they were committed; as the United Kingdom had not ratified the Torture Convention until 1988, only events in Chile after 1988 could then be extraditable crimes. This was due to the application of the principle of double criminality: the crime had to be one under both UK and Spanish law at the time it was committed. Conspiracy in Spain to murder someone in Spain was also found to be an extraditable crime. Because of the application of the principle, then, only a few of the many crimes for which Pinochet was alleged to have been responsible constituted crimes for which he could be extradited. On the basis of the decision, Pinochet was to have been extradited to Spain. However, in light of concerns about Pinochet's health and his mental fitness to stand trial, the British home secretary ultimately ordered him returned to Chile in March 2000.

Proceedings in Chile

When Pinochet returned to Chile, he was not able to escape attempts to prosecute him for past abuses. Charges were filed for a number of killings of political prisoners in 1973. However, Pinochet's parliamentary immunity based on his "senator for life" status was an obstacle to his prosecution, though it was removed ultimately by the Chilean courts. A judge charged Pinochet with kidnapping and ordered his arrest, but this decision was overruled by the Supreme Court in 2000 on procedural grounds – that his house arrest had been improperly ordered. Several further proceedings followed, but never reached fruition. Pinochet died in Chile in December 2006 while under house arrest.

Beyond *Pinochet*: other critical cases

We have focused on the *Pinochet* cases because they are familiar, and raise important issues such as official immunities, but advances in universal jurisdiction have been more dramatic in other cases. We discuss here a number of other cases that have been brought in Spain and Belgium (see "Further reading" and "Official documents and sources" at the end of this chapter for more detail).

As discussed, Pinochet was not ultimately extradited to Spain but was returned home for reasons of health. By contrast, Spain has been able to pursue cases against former members of Argentina's junta such as Adolfo Scilingo and Miguel Cavallo, who were responsible for disappearances, torture, and killing during military rule in that country from 1977 to 1983. Scilingo was already present in Spain voluntarily when his arrest was ordered; he was subsequently sentenced to 640 years in prison. While his convictions for genocide, torture, and terrorism were overturned, those for his role in murder and illegal detention were upheld in 2007. This was because torture was not yet defined as a crime in Spanish law when Scilingo allegedly committed those acts; however, those acts did fall within the definition of crimes against humanity in customary law. In the case of Cavallo, Spain issued an extradition request to Mexico, and Mexico duly complied, assisting in the extradition of an Argentine not back to Argentina, but to Spain. In March 2008, Spain transferred Cavallo to Argentina, where he is being tried.

Also, as we saw in Chapter 7, in February 2008 a Spanish judge indicted 40 high-ranking Rwandan Tutsi military officials for crimes committed during the 1994 conflict and genocide in Rwanda, sparking an outcry from the government (see Box 7.4). The government, controlled by the Rwandan Patriotic Front (RPF), a Tutsi former rebel group, rejects any claims that its troops committed crimes during the conflict, and presents RPF members rather as heroes who brought a halt to the genocide. Political pressure is alleged to have prevented the International Criminal Tribunal for Rwanda (ICTR), discussed in Chapter 10, from pursuing any such cases, although it has investigated allegations of crimes by the RPF. Philip Reyntjens, a former employee of the ICTR, calls its failure to prosecute any Tutsis a "perverse game of victor's justice." He says the only chance of a trial for members of the RPF is in other countries.

Spain is of course not the only state that has actively pursued cases through the exercise of universal jurisdiction. Belgium has as well, although it has radically limited its legislation in response to political pressure following high-profile attempts to bring cases against Ariel

Sharon and US officials. In 2006, Belgium issued a request to Senegal for the extradition of ex-Chadian dictator Hissène Habré, who had been in exile in Senegal since 1990. Habré had been in fact indicted in Senegal in 2001 for crimes, such as torture, allegedly committed while he was dictator of Chad, but the Senegalese courts declined to try him. In response to the Belgian request, the Senegalese president indicated that he would never extradite Habré to Belgium. The political controversy was taken up by the **African Union** (AU), which tasked a group of African jurists to examine the issue. The expert panel determined that Habré must be tried, and that Senegal would be the most appropriate location. The experts found not only that the Senegalese courts had jurisdiction over the case, but also that Senegal had an obligation to act in response to allegations of torture in accord with its duties under the Torture Convention. In addition, the expert panel found that several other locations would also be feasible, including Chad or any other African nation that had ratified the Torture Convention.

Legal limits to universal jurisdiction

However, at the same time, some restrictions have been imposed on the exercise of universal jurisdiction by the International Court of Justice. In two instances where courts of European countries (Belgium and France) have sought to exercise jurisdiction over criminal charges against sitting officials of African states engaged in or emerging from conflict (the Democratic Republic of Congo [DRC] and its neighbor the Republic of Congo), those states challenged that jurisdiction before the ICJ. The ICJ issued a ruling in one of the cases that restricts the exercise of universal jurisdiction, and provides some clarity as to the status of official immunities.

DRC v. Belgium

In April 2000 a Belgian magistrate issued an international arrest warrant for the Democratic Republic of Congo's minister of foreign affairs, Yerodia Ndombasi, for crimes alleged to constitute "serious violations of international law." The DRC filed a case before the International Court of Justice challenging Belgium's jurisdiction and seeking provisional measures to discharge the warrant immediately on the grounds that Belgium's attempt to arrest Yerodia constituted a violation of its international legal obligations. The DRC argued that there was no evidence of jurisdiction based on any of the normal tools of extraterritorial jurisdiction: territory, *in personam* jurisdiction, or harm to the security or dignity of Belgium. The DRC contended that while several treaties created universal jurisdiction, they did so *only* where the alleged perpetrator was on the territory of the state seeking jurisdiction. It further argued that Belgium had violated the principle of sovereign legal equality, and asserted that Yerodia was protected by diplomatic immunity.

In February 2002 the ICJ issued its decision in the case, finding that Belgium had indeed violated its own legal obligations toward the DRC in its failure to respect the immunity from criminal jurisdiction enjoyed by an *incumbent* minister under international law. However, it did not reject the principle per se, but only its exercise in this instance. Instead, the ICJ indicated that the warrant would have undermined the conduct of foreign relations by the minister (see Box 11.3). The court thus issued an order that Belgium cancel the international arrest warrant. However, one line in the judgment did indicate that this immunity was only in relation to national courts, not international courts.

Box 11.3 **Universal jurisdiction and immunity**

CASE CONCERNING THE ARREST WARRANT OF 11 APRIL 2000
(DEMOCRATIC REPUBLIC OF THE CONGO v. BELGIUM)
JUDGMENT OF 14 FEBRUARY 2002

54. The Court accordingly concludes that the functions of a Minister for Foreign
Affairs (are such that, throughout the duration of his or her office, he or she when
abroad enjoys full immunity from criminal jurisdiction and inviolability. That
immunity and that inviolability protect the individual concerned against any act
of authority of another State which would hinder him or her in the performance of
his or her duties.

55. In this respect, no distinction can be drawn between acts performed by a Minister
for Foreign Affairs in an "official" capacity, and those claimed to have been
performed in a "private capacity," or, for that matter, between acts performed
before the person concerned assumed office as Minister for Foreign Affairs and
acts committed during the period of office. Thus, if a Minister for Foreign Affairs
is arrested in another State on a criminal charge, he or she is clearly thereby
prevented from exercising the functions of his or her office.

The reasoning of the ICJ meant that efforts to pursue a case against Israeli leader Ariel
Sharon while he was in office were dropped. The judgment clarifies limits upon the exercise
of universal jurisdiction imposed by diplomatic immunity so long as the accused remains in
an office of diplomatic importance (although the parameters of what offices are significant
has not been articulated), but gray areas remain. In particular, whether immunities attach to
former diplomats or heads of state for acts undertaken in office has not been addressed,
although the logic in the *Pinochet* cases, which has precedent only in the United Kingdom,
would dictate that only legitimate acts are covered by any official immunity.

Republic of Congo v. France

Similar issues arose in a case brought against France, which has not been decided but could
eventually result in a more direct pronouncement on the legality and extent of universal
jurisdiction by the ICJ. Judicial proceedings were initiated in France against the sitting
president, Denis Sassou Nguesso, of the Republic of Congo, and against the sitting interior
minister, for torture and crimes against humanity under Articles 689-1 and 689-2 of the
French Code of Criminal Procedure. The Republic of Congo brought a case against France
at the ICJ, challenging its attempts to initiate investigations, and sought provisional measures
to compel France to suspend judicial proceedings. The Republic of Congo argued that a
sitting head of state, or cabinet minister, is immune from any "act of authority" by another
state that would hinder them in the exercise of their duties, and further that the "unilateral"
exercise by a state of universal jurisdiction is a violation of the sovereign equality enshrined
in Article 2(1) of the UN Charter. This constituted a more direct challenge to the principle of
universal jurisdiction than that raised by the DRC in the *Yerodia* case. The ICJ rejected the

Republic of Congo's request for provisional measures in 2003, on the grounds that France recognized official immunities and thus had made it clear there was no risk that the case would go forward while the officials were in office.

Civil accountability

The Alien Tort Claims Act

The Alien Tort Claims Act, passed in 1789, established US federal district court jurisdiction over "any civil action by an alien for a tort only committed in violation of the law of nations or a treaty of the United States." Because there is virtually no legislative history, it is unclear what the original purpose of the ATCA was, although some argue that it was meant only to address piracy, slave-trading, and attacks on foreign diplomats, while others offer a wider interpretation. Today, cases interpreting the act have enabled *civil* claims to be brought for acts beyond this limited list; however, *criminal* charges cannot be brought. Courts have interpreted "the law of nations" to be customary international law – a norm is so considered for the purposes of ATCA cases when it is "specific, universal, and obligatory." Like universal jurisdiction, civil accountability under the ATCA has proven controversial, particularly as judgments have been rendered against corporate actors.

The landmark Filartiga *case*

While the ATCA is over 200 years old, it was rarely invoked until 1980, when a federal court issued a historic decision. In a case brought against a Paraguayan police inspector-general that arose from the torture and murder of Paraguayan citizen Joelito Filartiga, a New York appellate court determined that human rights violations such as torture could constitute violations of the law of nations for the purposes of the ACTA. *Filartiga v. Peña-Irala* was a landmark case in establishing a reading of the ATCA never previously discussed, but falling within the language of the statute. Subsequent jurisprudence has established that extrajudicial execution, disappearances, war crimes and crimes against humanity, and genocide are also acts contrary to the law of nations for the purposes of interpreting the statute.

Kadic v. Karadžić

As we saw in Chapter 4, nonstate armed groups and their leaders may fall through the cracks of international humanitarian law and international human rights law. Internal armed conflicts could not traditionally be the sites of **grave breaches**, even though the same acts could have constituted grave breaches in international armed conflict. Also, human rights obligations are undertaken exclusively by states – by signing treaties or once they become customary law – and in some instances appear on their face to require official action, implying action by state actors rather than **nonstate actors**.

Radovan Karadžić, the leader of Bosnian Serbs during the conflicts in the former Yugoslavia (discussed in Chapter 5), has been accused of bearing direct and indirect responsibility for a wide range of abuses during that time. He was indicted by the International Criminal Tribunal for the Former Yugoslavia (ICTY) (discussed in Chapter 10) and after years in hiding was arrested in mid-2008. However, over a decade earlier in the United States he was the subject of a civil suit for a range of abuses. In the *Kadic v. Karadžić* case, attorneys acting on Karadžić's behalf objected that US courts lacked subject-matter jurisdiction, because Karadžić, as a nonstate actor, could not have committed the crimes alleged, which were not attributable to a state. While a lower court held that acts committed by nonstate actors do not violate the law of nations, a US appellate court found that Karadžić could be found liable for genocide, war crimes, and crimes against humanity in his private capacity, and for other violations in his capacity as a state actor. Because he exercised effective control of a territory as the head of Republika Srpska, his regime could satisfy the criteria of a state, and, in the alternative, he might be found to have acted in collaboration with a recognized state, then Yugoslavia. The case was thus an important step forward in treating an individual – head of a nonstate armed group but not of an internationally recognized state – as an official actor for the purposes of international criminal accountability. A similar issue was confronted by the ICTY in the *Tadić* jurisdiction case, discussed in Chapter 10.

Corporations as targets of litigation

More recently, corporations have also been held liable under the ATCA, either for direct commission of abuses or, more frequently, for complicity in abuses. Transnational corporations have been the subject of increasing attention by human rights advocates precisely because of the difficulty of regulating them internationally, and because many of them engage in, or are complicit in the perpetration of, significant human rights violations, particularly when they operate in conflict-affected countries. However, finding the appropriate links and legal personality to establish jurisdiction over corporations has proven difficult. During the negotiations for the Rome Statute for the International Criminal Court, it was proposed that jurisdiction be extended to both legal and natural persons. However, legal persons (such as corporations) were ultimately excluded from the Court's jurisdiction. This means that subjecting corporations to criminal sanctions in international law remains impossible, subject to any revisions in the Rome Treaty. Given the difficulty of prosecuting corporations directly before the ICC, the use of the ATCA has proven attractive for filing cases against corporations in the United States.

Numerous cases have extended the *Filartiga* line of reasoning to pursue corporate accountability for crimes committed directly or when corporations act in complicity with state actors in violation of human rights. For corporate complicity or aiding and abetting a government to be found, in civil cases, it is not sufficient to have simply operated in a country where widespread abuses occurred. Rather, it is necessary that specific projects were connected with specific violations, and that the corporation knew or should have known that such violations would occur.

A crucial corporate case was *Doe v. Unocal*, brought against Unocal, a California-based petroleum company, on behalf of 15 Burmese villagers for abuses such as forced labor, rape, torture, and murder perpetrated by the Burmese military, which had been hired by Unocal to protect and assist its construction of a pipeline. The case was also brought against the Burmese government and the French company Total. While cases against the state authorities and subsidiaries were dismissed, those against Unocal were not. The court found that corporations could be liable not only for their own actions, but also for actions of their partners or joint venturers, including governments. Unocal was found to be complicit in these acts because it hired the military for security and other support with full knowledge of its history of serious human rights abuses. Unocal appealed and then, just before the appellate court was to begin its review of the case, settled with a group of villagers for an undisclosed sum.

As discussed in Chapter 7, the Canadian oil company Talisman Energy has faced similar allegations and a lawsuit for its alleged complicity with abuses in Southern Sudan. In 2001 the Presbyterian Church of Sudan filed a case under the ATCA against Talisman. The case alleges that the company assisted the government's military assaults on minority villages in order to help the government clear the way for Talisman's oil exploration. Talisman attempted several times to have the case dismissed; in its last attempt, in 2003, the judge held that because the alleged acts of genocide, war crimes, torture, and enslavement constituted violations of international law, plaintiffs had actionable ATCA claims. The judge further found that under international law, Talisman could be alleged to have aided and abetted these acts; the case is on appeal at the time of this writing (see Box 8.3).

Limits to the ATCA: the Sosa case

However, while civil liability through the ATCA has resulted in landmark judgments against individuals and, to a lesser degree, against corporations, there are limits due to strong political opposition both from the US government under George W. Bush, and from corporations. The Bush administration argued that ATCA cases potentially undermine the "war on terror." It also argued that ATCA is nothing more than a jurisdictional grant. The US Supreme Court concurred with the latter point in considering the scope of the ATCA in 2004. Its decision in *Sosa v. Alvarez-Machain* found that the ATCA does not create a new cause of action and is merely a jurisdictional grant. The Court also suggested that there are limits to what the law can construe as violating the "law of nations" for the purposes of the act. While the exact scope is unclear, the Court indicated that extrajudicial kidnapping would not fall within the law, and suggested that the law might be restricted to its supposed original intent: protection of diplomats and responding to piracy. This judgment does not repeal the earlier decisions, but leaves open the possibility that courts could restrict application of the ATCA.

Civil liability in the United Kingdom

The United States is not the only country in which civil accountability may be imposed for abuses. The United Kingdom does not have a statute like the ATCA, though this has not prevented its courts from deciding civil cases against foreign state officials for torture, in situations similar to those that are addressed by many ATCA cases. In October 2004 the Supreme Court of Judicature issued a decision regarding immunity in two civil cases

Table 11.1 Landmark Alien Tort Claims Act cases: extension and limitation

Case	Venue	Issue	Development
Filartiga v. Peña-Irala (1980)	US Federal Court of Appeals	Torture by noncitizen of noncitizen	Law of nations includes human rights law; torture now banned as part of customary international law
Kadic v. Karadžić (1995)	US Federal Court of Appeals	Extent of state actor requirement; color of law requirement	Liability of nonstates actors established; appears limited to actors that have effective control
Doe v. Unocal (1997–2004)	US Federal District Court/ Court of Appeals	Complicity for acts of others	Corporations can be complicit for acts of joint venturers; case appealed, then settled out of court
Sosa v. Alvarez-Machain (2004)	US Supreme Court	Extent of law of nations for ATCA	ACTA contracted to include only *clearly established* violations of law of nations; implications still unclear

involving alleged torture by foreign officials. In both cases, *Jones v. The Ministry of the Interior* and *Mitchell v. Al-Dali*, British and/or Canadian citizens claimed that they had been tortured by Saudi officials, and brought civil claims for damages arising from the alleged torture, including "aggravated and exemplary damages for assault and battery, trespass to the person, torture, and unlawful imprisonment." The government of Saudi Arabia sought to challenge the suits on the grounds of immunity under the United Kingdom's State Immunity Act of 1978. The Court distinguished between official acts and acts that could not be viewed as in pursuit of official functions, and the distinction between official and private acts, before turning to the crime of torture, which is by definition an act that occurs in an "official" capacity. The Court reviewed a range of recent cases, including the *Pinochet* cases and US ATCA cases, and determined that official immunity for official acts could not preclude prosecution for systematic torture. The Court also considered the extent of civil immunity and held, building upon reasoning in relevant criminal cases, as well as in *Sosa v. Alvarez-Machain*, and other US practice, that even if the Saudi government was immune from civil suits, Saudi officials were not.

Transnational accountability after (or during) conflict

This chapter has examined two tools for transnational accountability after, or indeed during, conflict, by which victims may seek redress through criminal or civil processes in the courts of another country. In many instances, after conflict, or while conflict still rages, it may be difficult for domestic courts to act, and where the ICC or other international or internationalized courts do not have jurisdiction, such transnational processes may provide the only feasible venue. It is therefore worthwhile, when considering options for accountability for gross violations of human rights and international humanitarian law during conflict, where other venues such as domestic courts or ad hoc or permanent international courts are not available, to also consider transnational accountability processes.

Table 11.2 Domestic accountability abroad

	Type of justice	Countries	Key cases
Universal jurisdiction	Criminal	Canada; multiple European countries including Spain and Senegal	*Pinochet* and many more
US ATCA	Civil	United States	*Filartiga v. Peña-Irala* and many more
UK civil cases	Civil	United Kingdom	*Jones v. The Ministry of the Interior*

Key points

- Accountability for past abuses may be sought not only in the country where crimes occurred or in international courts, but also in national courts of other states.
- Such accountability may involve criminal charges or civil claims.

- Criminal accountability through universal jurisdiction is controversial, but actively practiced in a number of European jurisdictions.
- Civil claims are widespread in the United States under the Alien Tort Claims Act (ACTA), and may include claims against multinational corporations.

Discussion questions

- What limitations did the International Court of Justice impose upon universal jurisdiction in the *DRC v. Belgium* case?
- What was the original purpose of ATCA and do you think its use to address human rights abuses is consistent with it?
- How can corporations be held responsible for crimes committed by other actors?
- What are some specific potential problems with the use of either civil or criminal accountability in the courts of other nations?
- Considering the four country studies presented in Part II of this book – the former Yugoslavia, Sierra Leone, the Democratic Republic of Congo, and Sudan – can you think of specific cases that might be brought through universal jurisdiction or civil accountability?

Further reading

Aceves, William J., "*Doe v. Unocal* 963 F. Supp. 880," *American Journal of International Law* 92, no. 2 (April 1998): 979–87.

Ballentine, Karen, and Heiko Nitzschke, eds., *Profiting from Peace: Managing the Resource Dimensions of Civil War* (Boulder: Lynne Rienner, 2005).

Bouwknegt, Thijs, and Sebastiaan Gottlieb, "Spain Indicts 40 Rwandan Soldiers" (2008), http://www.radionetherlands.nl/currentaffairs/080208-rwanda-indictment.

Burley, Anne-Marie, "The Alien Tort Claims Statute and Judiciary Act of 1789: A Badge of Honor," *American Journal of International Law* 83, no. 2 (1989): 461–93.

Macedo, Stephen, ed., *Universal Jurisdiction: National Courts and the Prosecution of Serious Crimes Under International Law* (Philadelphia: University of Pennsylvania Press, 2004).

Martin-Ortega, Olga, "Business and Human Rights in Conflict," *Ethics and International Affairs* 22, no. 3 (2008): 273–83.

Reydams, Luc, *Universal Jurisdiction: International and Municipal Legal Perspectives* (Oxford: Oxford University Press, 2003).

Sriram, Chandra Lekha, *Globalizing Justice for Mass Atrocities: A Revolution in Accountability* (London: Routledge, 2005).

Official documents and sources

Alien Tort Claims Act, Title 28, Pt. IV, Chap. 85, Sec. 1350, http://www4.law.cornell.edu/uscode/28/1350.html.

Doe v. Unocal, http://homepage.ntlworld.com/jksonc/docs/filartiga-630F2d876.html.

Filartiga v. Pena Irala, http://homepage.ntlworld.com/jksonc/docs/filartiga-630F2d876.html.

Kadic v. Karadžić, 70 F.3rd 232 (2nd Cir. 1995), Rehearing Denied, 74 F.3rd 377 (2nd Cir. 1996), Cert. Denied 518 U.S. 1005 (1996).

Sosa v. Alvarez-Machain, http://a257.g.akamaitech.net/7/257/2422/29june20041115/www.supreme courtus.gov/opinions/03pdf/03-339.pdf.
Regina v. Bartle and the Commissioner of Police for the Metropolis and Others Ex Parte Pinochet, 38 I.L.M. 581 (H.L. 1999).
Wiwa v. Royal Dutch Shell, http://www.derechos.org/nizkor/econ/shell28feb02.html.

12 Hybrid tribunals

The development of hybrid tribunals

Given the expense and scale of the **International Criminal Tribunal for Rwanda** (ICTR) and the **International Criminal Tribunal for the Former Yugoslavia** (ICTY), it is unlikely that further international tribunals will be created, especially in light of the establishment of the **International Criminal Court** (ICC). However, the ICC will not be able to address all possible cases, both because it will not have sufficient resources and because it may not have temporal or territorial jurisdiction over all cases of interest. "Hybrid" or "mixed" tribunals, a recent development in international attempts to seek accountability for serious crimes, are an alternative. They are so called because they involve both domestic and external judges, as well as a mixture of domestic and international law, and are most often located in the country where the conflict took place.

Hybrid tribunals have been established for Kosovo, Timor-Leste, Bosnia, Sierra Leone, Cambodia, and Lebanon. The United States suggested that such a mechanism would be appropriate to address the situation in Darfur, preferring it to the **UN Security Council** referral to the ICC, but ultimately engaged in negotiation over a compromise resolution that limited jurisdiction over nationals of nonstate parties. Although hybrid tribunals have also been suggested as a possibility for Afghanistan and Iraq, the Supreme Iraqi Criminal Tribunal is fully domestic.

Defining a hybrid tribunal

Unlike the international ad hoc criminal tribunals or the ICC, a hybrid tribunal is not purely a creation of the international community, employing solely international law and international prosecutors and judges. It is also distinct from domestic processes such as prosecutions, in that it does not solely use domestic judges and law. Instead, it is an attempt to address the limitations of domestic and of international models. There is no particular model that hybrid tribunals follow, but rather each institution deploys a different mix of domestic and international law, and domestic and international judges and staff.

Combining national and international justice

Supporters of hybrid tribunals argue that such mechanisms combine the best of both national and international justice. They expect that the combination of domestic and international judges can avoid the risks of political manipulation and potential bias that domestic courts face. They also suggest that the combination of domestic and international law can avoid the use of domestic laws that do not meet international standards, ensuring that hybrid tribunals are better suited to the needs of countries emerging from conflict. Because hybrid tribunals are located in the countries where the conflicts occurred, trials take place relatively close to where the crimes were committed, which should in principle make it easier to obtain information and witnesses. Presence in the country of conflict, advocates argue, should also in principle serve to inform and educate the populace at large, enable a sense of participation in the process, and, ideally, promote reconciliation. Several hybrid tribunals also have specific mandates to help to build the capacity of collapsed domestic legal institutions. Although each hybrid tribunal is unique, they can be described generally as either domestic courts with international elements or international courts with domestic elements.

This chapter examines the hybrid tribunals created for Kosovo, Timor-Leste, and Cambodia, as well as the Special Court for Sierra Leone in greater depth, building on the discussion in Chapter 6.

Table 12.1 Hybrid tribunals to date

Tribunal	Type
"Regulation 64" Panels, Kosovo, established in 2000	Domestic court, special court within, with significant international elements
Special Panels for Serious Crimes, Timor-Leste, established in 2000	Domestic court, special court within, with significant international elements
War Crimes Chamber, Bosnia, established in 2005	Domestic court, special court within, with significant international elements
Special Court for Sierra Leone, established in 2002	International court with domestic elements
Extraordinary Chambers in the Courts of Cambodia; agreement reached between UN and Cambodian government in 2003 and became operational in 2006	Domestic courts with international judges
Special Tribunal for Lebanon, established in 2007	International court with domestic elements

Kosovo

Background

As is examined in greater detail in Chapter 5, escalating tension and violence between ethnic Albanians and Serbians in the mid-1990s culminated in the Kosovo Liberation Army (KLA) targeting Serbs. In 1998, Slobodan Milošević retaliated through an ethnic cleansing campaign against Kosovar Albanians, and in March 1999 rejected a peace deal. This led to a three-month airstrike by the **North Atlantic Treaty Organization** (NATO), and Serbia was forced to withdraw in June 1999. Creation of the UN Interim Administration Mission in Kosovo (UNMIK) was authorized through a **UN Security Council resolution**, Resolution 1244, in 1999. This resolution provided UNMIK with a broad mandate to provide

> an interim administration for Kosovo under which the people of Kosovo can enjoy substantial autonomy within the Federal Republic of Yugoslavia, and which will provide

transitional administration while establishing and overseeing the development of provisional democratic self-governing institutions to ensure conditions for a peaceful and normal life for all inhabitants of Kosovo.

Mandate and structure

Although the ICTY did have jurisdiction over crimes during the Kosovo conflict, it had a limited capacity to try cases. However, the **United Nations** (UN), the Organization for Security and Cooperation in Europe (OSCE), and international nongovernmental organizations realized that there were significant problems with the Kosovar courts. There were few Serb judges left, and there was risk of ethnic bias as well as intimidation of Albanian judges. As a result, Serbs were often detained for crimes for which Albanians would be released. UNMIK Regulation no. 2000/6, passed in February 2000, gave the **Special Representative of the Secretary-General** (SRSG) the power to appoint an international judge and an international prosecutor to assist in the administration of justice. It was hoped that this would improve the situation and secure a foundation for due process. The first international judge and prosecutor were appointed in Mitrovica district in February 2000. UNMIK Regulation no. 2000/64, passed in December 2000 (see Box 12.1), then gave the SRSG the right to appoint enough judges to form the majority in any decisions. These were known as Regulation 64 panels.

Box 12.1 **UNMIK Regulation no. 2000/64**

UNMIK Regulation no. 2000/64
December 15, 2000

On Assignment of International Judges/Prosecutors and/or Change of Venue

The Special Representative of the Secretary-General . . .
Hereby promulgates the following:

Section 1
Recommendation for Assignment of International Judges/Prosecutors and/or Change of Venue

1.1 At any stage in the criminal proceedings, the competent prosecutor, the accused or the defence counsel may submit to the Department of Judicial Affairs a petition for an assignment of international judges/prosecutors and/or a change of venue where this is considered necessary to ensure the independence and impartiality of the judiciary or the proper administration of justice.

1.2 At any stage in the criminal proceedings, the Department of Judicial Affairs, on the basis of the petition referred to in section 1.1 above or on its own motion, may submit a recommendation to the Special Representative of the Secretary-General.

. . .

1.3 The Special Representative of the Secretary-General shall review a recommendation submitted by the Department of Judicial Affairs and signify his approval
or rejection thereof. . . .

Section 2
Designation of International Judges/Prosecutors and/or New Venue

2.1 Upon approval of the Special Representative of the Secretary-General . . . the
Department of Judicial Affairs shall expeditiously designate:

(a) An international prosecutor
(b) An international investigating judge; and/or
(c) A panel composed only of three (3) judges, including at least two international judges, of which one shall be the presiding judge, as required by the
particular stage at which the criminal proceeding has reached in a case.

The Regulation 64 panels differed from other hybrid models in that the international judges
and prosecutors worked on a broad range of cases, not only serious crimes. Since their role
was to support domestic trials and ensure prevention of ethnic bias, they worked exclusively
with domestic law, using international law only where it was a part of the applicable domestic
law. They were able to try **genocide** and **war crimes** due to the fact that these crimes were
incorporated within the domestic code.

There were no clear criteria to determine which cases should have international judges
and prosecutors, in order to ensure that they could be appointed to a broad range of cases
to guarantee impartiality. In contrast to normal panels, which consisted of two professional
and three lay judges, Regulation 64 panels had three professional judges and at least two
international judges.

Evaluation

The Regulation 64 panels were first assigned to pending cases concerning war crimes. There
were a number of Serbs already in detention when Regulation 64 came into effect. Also in
this backlog of cases was a high-profile case against former KLA leaders. Subsequent
proceedings dealt increasingly with cases that were considered particularly difficult for
security or political reasons, such as cases involving organized crime and corruption, which
were also tied to terrorism and interethnic violence.

Selection of cases

The appointment of international judges and prosecutors was completely at the discretion of
the SRSG, as detailed in Article 1.3 of UNMIK Regulation no. 2000/64 (see Box 12.1). This
discretion, combined with a lack of guiding criteria, meant that these appointment decisions
could potentially be political, rather than decided on the merits of the cases. There has been
criticism that UNMIK was in a position to influence the justice process, with **Amnesty
International** claiming that international judges and prosecutors were subject to executive
interference. International judges and prosecutors were not accountable to an independent
body, unlike local judges, who were regulated by the Kosovo Judicial and Prosecutorial

Council. Whether true or not, there was a perception of political interference on behalf of Serbs, which was potentially damaging to the work of the Regulation 64 panels.

Lack of cooperation

Most Serb perpetrators fled to Serbia following the conflict. There were problems regarding the extradition of indicted individuals from Serbia, due to both Kosovo's status as a UN protectorate and internal Serbian politics. This added to the perception that only Albanians were being prosecuted.

Problems with recruitment of international judges and prosecutors

There were also difficulties in attracting qualified staff. Because Regulation 64 panels worked only on domestic cases, international judges were sometimes unaware of applicable law, lacked substantive knowledge of **international humanitarian law** and **international human rights law**, or lacked experience with criminal prosecutions.

Due process

While international judges and prosecutors were relatively well resourced, there was concern that local defense lawyers did not have sufficient resources, potentially undermining the possibility of ensuring a fair trial. There were also difficulties with language: proceedings of trials conducted in English were often available only in summary translation; judgments too were not easily accessible.

Lack of focus on war crimes

There was an increasing focus on cases dealing with organized crime, and between 2002 and 2007 only six new cases concerning war crimes were opened. This shift in focus meant that many atrocities committed during the conflict were not being prosecuted. This shift was criticized as reflecting international interest in combating terrorism and corruption, rather than reflecting local demands for justice.

Legacy

The Regulation 64 panels were an innovative way of dealing with a justice system incapable of investigation and prosecution of serious crimes after conflict. Although it was hoped that the inclusion of international judges and prosecutors would help the domestic system, through capacity building of prosecutors, defense lawyers, and judges, there is concern that, in practice, the domestic justice system is still no better equipped. The lack of progress is demonstrated by the fact that after the withdrawal of UNMIK after seven years, the international component is to be continued under the European Union Rule of Law Mission to Kosovo (EULEX). The EULEX program plans to provide more mentoring than that previously provided by UNMIK, and has a larger number of international judges (40) and prosecutors (20).

Timor-Leste

Background

Timor-Leste (East Timor) was a Portuguese colony from the beginning of the seventeenth century until 1974. During the process of self-determination, with political parties divided over whether Timor-Leste should become fully independent, integrate with Indonesia, or maintain relations with Portugal, civil war broke out. In December 1975, Portugal withdrew completely as Indonesia invaded and annexed Timor-Leste; in 1976, Indonesia declared Timor-Leste its 27th province. Until 1999 the Armed Forces of Indonesia (Tentara Nasional Indonesia [TNI]) carried out military campaigns against nationalist guerrilla fighters from the Revolutionary Front for an Independent East Timor (Frente Revolucionária de Timor-Leste Independente [FRETILIN]). The TNI targeted not only combatants, but also huge numbers of civilians, killing many and displacing even more. The TNI carried out widespread human rights abuses, including **torture** of FRETILIN supporters, rape, disappearances, and massacres. Following the resignation of Indonesia's President Suharto in 1998, his replacement, Jusef Habibie, suggested that Timor-Leste could be given a special status of limited autonomy. This approach was unacceptable to the TNI, which encouraged widespread intimidation and violence toward the general population through support of prointegration militias.

In May 1999, Indonesia and Timor-Leste agreed that a referendum would be held to decide whether Timor-Leste would have special autonomy or be completely independent. The referendum took place on August 30, 1999, with 78 percent of voters supporting independence and rejecting the proposed autonomy. This was followed by a campaign of "scorched earth" tactics by the pro-integration militias and the TNI, resulting in the deaths of many civilians and the displacement of thousands. In response, the Security Council authorized a multinational force, the International Force for East Timor (INTERFET), to restore peace and security. The TNI and the Indonesian police withdrew, and on September 28, 1999, Portugal and Indonesia agreed to transfer authority in Timor-Leste to the United Nations. In October 1999 the Security Council established the UN Transitional Administration in East Timor (UNTAET), authorized by Resolution 1272, to administer the country through the transition to independence. Having legislative and executive powers, including the administration of justice, UNTAET effectively acted as the government of the country. Timor-Leste became independent in 2002.

Mandate and structure

Once UNTAET was established, there were calls for an international ad hoc tribunal like the ICTY or ICTR, but this option was not seriously considered by the UN, in part because of emergent criticisms of those institutions (see Chapter 10). UNTAET created the Serious Crimes Unit (SCU) to investigate and lead prosecutions, and created the Special Panels for Serious Crimes to try the suspects. UNTAET established the Special Panels through its own Regulation no. 2000/15 (see Box 12.2), but they were placed within the domestic legal framework – within the Dili district court.

The Special Panels had exclusive jurisdiction for serious crimes, war crimes, genocide, and **crimes against humanity** committed from January 1 to October 15, 1999. They also had exclusive jurisdiction, and therefore primacy over domestic courts, for the national crimes of murder and sexual offenses committed within this time period.

Box 12.2 **UNTAET Regulation no. 2000/15**

UNTAET Regulation no. 2000/15
June 6, 2000

On the establishment of panels with exclusive jurisdiction over serious criminal offences

Section 1
Panels with jurisdiction over serious criminal offences

1.1 . . . there shall be established panels of judges (hereinafter: "panels") within the District Court in Dili with exclusive jurisdiction to deal with serious criminal offences

1.3 The panels . . . shall exercise jurisdiction . . . with respect to the following serious criminal offences:

   (a) Genocide
   (b) War Crimes
   (c) Crimes against Humanity
   (d) Murder
   (e) Sexual Offences; and
   (f) Torture

1.4 At any stage of the proceedings, in relation to cases of serious criminal offences . . . a panel may have deferred to itself a case which is pending before another panel or court in East Timor.

Each Special Panel had one domestic and two international judges. The same type of judicial mechanism was added to the Court of Appeal in Dili, although in some cases three international judges and two domestic judges could be appointed. There was only one Special Panel until mid-2003, and then a second and third panel were subsequently established.

Evaluation

The Special Panels and SCU did achieve some success. The SCU indicted over 400 people, with all charges involving crimes against humanity or violations of domestic law. Between 2002 and 2005 the Special Panels carried out 55 trials, which resulted in the convictions of 83 people. However, there were challenges to the process.

Gaps between domestic and international law

The Special Panels had exclusive jurisdiction for certain crimes under domestic law (murder and sexual crimes) between January and October 1999. However, outside this time period there was inconsistency in determining how crimes would be prosecuted, because the Timorese courts had jurisdiction only from October 25, 1999, the date that UNTAET was established. Crimes that occurred before January 1, 1999, would be under the jurisdiction of Indonesian courts. Further, because the Special Panels were prosecuting murder and sexual crimes under domestic law, they had jurisdiction only over the territory of Timor-Leste. This meant that rapes and murders committed in camps in West Timor between January and October 1999 were outside the jurisdiction of the Special Panels. Again, domestic courts could not prosecute these crimes, because their jurisdiction began only on October 25, 1999. Finally, domestic legislation concerning these crimes did not necessarily meet international standards; for example, the definition of rape meant that it was only a crime when the victim was female.

Lack of cooperation

Despite the signing of a memorandum of understanding between the Indonesian government and UNTAET, there was never any cooperation by the Indonesian government with the Special Panels. This created a difficult obstacle to the work of the Special Panels. Most of the accused were in Indonesia, and the Timorese government was not able to arrest them. As a result, the Special Panels were not able to target those who were most responsible for the atrocities; only people from Timor-Leste were convicted, and most perpetrators remain free and have even been promoted to higher military and political appointments in Indonesia.

The work of a hybrid tribunal is drastically limited if it cannot reach indicted suspects in a country that will not cooperate. An international tribunal such as the ICTY or ICTR, authorized under Chapter VII of the **UN Charter**, has greater capacity to access suspects, as all countries are obliged to cooperate. If the Special Panels had been established in this way, greater international pressure could have been brought to bear on Indonesia.

Organizational problems

In the absence of a Chapter VII commitment, funding for the Special Panels was provided only on a voluntary basis, and thus the budget of the panel was limited. There were difficulties with staffing and recruitment. The judges, in particular, were not well paid, and it was difficult to appoint them according to the language criteria established by the government. Thus, many judges had little experience in international criminal law. Similarly, defense counsels lacked skills in representation, potentially undermining the right of the accused to a fair trial.

Lack of an integrated reconciliation strategy

The Commission for Reception, Truth, and Reconciliation (CAVR) not only acted as a **truth commission**, working to create a narrative of the events and human rights abuses between 1974 and 1999, but also involved community reconciliation procedures. The community reconciliation mechanism was nonjudicial, with people taking part in local hearings to confess their crimes. However, only lesser crimes could be included within the reconciliation process, and serious crimes were not addressed. All those who wished to take part in the reconciliation process were required to submit a statement to the SCU, which decided whether the individual could take part or whether it, the SCU, had jurisdiction and should prosecute the crime. However, it was evident that the SCU, with its limited resources would never be able to prosecute all perpetrators of serious crimes. This led to a confusing situation, with individuals excluded from both processes if the SCU could not prosecute. Those who participated in the reconciliation process felt that those who had committed worse crimes had effectively been allowed to act with **impunity** because the Special Panels and SCU lacked the capacity to try them all.

Legacy

In 2006 the UN Integration Mission in Timor-Leste (UNMIT) created the Serious Crimes Investigation Team (SCIT) to carry on the investigative functions of the SCU. However, the SCIT has a more limited mandate – to investigate, not to prosecute; the latter responsibility lies with the domestic office of the prosecutor. The SCIT began work in February 2008, and has prioritized cases from those still pending before the SCU.

Cambodia

Background

The Khmer Rouge, led by Pol Pot, invaded and gained control of Cambodia in April 1975, and for four years the country suffered repressive rule. The Khmer Rouge forced millions of people into rural areas to start a communist agrarian society. Human rights abuses were widespread, with hundreds of thousands of people tortured and executed, including individuals belonging to religious and ethnic minorities, intellectuals, and members of other political parties. One of the most notorious prisons was a former high school in Phnom Penh named Security Prison 21 (S-21), or Tuol Sleng, where thousands of people were imprisoned, tortured, and killed.

The number of people killed through starvation, forced labor, as well as execution is estimated at over 1.5 million. The Vietnamese managed to invade and capture Phnom Penh in January 1979, forcing the Khmer Rouge to retreat to an area bordering Thailand. The Khmer Rouge engaged in guerrilla warfare for another 20 years, resulting in the displacement of hundreds of thousands of people. In 1981 the Kampuchean People's Revolutionary Party won National Assembly elections, but the international community did not recognize the government. The Vietnamese withdrew in 1989, and a peace agreement was signed in 1991 in Paris. The UN Transitional Authority in Cambodia (UNTAC) was established by Security Council Resolution 745. UNTAC ensured that a free and fair general election was held in 1993, which was won by the National United Front for an Independent, Neutral, Peaceful, and Cooperative Cambodia (Front Uni National pour un Cambodge Indépendant, Neutre, Pacifique, et Coopératif [FUNCINPEC]). Following the election, the monarchy was restored and the country was renamed the Kingdom of Cambodia. In 1994, thousands of guerrillas surrendered to a government **amnesty**, and in 1996 the deputy of the Khmer Rouge, Ieng Sary, was granted amnesty by the country's king. Pol Pot died in 1998.

Mandate and structure

In 1997 the Cambodian government asked the UN for assistance in establishing a tribunal to prosecute the Khmer Rouge. A long period of negotiation over the structure and mandate of the tribunal followed. In 1998 a UN group of experts was appointed, which recommended that a UN tribunal be established under Chapter VI or VII of the UN Charter, similar to the ICTY and ICTR. The United Nations and many states supported this approach because of fears that the Cambodian justice system was susceptible to corruption and manipulation, and that it was not fully independent of the government. However, the Cambodian government insisted that the tribunal be located within Cambodia. A Cambodian task force put forward the suggestion of a domestic process with international involvement and a supermajority system requiring the support of one international judge. Several UN member states – the United States, France, Japan, Australia, and India – supported this proposal. The United Nations and the Cambodian government began lengthy negotiations concerning the establishment and operation of the tribunal. The Cambodian National Assembly approved a law in 2001 to create the Extraordinary Chambers in the Courts of Cambodia (ECCC) in order to bring genocide charges against Khmer Rouge leaders for crimes committed between 1975 and 1979. However, the United Nations had many concerns with the law, fearing that the ECCC process would be too weak to succeed, and withdrew when negotiations with the Cambodian government broke down. The negotiations started again in 2003 and an agreement was finally reached on May 13 of that year. After waiting for funding from voluntary contributions from UN member states, the United Nations announced on April 19, 2005, that the ECCC was ready to proceed.

The ECCC is constituted within the Cambodian legal system, but includes domestic and international judges. While Cambodian judges will outnumber international judges in both the trial chamber and the supreme court, which has generated concerns about bias, voting is to be conducted on the basis of supermajority, so that domestic judges will not be able to simply outvote the international judges (see Box 12.3). Therefore, the Cambodian judges will not be able to make a majority decision on their own, but rather will require the support of one international judge. It is hoped that this will prevent political interference.

Box 12.3 The Law on the Establishment of the Extraordinary Chambers

Law on the Establishment of Extraordinary Chambers in the courts of Cambodia for the prosecution of crimes committed during the period of Democratic Kampuchea (with inclusion of amendments as promulgated on 27 October 2004)

Chapter I
General Provisions
Article 1
The purpose of this law is to bring to trial senior leaders of Democratic Kampuchea and those who were most responsible for the crimes and serious violations of Cambodian penal law, international humanitarian law and custom, and international conventions recognized by Cambodia, that were committed during the period from 17 April 1975 to 6 January 1979.

Chapter II
Competence
Article 2
Extraordinary Chambers shall be established in the existing court structure, namely the trial court and the supreme court to bring to trial senior leaders of Democratic Kampuchea and those who were most responsible for the crimes and serious violations of Cambodian laws related to crimes, international humanitarian law and custom, and international conventions recognized by Cambodia, that were committed during the period from 17 April 1975 to 6 January 1979.

Senior leaders of Democratic Kampuchea and those who were most responsible for the above acts are hereinafter designated as "Suspects."

Chapter III
Composition of the Extraordinary Chambers
Article 9
The Trial Chamber shall be . . . composed of five professional judges, of whom three are Cambodian judges with one as president, and two foreign judges; and before which the Co-Prosecutors shall present their cases. . . .

The Supreme Court Chamber, which shall serve as both appellate chamber and final instance, shall be . . . composed of seven judges, of whom four are Cambodian judges with one as president, and three foreign judges. . . .

Chapter V
Decisions of the Extraordinary Chambers
Article 14
1. The judges shall attempt to achieve unanimity in their decisions. If this is not possible, the following shall apply:
   a) a decision by the Extraordinary Chamber of the trial court shall require the affirmative vote of at least four judges;
   b) a decision by the Extraordinary Chamber of the Supreme Court shall require the affirmative vote of at least five judges.
2. When there is no unanimity, the decision of the Extraordinary Chambers shall contain the opinions of the majority and minority.

Source: Council of Jurists and the Secretariat of the Task Force, unofficial translation, revised August 26, 2007.

The ECCC is part of the Cambodian court system and uses both Cambodian and international law. The court has jurisdiction over crimes committed between April 17, 1975, and January 6, 1979, specifically genocide as defined in the **Genocide Convention**, crimes against humanity as defined in the Rome Statute, **grave breaches** of the **Geneva Conventions**, torture, homicide, religious persecution, and destruction of cultural property.

Evaluation

Five suspects have been indicted and arrested, and are now in detention. The first individual to stand trial before the ECCC will be Kaing Guek Eav (Duch), the head of the S-21 prison. He is charged with crimes against humanity (murder, extermination, enslavement, imprisonment, torture, rape, persecution on political grounds, and other inhumane acts) and grave breaches of the Geneva Conventions (willful killing, torture or inhumane treatment, willfully causing great suffering or serious injury to body or health, willfully depriving a prisoner of war or civilian of the rights of fair and regular trial, and unlawful confinement of a civilian). Ieng Sary, former Deputy Prime Minister and former Foreign Minister, has also been charged with crimes against humanity and war crimes, but there have been challenges to this charge. In 1979 he was convicted of genocide by the People's Revolutionary Tribunal (backed by the Vietnamese), but was pardoned in 1996 by royal decree and granted amnesty. Sary's lawyers argue that he cannot be tried twice for the same crime (double jeopardy). No decision has yet been reached on this objection. The other three accused in detention are Khieu

Samphan, president during the Khmer Rouge occupation and charged with crimes against humanity and war crimes; Nuon Chea, second in command to Pol Pot and charged with crimes against humanity and war crimes; and Ieng Thirith, Minister of Social Affairs and charged with crimes against humanity.

It remains to be seen how the ECCC trials will proceed. The ECCC is funded by voluntary contributions, and there have been calls from international organizations to condition further funding of the ECCC on resolution of concerns that have emerged about corruption. There is insufficient capacity for translation of documents into all official ECCC languages: Khmer, French, and English. Importantly, it is unclear what will happen if a supermajority is not reached in a given case.

Although it is difficult to prosecute crimes committed three decades ago, particularly in terms of gathering evidence and the age of the accused and witnesses, no other **transitional justice** processes have taken place in Cambodia. The ECCC may represent the only opportunity to address the country's abusive past.

Sierra Leone

Background

As discussed in Chapter 6, conflict between the government of Sierra Leone and the Revolutionary United Front (RUF) broke out in 1991 and endured for over a decade, leading to some 50,000–75,000 deaths and widespread atrocities, including mutilation and sexual violence. The conflict also involved widespread use of child combatants – often abducted and drugged – who were in many instances both victims and perpetrators of abuses. The first real possibility of peace came when negotiations in 1999 resulted in the Lomé Agreement between the government and the RUF, as well as a Security Council-mandated **peacekeeping** force, the UN Assistance Mission in Sierra Leone (UNAMSIL), was authorized by Resolution 1270. The United Nations, which acted as a "moral guarantor" of the peace agreement, issued a reservation objecting to an amnesty provision that it did not consider to cover international crimes. Notwithstanding the agreement, fighting and atrocities resumed, and the RUF staged attacks on UNAMSIL. In May 2000, notorious RUF leader Foday Sankoh was captured, provoking discussions about the appropriate venue to try him and other perpetrators. In June the government asked the UN to establish an international court to try such cases.

Mandate and structure

The Special Court for Sierra Leone (SCSL) was an entirely new court, distinct from the judicial system of the country. The United Nations created the SCSL through Security Council Resolution 1315 in August 2000, following an agreement with the government of Sierra Leone.

The SCSL statute (see Box 12.4), completed on January 16, 2002, gives the court the power to prosecute persons who bear the greatest responsibility for serious violations of national and international humanitarian law since November 30, 1996. The crimes under the jurisdiction of the SCSL include crimes against humanity, violations of **Common Article 3** and Additional Protocol II of the Geneva Conventions, other serious violations of international humanitarian law, and crimes under national law.

Box 12.4 **The statute of the Special Court for Sierra Leone**

... established by an Agreement between the United Nations and the Government of Sierra Leone pursuant to Security Council resolution 1315 (2000) of 14 August 2000. . . .

Article 1
Competence of the Special Court
1. The Special Court shall . . . have the power to prosecute persons who bear the greatest responsibility for serious violations of international humanitarian law and Sierra Leonean law committed in the territory of Sierra Leone since 30 November 1996. . . .

Article 2
Crimes against humanity

Article 3
Violations of Article 3 common to the Geneva Conventions and of Additional Protocol II

Article 4
Other serious violations of international humanitarian law
. . .
c.   Conscripting or enlisting children under the age of 15 years into armed forces or groups or using them to participate actively in hostilities

Article 5
Crimes under Sierra Leonean law
Offences relating to the abuse of girls under the Prevention of Cruelty to Children Act

i.   Abusing a girl under 13 years of age. . . .
ii. Abusing a girl between 13 and 14 years of age. . . .
iii. Abduction of a girl for immoral purposes. . . .

Offences relating to the wanton destruction of property under the Malicious Damage Act

i.   Setting fire to dwelling, houses, any person being therein
ii. Setting fire to public buildings
iii. Setting fire to other buildings

Article 7
Jurisdiction over person of 15 years of age
1.   The Special Court shall have no jurisdiction over any person who was under the age of 15 at the time of the alleged commission of the crime . . .

Article 8
Concurrent jurisdiction

1. The Special Court and the national courts of Sierra Leone shall have concurrent jurisdiction.
2. The Special Court shall have primacy over the national courts of Sierra Leone. . . .

Article 10
Amnesty
An amnesty granted to any person falling within the jurisdiction of the Special Court in respect of the crimes referred to in articles 2 to 4 of the present Statute shall not be a bar to prosecution.

The SCSL's first trial chamber, in Freetown, consists of two international judges appointed by the **UN Secretary-General**, based on nominations from UN member states, and one appointed by the government of Sierra Leone. The second trial chamber, in The Hague (established solely to try Charles Taylor), has two international judges appointed by the UN Secretary-General and one appointed by the government of Sierra Leone. The SCSL's appeals chamber consists of two international judges appointed by the UN Secretary-General and two judges appointed by the government of Sierra Leone.

Evaluation

The question of immunity for Charles Taylor

As discussed in Chapter 6, the conflict in Sierra Leone was not confined to that country, but was also affected by conflicts and political leaders elsewhere. In particular, Charles Taylor, President of Liberia at that time, was heavily involved, through support to the RUF. In 2003 the prosecutor of the SCSL unsealed an indictment against him while Taylor was attending **peace negotiations** in Ghana for his own country. Rather than arrest Taylor, Ghana allowed him to leave the country. This was in part out of concern that arresting him would be a diplomatic affront, but also out of fear that it might undermine the Liberian peace process. Taylor went into hiding in Nigeria, which granted him asylum and refused to surrender him to the SCSL. The Nigerian High Court, however, said that it would honor a request for extradition from any permanent Liberian government once it was installed, rather than from the interim government in power at the time.

Taylor claimed he was immune from prosecution because at the time of the indictment he was President of Liberia and enjoyed immunity as head of state. The SCSL rejected this challenge to jurisdiction on immunity grounds, invoking the decision of the **International Court of Justice** (ICJ) in the *Yerodia* case (discussed in Chapter 11), in which the ICJ stated that while national courts must respect official immunity, international courts need not. The Special Court considered itself to be an international court created by agreement between the government of Sierra Leone and the UN rather than a domestic court, and thus that it had jurisdiction.

After President Ellen Johnson-Sirleaf was elected in the 2005 Liberian national elections, she requested Taylor's extradition from Nigeria. He attempted to escape but was captured at the Cameroon border. The UN Mission in Liberia (UNMIL) had been mandated under Security Council Resolution 1638 to take responsibility for his "apprehension, detention and transfer to the Special Court for Sierra Leone, in the event of his return to Liberia." Taylor was taken into custody by the SCSL on March 29, 2006, and transferred to The Hague on June 20.

Taylor's trial was moved to the ICC in The Hague because it was feared that holding the trial in Sierra Leone might threaten peace and stability in the country. However, the SCSL retains exclusive jurisdiction over the case. Taylor was originally indicted on 11 charges, for alleged acts that constitute crimes against humanity, violations of Common Article 3 and Additional Protocol II of the Geneva Conventions, and other violations of international humanitarian law, including murder, physical violence, rape and sexual slavery, use of child soldiers, abductions and forced labor, and looting. His trial began on June 4, 2007, and should conclude in 2009.

The problem of the blanket amnesty

There was also a potential technical legal problem with the blanket amnesty included in the Lomé Agreement. This amnesty was raised by defendants seeking to challenge the jurisdiction of the SCSL, claiming that the amnesty was still in force and reduced the court's temporal jurisdiction to crimes committed only after the signing of the peace accord in 1999. However, Article 10 of the court's statute (see Box 12.4) provides that any amnesty for the crimes covered in the statute would not be a bar to prosecution. Furthermore, the amnesty's validity can be challenged on several grounds. First, the UN reservation at the time stated that the amnesty could not cover international crimes such as genocide, crimes against humanity, war crimes, or other serious violations of international humanitarian law. Thus, even if the amnesty were valid, it would be valid only in respect of domestic crimes. Further, the UN was not party to the 1999 agreement, but rather (along with a number of other institutions and governments) agreed to act as guarantor of the agreement. The government of Sierra Leone was in a different position. It was a party to the Lomé Agreement, and also entered into a contract with the UN for the creation of the SCSL. Nonetheless, the government argued, as have others, that the amnesty provision, along with the rest of the peace accord, was nullified by the continued violation of the accord by the RUF. In March 2004 the Special Court found that the Lomé Agreement could not be considered a treaty, and that the amnesty contained in the peace accord would therefore have only domestic effect and could have no effect upon an international court.

Perceptions of the court as driven by the government

As discussed in Chapter 6, Sam Hinga Norman was seen by many in Sierra Leone as a hero, and defender of a democratically elected government. Many objected to his indictment in March 2003 for war crimes, crimes against humanity, and recruitment of child soldiers. Cadres of the Civil Defense Forces (CDF), and some domestic human rights advocates, saw the indictment as proof that the SCSL was biased in favor of the government. Although many Sierra Leoneans approved of the creation of the SCSL, some wanted the court to address only the actions of the Armed Forces Revolutionary Council (AFRC) and the RUF, and resented the fact that former CDF fighters were being called to account. There were even concerns that CDF fighters might seek to destabilize the country. Others argued that Hinga Norman was being made a scapegoat and that if he was responsible for the excesses of his forces, then President Kabbah, to whom he had reported, should also be tried. Hinga Norman died in February 2007 during his trial. The SCSL tried two other CDF leaders and found them guilty of war crimes in a controversial trial that even the prosecutor admitted had been challenging. The prosecutor stated, however, that even though the CDF had sought to restore a democratically elected government, its crimes could not be justified.

Limitations on the court's ability to extradite suspects

The SCSL is dependent on other countries to agree to extradite the accused. This means that indictees who seek asylum elsewhere can evade prosecution if the sheltering states do not choose to extradite them. The lack of power to compel extradition is a problem precisely because the Sierra Leonean conflict had regional dimensions. However, the jurisdiction of the Special Court is limited to the territory of Sierra Leone, meaning that even if it had the power to compel extradition, it could not consider cases arising from events taking place outside the country, even if they involved atrocities related to the conflict. Although Charles Taylor was finally arrested after three years at large, another serious perpetrator, Johnny Paul Koroma, has continued to elude the court. Another key perpetrator, Foday Sankoh, died in detention.

Funding problems

The SCSL has had difficulty securing funding, which could impact the court's capacity to carry out its work. Its budget was to be US$30.2 million for its first year of operation and US$84.4 million for the next two years, but has averaged only about $25 million annually.

The SCSL's relationship with the Truth and Reconciliation Commission

The Special Court was established at about the same time as the Truth and Reconciliation Commission (TRC). In principle, their responsibilities did not overlap, as the role of the TRC was not to prosecute crimes, but rather to investigate the causes, nature, and extent of the violence, and also to make recommendations regarding reparations and legal, political, and administrative reform. There was a risk that evidence disclosed to the commission, which had a different remit and different evidentiary requirements, might be used by the court, but the SCSL prosecutor made it clear that this was not an option. Some may not have believed him, and may have refused to testify before the commission. There was also tension between the two institutions when, in an attempt to avoid disrupting stability and undermining its own proceedings, the SCSL did not allow Hinga Norman to testify publicly before the TRC.

Legacy

Despite the many limits to the SCSL, including to its capacity and mandate, and the danger that key trials such as those of CDF members and Taylor would destabilize the country or even the region, the court has successfully prosecuted key perpetrators. The SCSL's strategy has been to prosecute only those most responsible for the crimes, focusing on all parties involved in the conflict: Taylor and members of the CDF, AFRC, and RUF. It has indicted 13 people and arrested 12, with Johnny Koroma still at large. Three accused have died: RUF leader Foday Sankoh, former RUF battlefield commander Sam Bockarie, and Hinga Norman. In sum, nine people remain on trial or have been convicted, a significant achievement in imposing accountability for atrocities committed during the conflict.

The SCSL has reached landmark convictions on the use of child soldiers. In June 2007 in the trial of three members of the AFRC, the court found them guilty of the recruitment and use of child soldiers as a war crime. The court also convicted the three accused of war crimes based on charges of sexual violence, particularly taking young girls as forced "wives." This was the first time that an international tribunal ruled on the use of both child soldiers and sexual violence, resulting in an expansion of international criminal jurisprudence to include these violations.

Also important is the SCSL's indictment of Taylor as a sitting head of state. However, holding his trial in The Hague makes it more difficult to ensure that the people of Sierra Leone are connected to the outcome.

The future of hybrid tribunals

While it was hoped that hybrid tribunals would combine the best of international and domestic justice, they have serious limitations. Hybrid tribunals have been limited precisely because they are partially domestic courts, in contrast to ad hoc tribunals. Because hybrid tribunals are not created by Security Council resolutions under Chapter VII of the UN Charter, they do not have the authority of ad hoc tribunals to demand extradition of suspects from other countries, nor are they entitled to compulsory UN contributions by member states. As a consequence of the latter, the budgets of hybrid tribunals are much more limited, in some instances totaling less for their entire mandates than the biennial budgets of the ICTY and ICTR. Conversely, hybrid tribunals also suffer from being partially international, since they are viewed by some as foreign courts. In particular, the limited allocation of funds for translation appears to have exacerbated this perception. Although trials undertaken by hybrid tribunals are inherently logistically complex, it seems that many of the lessons from the experiences of the ICTR and ICTY concerning staffing and organization have not been adequately learned.

Nevertheless, these trials offer another venue for seeking accountability in a postconflict context in which the domestic judicial system is likely to be severely underfunded, corrupt, biased, or incapable of processing cases. Where it seems unlikely that legitimate cases could be pursued by the domestic system, or if the ICC is unable to do so because of jurisdictional limitations, hybrid courts can still provide a measure of justice. Some, although not all, of the difficulties identified here could potentially be addressed with more money, commitment, and support from the international community.

Key points

- Hybrid tribunals combine domestic and international systems of justice to provide a mixed court system.
- The organization of a hybrid tribunal depends on the context, and can range from insertion of international judges into a domestic system, such as in Kosovo, to the creation of a special court, such as in Sierra Leone.

- Supporters of hybrid tribunals maintain that they combine the benefits of international tribunals, such as impartiality and legitimacy, with the strengths of the domestic courts, including ownership by the local populace and efficiency.
- In practice, experience in Kosovo, Timor-Leste, and Sierra Leone has been mixed, and it remains to be seen how trials through the court in Cambodia will function.
- Despite difficulties, hybrid tribunals will probably continue to be used in the future to provide a measure of justice and potentially assist with rehabilitation of the domestic system.

Discussion questions

- What are the potential benefits and limitations of hybrid tribunals?
- What should the relationship of hybrid tribunals be to other domestic processes, such as truth commissions?
- What is the difference between tribunals that are largely national, with international elements grafted onto them, such as the one in Kosovo, and tribunals that are international with a domestic element such as that in Sierra Leone?
- What are the specific legal objections that have been raised to hybrid tribunals?
- Compare the experiences of two hybrid tribunals, including their capacity to enhance **peacebuilding** in their respective countries.

Group exercise

Evaluate the different permutations of hybrid tribunals and determine which arrangement would be appropriate for Afghanistan. Consider the actors involved during the period from the Soviet invasion of the country in 1979 to the fall of the Taliban in 2001, keeping in mind that many of them still hold positions of power today.

Further reading

Amnesty International, *Kosovo (Serbia): The Challenge to Fix a Failed UN Justice Mission* (London, January 2008).

Cambodian Genocide Program, http://www.yale.edu/cgp.

Hartmann, Michael E., *International Judges and Prosecutors in Kosovo: A New Model for Post-conflict Peacekeeping* (Washington, DC: US Institute for Peace, October 2003).

Kerr, Rachel, and Eirin Mobekk, *Peace and Justice: Seeking Accountability After War* (Cambridge: Polity, 2007), chap. 4, "Internationalized Courts."

Open Society Justice Initiative, "The Extraordinary Chambers," *Justice Initiatives* (Spring 2006), http://www.osji.org/db/resource2?res_id=103182.

——, "Recent Developments at the Extraordinary Chambers in the Courts of Cambodia" (regular updates), http://www.justiceinitiative.org/activities/ij/krt.

Perriello, Tom, and Marieke Wierda, *Lessons from the Deployment of International Judges and Prosecutors in Kosovo* (New York: International Center for Transitional Justice, March 2006).

Reiger, Caitlin, and Marieke Wierda, *The Serious Crimes Process in Timor-Leste: In Retrospect* (New York: International Center for Transitional Justice, March 2006).

Sriram, Chandra, *Globalizing Justice for Mass Atrocity: A Revolution in Accountability* (London: Routledge, 2005).

Track Impunity Always (TRIAL), http://www.trial-ch.org.

Worden, Scott, and Emily Wann, *Special Court of Sierra Leone Briefing: The Taylor Trial and Lessons from Capacity-Building and Outreach* (Washington, DC: US Institute of Peace, August 2007).

Official documents and sources

Extraordinary Chambers in the Courts of Cambodia, http://www.eccc.gov.kh.

Special Court for Sierra Leone, http://www.sc-sl.org.

United Nations, *Report of the Secretary-General on the establishment of a Special Court for Sierra Leone* (4 October 2000), UN Doc. S/2000/915.

——, *Report of the Secretary-General on the Khmer Rouge Trials* (August 27, 2007), UN Doc. A/62/304.

United Nations assistance to the Khmer Rouge trials, http://www.unakrt-online.org/01_home.htm.

United Nations Transitional Administration in East Timor (UNTAET), http://www.un.org/peace/etimor/etimor.htm.

13 The International Criminal Court

Background

Attempts to address serious crimes after war date from the end of World War I, when the Versailles Treaty provided for criminal responsibility of German state officials. After the end of World War II the establishment of a permanent international criminal court was part of the agenda of the **United Nations** (UN) and some international lawyers. From 1948 the International Law Commission (ILC), the UN body devoted to the progressive development and codification of international law, worked to develop two aspects of international criminal law: the drafting of a code of **crimes against humanity**, and the drafting of a statute for the establishment of an international criminal court. In 1954 the ILC produced the Draft Code of Offences Against the Peace and Security of Mankind, which was updated several times until its final draft was completed in 1996.

Work on an international criminal court was deferred pending the adoption of the draft code and an agreed definition of the crime of aggression. The UN appointed a special rapporteur to draft the statute for the future court, for submission to the ILC. Even though the ILC produced a draft statute in 1951, which was revised in 1953, the political climate was not yet right for such an agreement, and the initiative was shelved. The process started again in 1989, and five years later, in 1994, the ILC prepared a draft statute that served as the starting point for the Preparatory Committee for the Establishment of an International Criminal Court, which began its work in 1996. In 1998 the preparatory committee submitted a final draft statute to the United Nations Conference of Plenipotentiaries on the Establishment of an International Criminal Court, which in July of that year adopted the draft as the final statute of the **International Criminal Court** (ICC), known as the Rome Statute.

The rationale for the establishment of the ICC comes from a conviction that emerged during the Nuremberg and Tokyo Tribunals: that, in the words of Antonio Cassese, "never again could tyranny and the attendant disregard for human dignity be allowed to go unchecked and unpunished." Prior to the establishment of the ICC, the international community had undertaken only ad hoc attempts in its pursuit of criminal accountability: through the Nuremberg and Tokyo Tribunals, and through the tribunals for the former Yugoslavia and Rwanda. Such ad hoc approaches were obviously limited, and subject to a variety of criticisms. The Nuremberg and Tokyo Tribunals were criticized for violating the principles of *nullem crimen sine lege* and *nulla poena sine lege*. The ad hoc tribunals created in 1993 and 1994 for the former Yugoslavia and Rwanda, respectively, were limited in their territorial and temporal jurisdiction, and raised questions about why similar institutions were not created in response to other situations involving serious violations of **international humanitarian law** and **international human rights law**. In the interim period the international community had been immersed in the Cold War, which prevented any consensus for creating more comprehensive accountability measures. The end of the tension between East and West, together with the new balance in the **UN Security Council**, provided the context for establishment of the ad hoc tribunals. These tribunals helped to create political momentum for the idea of a permanent court. The international community recognized the necessity of such a court after the proliferation of bloody internal armed conflicts in Eastern and Central Europe following the fall of the Berlin Wall, and elsewhere in the world, which demonstrated that cruelty and human rights abuses had not ended with World War II.

There was broad support for an international forum in which to try the most serious crimes against humanity, with 160 states and, perhaps equally noteworthy, some 250 nongovernmental organizations participating in the negotiations. These organizations arguably had a significant influence in shaping of the Rome Statute, and in encouraging its rapid ratification. The statute entered into force relatively quickly, on July 1, 2002, following its sixtieth ratification.

As of April 2009, 108 states have signed and ratified the Rome Statute. However, several highly influential countries, such as the United States, Russia, and China, have not. The United States played an important role during the Rome negotiations and originally did sign the statute, but then, on May 6, 2002, famously "unsigned" the law and has since fiercely opposed the ICC. The arguments put forth by the United States for such opposition are discussed later in the chapter.

The Rome Statute requires, in Article 123, that a review conference be held seven years after its entry into force. This conference will take place in 2010, a delay of one year.

Structure of the Court

The International Criminal Court sits in The Hague, in the Netherlands. It comprises four organs: the Presidency, the Chambers, the Office of the Prosecutor, and the Registry. Philippe Kirsch, a Canadian, is the first judge to occupy the position of President of the Court. Akua Kuenyehia, from Ghana, and Rene Blattmann, from Bolivia, are the First and Second Vice Presidents, respectively. The Chambers are organized into three divisions: Pre-Trial, Trial, and Appeals. The First Vice President and six other judges sit in the Pre-Trial Chamber. The Second Vice President and five other judges sit in the Trial Chamber. The President and four other judges sit in the Appeals Chamber.

The Office of the Prosecutor (OTP) is in charge of examining information received on crimes committed within the jurisdiction of the Court, and examining referrals to the Court. The OTP also conducts the investigations that may lead to prosecutions before the Court. The head of the OTP is Luis Moreno Ocampo, who took office on June 16, 2003.

The 18 judges of the Court were elected in February 2003. Seven of them were female. They were all nationals of states party to the Rome Statute; seven were from Western European and other states, four were from Latin American and Caribbean states, three were from Asian states, three were from African states, and one was from Eastern Europe.

Judges can be appointed for terms of three, six, and nine years. Three- and six-year terms can be renewed up to nine years, which is the maximum period a judge can hold office.

Jurisdiction of the Court

The International Criminal Court has jurisdiction over a limited set of crimes committed after the Rome Statute entered into force (July 1, 2002). This temporal limitation leaves countless crimes committed in the framework of contemporary conflicts outside the jurisdiction of the Court. In practice, this limitation has proved frustrating for human rights victims and advocates alike. This frustration is based on a lack of understanding of the ICC's mandate and its limited role in responding to human rights abuses.

The four crimes over which the ICC has jurisdiction, as listed in the Rome Statute, are **genocide**, crimes against humanity, **war crimes**, and aggression. The crime of aggression, while included in Article 5(1), has yet to be defined. The Court will not be able to exercise jurisdiction over that crime until a definition has been agreed.

The Rome Statute has been criticized for defining the jurisdiction of the Court in rather conservative terms. Some commentators and nongovernmental organizations consider this conservative jurisdiction a missed opportunity to develop international humanitarian law more progressively, through widening the definition of some international crimes or over-coming the distinction between international and internal conflicts. The statute basically adopts the definitions of genocide, crimes against humanity, and war crimes that are already present in customary and conventional law, as discussed in Chapter 4. These definitions (Articles 6–8) should be read in conjunction with the "Elements of Crimes" (Article 9), adopted by the Assembly of State Parties on September 9, 2002.

Crimes under ICC jurisdiction

Genocide

The International Criminal Court follows the same definition of genocide established in the **Genocide Convention**, identical to the concept established by customary international law: a set of acts committed with the *intent* to destroy, in whole or in part, a national, ethnic, racial, or religious group. These acts, listed in Article 6 of the Rome Statute, are killing members of a group; causing serious bodily or mental harm to members of a group; deliberately inflicting on a group conditions of life calculated to bring about its physical destruction in whole or in part; imposing measures intended to prevent births within a group; and forcibly transferring children of one group to another group.

The Genocide Convention includes among punishable acts not only genocide itself but also conspiracy to commit genocide, direct and public incitement to commit genocide, attempt to commit genocide, and complicity in genocide. However, Article 6 of the Rome Statute does not refer to any of these crimes. During drafting negotiations there was a lack of agreement on the treatment of complicity; and other aspects of genocide crimes, such as attempt and incitement, are already dealt with in Article 25, where the grounds for individual criminal responsibility for all the crimes are laid out.

As in the Genocide Convention, Article 6 of the Rome Statute does not specify the actual harm that needs to be done to a group in order to give rise to responsibility. The definition refers only to the *intent* to destroy a group *in whole or in part*. In theory, the customary international rule, as codified in Article 6, does not require that the victims of genocide be numerous; in principle, genocide can be found even if only a small number of persons have been killed. However, in practice, genocide has been found only when victims are numerous.

Crimes against humanity

The definition of crimes against humanity in the Rome Statute builds upon customary international law. Observers have praised the statute's definition for clarifying and broadening the scope of the customary definition in some aspects; but it is also limiting in other aspects.

Crimes against humanity comprise a number of acts, as part of a widespread or systematic attack directed against any civilian population. They thus cover a host of atrocities that might not be covered by war crimes, because official armed conflict may not be present. The specific acts are listed in Article 7(1): murder; extermination; enslavement; deportation or forcible transfer of a population; imprisonment or other severe deprivation of physical liberty in violation of fundamental rules of international law; **torture**; rape, sexual slavery, enforced prostitution, forced pregnancy, enforced sterilization, or any other form of sexual violence of comparable gravity; persecution against any identifiable group on political, racial, national, ethnic, cultural, religious, gender, or other grounds that are universally recognized as impermissible under international law in connection with any of the acts that constitute crimes under the jurisdiction of the Court; enforced disappearance of persons; the crime of apartheid; and any other inhumane acts of similar character undertaken to intentionally cause great suffering or injury to the body or mental or physical health of a person. As we see, these acts include "ordinary" crimes such as murder, but it is the context – the widespread or systematic attack directed against any civilian population – that qualifies them as crimes against humanity. The Rome Statute defines "attack directed against any civilian population" as a course of conduct involving multiple commissions of the mentioned acts against any such population pursuant to or in furtherance of a state or organizational policy to commit such attack (Article 7.2[a]).

War crimes

War crimes are defined in the Rome Statute in great detail. The statute advances the definition of war crimes by extending it to offenses committed in internal armed conflicts; however, it still distinguishes between the two contexts.

The statute establishes jurisdiction over war crimes, in particular, when committed as part of a plan or policy, or as part of a large-scale operation (Article 8.1). It draws heavily upon the definitions of war crimes arising from within the four **Geneva Conventions**. As is discussed in Chapter 4, not all acts outlawed or regulated by the Geneva Conventions constitute war crimes, only those that are enumerated as **grave breaches**. The Rome Statute defines three categories of war crimes: grave breaches of the Geneva Conventions (Article 8.2[a]), other serious violations of the laws and customs applicable in international armed conflicts under international law (Article 8.2[b]), and serious violations of **Common Article 3** of the four Geneva Conventions (Article 8.2[c–e]):

The first category includes the following acts: willful killing; torture or inhuman treatment, including biological experiments; willfully causing great suffering or serious injury to body or health; extensive destruction and appropriation of property not justified by military necessity and carried out unlawfully and wantonly; compelling a prisoner of war or other protected person to serve in the forces of a hostile power; willfully depriving a prisoner of war or other protected person of the right to a fair and regular trial; unlawful deportation, transfer, or confinement; and hostage-taking. As grave breaches of the Geneva Conventions, these crimes can only be committed in the context of international armed conflicts.

The second category, acts that constitute serious violations of the laws and customs applicable in international armed conflicts, includes the following: intentional attacks against civilian populations (and their facilities) who do not take part in the hostilities, such as relief workers and **peacekeeping** personnel; intentionally launching attacks that will cause incidental loss of life or injury to civilians; and improper use of a flag of truce, or the flag of the United Nations.

Finally, the third category of war crimes are related to noninternational armed conflict, those offenses enumerated in Common Article 3 of the Geneva Conventions. The Rome Statute therefore criminalizes acts – not only against civilians, but also against combatants who have laid down arms or are injured – such as murder, torture, outrages upon personal dignity, hostage-taking, and extrajudicial execution. Other acts that are considered war crimes in the context of a noninternational armed conflict include attacks upon the civilian population, attacks upon designated relief workers and peacekeepers, pillaging, attacks upon religious sites, and conscription of children.

The Rome Statute makes a clear distinction between internal armed conflicts and internal disturbances and tensions. Article 8.2(d–f) includes acts committed in the context of riots, isolated and sporadic acts of violence, and other acts of a military nature. The described acts must occur within the territory of a state where a protracted armed conflict is present between governmental authorities and organized armed groups, or between such armed groups.

Preconditions for jurisdiction

In order for the Court to be able to exercise jurisdiction over an accused individual, there must be a nexus with a state party to the Rome Statute. This nexus may be territorial, or one of nationality. Therefore, the Court has jurisdiction over an individual when the offense has been committed on the territory of a state party (including aboard vessels or aircraft registered in that state), or when the individual is a national of a state party.

There is a possibility that a national of a nonparty state could be tried if the crimes he or she is accused of were committed on the territory of a state party. This has been a primary source of US opposition to the Court. The United States feared that the ICC would be in a position to bring a case against its personnel deployed in military operations abroad, and that they could potentially be subject to frivolous and politically motivated suits. The United States has also argued that the jurisdiction of the Court could jeopardize the willingness of countries to contribute to peacekeeping operations when their personnel could be made criminally responsible, and claimed that prosecutions could upset local compromises and amnesties promulgated in the framework of **peace negotiations**. In reaction to the entry into force of the Rome Statute, the United States threatened to veto the renewal of the ongoing peacekeeping operations in the Security Council if protections for personnel of nonstate parties were not promised, and also signed bilateral agreements with all UN member states to avoid jurisdiction over US nationals. These agreements made use of an option under Article 98 of the Rome Statute that establishes that the Court may not proceed with a request for surrender or assistance that would require the requested state to act inconsistently with an obligation under international law. Thus, if these member states were to surrender US nationals to the ICC, they would be breaching their legal obligation toward the United States as established in these bilateral agreements. Domestically, in 2002 the US Congress passed the American Servicemembers' Protection Act, which established a prohibition on cooperation with the ICC for all US courts, agencies, and entities of any state or local government, as well as a prohibition on any military assistance to parties to the Court. The act also placed restrictions on US participation in certain UN peacekeeping operations and granted the US president the power to authorize the use of any means necessary to free members of the US armed forces and other US nationals detained or imprisoned by or on behalf of the ICC.

Exercise of jurisdiction and the principle of complementarity

The Court can initiate prosecution and exercise jurisdiction either if a case is referred to the ICC prosecutor, or if the prosecutor himself decides to initiate one. Only state parties (Articles 13[a] and 14 of the Rome Statute) and the Security Council, acting under Chapter VII of the **UN Charter** (Article 13[b]), can refer a situation to the prosecutor, but the prosecutor can initiate a case *proprio motu* on the basis of any information he has over the crimes (Article 15). In principle, this allows anyone – an individual, a state, a nongovernmental organization – to submit a petition to the prosecutor seeking an investigation. Once the prosecutor has reviewed the information and has concluded that there is a reasonable basis to proceed with an investigation, the situation must be submitted to the Pre-Trial Chamber, the organ that has the power to authorize the official opening of an investigation. If the Pre-Trial Chamber refuses to authorize the investigation, the prosecutor can still request a reconsideration of the situation when new facts or evidence emerge. Out of the four cases that are now under investigation by the Court, one, regarding the situation in Sudan, was referred by the Security Council, while the other three, regarding the situations in the Democratic Republic of Congo (DRC), Uganda, and the Central African Republic, were self-referrals. As is discussed later in this chapter, the situation in the DRC was self-referred after the ICC prosecutor made public that he was prepared to initiate the investigation *proprio motu*.

This does not mean that the Court has jurisdiction over every possible international crime. A key criterion for jurisdiction is that the state in which the crimes have been committed or whose national has been accused of such crimes is unwilling or unable to prosecute. This is because the jurisdiction of the Court is based on the principle of **complementarity**. Therefore, the Court will not take up cases where a legitimate legal process is under way in a relevant national jurisdiction, or if the accusation has been seriously investigated and dismissed domestically.

The different avenues by which a case reaches the Court have an impact on the level of government cooperation with the investigations and proceedings, including the arrest of suspects and their surrender to the Court. Experience so far demonstrates this disparity, and it is likely that the Court will receive little cooperation from the government of Sudan concerning the situation in that country.

Finally, an investigation or prosecution may be blocked for 12 months by the Security Council, acting under Chapter VII of the UN Charter (Article 16 of the Rome Statute).

Applicable principles of international criminal law

The functioning of the International Criminal Court is subject to a host of general principles of criminal law (see Chapter 4). These principles, listed in Part 3 of the Rome Statute (Articles 22–33), comprise the following: *nullem crimen sine lege* (no crime without law); *nulla poena sine lege* (no punishment without law); nonretroactivity; no punishment of persons younger than age 18; irrelevance of official capacity (including that heads of state or government shall not enjoy immunity from jurisdiction); command responsibility (a military commander shall be criminally responsible for crimes committed by the forces under his or her effective command and control, or a result of his or her failure to exercise proper control); rejection of the superior orders defense; necessary presence of mental element (intention and knowledge in the commission of the offense); and grounds for excluding criminal responsibility based on lack of capacity to acknowledge the wrongfulness of acts (such as mistakes of fact or mistakes of law that negate the mental element required by the crime, the presence of mental disease or state of intoxication, and acting in self-defense or under threat of imminent death). The Rome Statute also states expressly the principle of presumption of innocence (Article 66).

Further, only natural persons can be prosecuted by the ICC. After much debate in the treaty negotiations, the suggestion that legal persons – such as corporations or other groups – could be prosecuted was rejected. Under the Rome Statute (Article 25), individual criminal responsibility arises when a person materially commits a crime; orders, solicits, or induces the commission of such crime; aids and abets or otherwise assists in the commission of the crime; or in some other way contributes to its commission or attempted commission by a group of persons acting with a common purpose (see Box 13.1).

Box 13.1 **The Rome Statute, Article 25**

Article 25: Individual Criminal Responsibility

1. The Court shall have jurisdiction over natural persons pursuant to this Statute.
2. A person who commits a crime within the jurisdiction of the Court shall be individually responsible and liable for punishment in accordance with this Statute.
3. In accordance with this Statute, a person shall be criminally responsible and liable for punishment for a crime within the jurisdiction of the Court if that person:

    (a) Commits such a crime, whether as an individual, jointly with another or through another person, regardless of whether that other person is criminally responsible;

    (b) Orders, solicits or induces the commission of such a crime which in fact occurs or is attempted;

    (c) For the purpose of facilitating the commission of such a crime, aids, abets or otherwise assists in its commission or its attempted commission, including providing the means for its commission;

    (d) In any other way contributes to the commission or attempted commission of such a crime by a group of persons acting with a common purpose. Such contribution shall be intentional and shall either:

    (i) Be made with the aim of furthering the criminal activity or criminal purpose of the group, where such activity or purpose involves the commission of a crime within the jurisdiction of the Court; or

    (ii) Be made in the knowledge of the intention of the group to commit the crime;

    (e) In respect of the crime of genocide, directly and publicly incites others to commit genocide;

    (f) Attempts to commit such a crime by taking action that commences its execution by means of a substantial step, but the crime does not occur because of circumstances independent of the person's intentions. However, a person who abandons the effort to commit the crime or otherwise prevents the completion of the crime shall not be liable for punishment under this Statute for the attempt to commit that crime if that person completely and voluntarily gave up the criminal purpose.

4. No provision in this Statute relating to individual criminal responsibility shall affect the responsibility of States under international law.

Punishments are also elaborated in the Rome Statute. International criminal tribunals do not now impose the death penalty, so the maximum term of imprisonment to which a person can be sentenced by the ICC is 30 years. Exceptionally, for particularly grave crimes life imprisonment is authorized. Imprisonment sentences are served at correctional facilities of the states that indicate their willingness to accept sentenced persons. Once prison sentences are ready to be enforced, the Court designates which state will house the prisoner. Those found guilty may also be fined, or be forced to forfeit property. Fines collected may be placed in the trust fund set up to compensate victims and families of victims.

Victim trust fund

Prior to establishment of the International Criminal Court, one of the main criticisms of the ad hoc tribunals had been their limited ability to address the needs of the victims of conflict, as discussed in Chapter 10. Aware of the potential obstacle that geographical distance poses to the participation of victims, with the ICC sitting in The Hague, the Rome Statute foresaw the need to function as a redress mechanism for victims and not exclusively as a punishment mechanism for perpetrators. Article 75 of the statute provides that the Court shall consider reparations for victims, including restitution, compensation, and rehabilitation, in its decisions. Such reparations are channeled through a victim trust fund, which was established by the Assembly of State Parties in 2002. It began its operations in early 2007. The main aim of the fund is to provide victims, including child soldiers, victims of rape, sexual assault, and other abuses, and those who have had their property and livelihood destroyed, the necessary help and compensation to enable them to rebuild their lives. The trust is funded by money collected through fines and forfeitures (Article 79), and by contributions from governments, international organizations, and individuals.

Functioning of the court: the first cases

Once the ICC prosecutor concludes that there is a reasonable basis on which to proceed with an investigation, he must seek authorization from the Pre-Trial Chamber. If the case appears to fall within the jurisdiction of the Court, on the basis of the prosecutor's supporting material, the Pre-Trial Chamber will authorize commencement of the investigation, without prejudice to subsequent consideration by the Court of its own jurisdiction and the admissibility of the case (Article 15). Once the formal investigation has been authorized, the prosecutor can ask the Pre-Trial Chamber to issue orders and warrants (Article 57), including warrants of arrest or summons to appear before the Pre-Trial Chamber. The Pre-Trial Chamber can issue a warrant of arrest when there are reasonable grounds to believe that a person has committed a crime within the jurisdiction of the Court, in order to ensure his or her appearance at trial, to ensure that he or she does not obstruct or endanger the Court's investigation or proceedings, or to prevent him or her from continuing to commit the crime of which he or she is accused, or from committing a related crime within the jurisdiction of the Court (Article 58). The state party that receives a request for arrest must immediately take steps to proceed with that arrest and then surrender the accused to the ICC (Article 59).

Once the accused has been surrendered to the Court, or appears before it voluntarily or under a summons, the Pre-Trial Chamber confirms the charges established by the prosecutor at a hearing in which the accused and his or her counsel are present. However, the Pre-Trial Chamber can hold such a confirmation hearing in the absence of the accused if he or she has waived the right to be present, or has fled or cannot be found, in which case the Pre-Trial Chamber appoints a defense counsel for the absent accused. At the confirmation hearing, the accused can object to the charges and the evidence and present his or her own evidence. Finally, on the basis of this hearing, the Pre-Trial Chamber determines whether there is sufficient evidence to believe that the person committed each of the crimes charged, and then confirms or declines to confirm those charges (Article 61).

After the charges have been confirmed, the case is initiated before the Trial Chamber. Trials are held in public, except in special circumstances requiring that certain proceedings take place in closed sessions (Article 64). The accused must be present during the trial. However, if his or her behavior is disruptive, the Trial Chamber has the power to remove the accused from the courtroom. In this case, the accused can observe the proceedings and instruct counsel from outside the courtroom (Article 63).

The first four cases under investigation by the ICC do not begin to encompass the scope of possible referrals, or indeed the myriad communications received by the Office of the Prosecutor suggesting that investigations be launched. In the first four years of its existence the OTP received 1,732 communications from 103 countries concerning situations in 139 countries around the world. Most of these communications were found to be manifestly outside the jurisdiction of the court – for temporal, subject-matter, or territorial reasons – but the OTP undertook intensive analysis of at least ten situations. During this process the OTP has maintained the confidentiality of its inquiries to protect the interests of those involved and the investigations themselves. In general, the OTP explains the reasons not to initiate an investigation only to the originators of the communications. However, in the cases of refusal to initiate investigations on Iraq and Venezuela, the prosecutor made his decisions public, in the interests of transparency. Other cases remain under analysis, for example the situation in Côte d'Ivoire.

The first four cases before the Court concern the situations in the Democratic Republic of Congo, Sudan, Uganda, and the Central African Republic. The conflicts in the DRC and Sudan are addressed in greater detail in Chapters 7 and 8, respectively.

Democratic Republic of Congo

The DRC is a party to the Rome Statute, which it signed on September 8, 2000, and ratified on April 11, 2002, when the conflict was still ongoing. This is the first situation for which the Office of the Prosecutor opened an investigation. The OTP began considering the possibility of initiating an investigation into the crimes committed in DRC territory, especially in the Ituri region, shortly after the entry into force of the Rome Statute. In September 2003, after informally investigating the situation for several months, the prosecutor announced that he was prepared to exercise his *proprio motu* powers and seek authorization from a Pre-Trial Chamber to start an official investigation of the case. He also made it clear that a referral and active support from the government of the DRC would be welcomed. In April 2004 the government of the DRC referred to the Court the crimes within its jurisdiction allegedly committed since July 1, 2002. This referral, unlike the initial investigation, does not limit itself to the Ituri region, but asks for the consideration of crimes committed "anywhere in the territory of the country." The investigation could also address crimes committed by any DRC faction, including, in theory, the DRC government, or foreign governments acting in the DRC, because this conflict was characterized by the involvement of the government and multiple militias and rebel groups, as well as the direct and indirect participation of several neighboring countries (see Chapter 7). So far, however, cases concerning the situation in the DRC have involved only crimes committed in the Ituri region.

Following the referral, an investigation was opened in June 2003 and the case was assigned to the Pre-Trial Chamber. In addition, two field offices were established to assist in the investigations, one in Bunia and one in Kinshasa.

The investigations to date have led to the arrest and transfer to The Hague of four senior militia leaders: Thomas Lubanga Dyilo, the leader of the Patriotic Congolese Union (Union Patriotique Congolais [UPC]), whose arrest warrant was issued on March 17, 2006; Germain Katanga, alleged commander of the Patriotic Resistance Force in Ituri (Force de Résistance Patriotique en Ituri [FRPI]), on October 17, 2007; Mathieu Ngudjolo, alleged former leader of the National Integrationist Front (Front des Nationalistes et Intégrationnistes [FNI]) and colonel in the DRC national army, on February 7, 2008; and Bosco Ntaganda, alleged former deputy chief of staff of the Patriotic Forces for the Liberation of Congo (Forces Patriotiques pour la Libération du Congo [FPLC]) and alleged current chief of staff of the National Congress for the Defense of the People (Congrès National pour la Défense du Peuple [CNDP]), an armed group active in North Kivu, on August 22, 2008.

The case against Thomas Lubanga has already reached the trial phase, making him the first person to stand trial before the ICC. The confirmation of charges hearing began in November 2006, and in January 2007 the Pre-Trial Chamber confirmed the charges and sent his case to trial. The Pre-Trial Chamber found sufficient evidence to establish substantial grounds to believe that Lubanga is criminally responsible as a co-perpetrator for enlisting, conscripting, and using children younger than age 15 to participate actively in hostilities. In July 2008 the Trial Chamber issued an order granting unconditional release of Lubanga on the grounds that the prosecution had not made available potentially exculpatory materials. The prosecution appealed this order and requested that the trial be resumed. Lubanga remains in custody.

The cases against Germain Katanga and Mathieu Ngudjolo Chui were joined together by the Pre-Trial Chamber in March 2008, as both defendants were charged with the same crimes. The charges were confirmed in July 2008. On September 2008 the case was sent to trial on seven counts of war crimes and three counts of crimes against humanity, including murder, sexual slavery, rape, using children to participate actively in hostilities, intentional attack against the civilian population, pillaging, and destruction of property.

Finally, Bosco Ntaganda was charged with three war crimes: enlisting, conscripting, and using children younger than age 15 to participate actively in hostilities.

Sudan

Just as Sudan reached a comprehensive peace agreement in its long-running civil war between north and south, violence exploded in Western Darfur, where Janjaweed militias with links to the government have been carrying out campaigns of intimidation and terror against the civilian population (see Chapter 8). The systematic nature of the attacks has led to their characterization as crimes against humanity, and possibly genocide.

The International Commission of Inquiry on Darfur, in its 2005 report to the **UN Secretary-General**, concluded that both the government of Sudan and the Janjaweed militias were responsible for serious violations of international human rights and international humanitarian law, amounting to international crimes. The commission did not determine that genocide had occurred, as it could not find evidence of an intent to destroy a group, in whole or in part. Rather, it largely accepted the claim by the government that these acts had been undertaken in the context of "counterinsurgency."

The government of Sudan had made clear that it would not refer a case to the ICC itself; it is a signatory to the Rome Statute but has not completed ratification. It even tried to shortcut the risk that a case might be referred by the UN Security Council by setting up "tribal" or "traditional" justice courts for Darfur, which by all accounts have not conducted any genuine proceedings.

In its report the Commission of Inquiry considered which venue might be most appropriate to address these crimes. It established that the Sudanese justice system was not fit to do so: specifically, it stated that the system was "unable and unwilling," the requisite language for complementarity. Given this situation, the Commission of Inquiry recommended that the Security Council refer the case to the ICC. The Security Council did so in Resolution 1593 on March 13, 2005 (see Box 13.2).

Box 13.2 **UN Security Council Resolution 1593 (March 31, 2005)**

The Security Council . . . *Acting* under Chapter VII of the Charter of the United Nations,

1. *Decides* to refer the situation in Darfur since 1 July 2002 to the Prosecutor of the International Criminal Court;
2. *Decides* that the Government of Sudan and all other parties to the conflict in Darfur, shall cooperate fully with and provide any necessary assistance to the Court and the Prosecutor pursuant to this resolution and, while recognizing that States not party to the Rome Statute have no obligation under the Statute, urges all States and concerned regional and other international organizations to cooperate fully;
3. *Invites* the Court and the African Union to discuss practical arrangements that will facilitate the work of the Prosecutor and of the Court, including the possibility of conducting proceedings in the region, which would contribute to regional efforts in the fight against impunity;
4. *Also encourages* the Court, as appropriate and in accordance with the Rome Statute, to support international cooperation with domestic efforts to promote the rule of law, protect human rights and combat impunity in Darfur;
5. *Also emphasizes* the need to promote healing and reconciliation and encourages in this respect the creation of institutions, involving all sectors of Sudanese society, such as truth and/or reconciliation commissions, in order to complement judicial processes and thereby reinforce the efforts to restore long-lasting peace, with African Union and international support as necessary;
6. *Decides* that nationals, current or former officials or personnel from a contributing State outside Sudan which is not a party to the Rome Statute of the International

> Criminal Court shall be subject to the exclusive jurisdiction of that contributing State for all alleged acts or omissions arising out of or related to operations in Sudan established or authorized by the Council or the African Union, unless such exclusive jurisdiction has been expressly waived by that contributing State.

The resolution was passed by a vote of 11 in favor, with no votes against and 4 abstentions. Among the abstaining countries was the United States, notable given its objections to the ICC in general. Given its permanent seat on the UN Security Council, it could have vetoed the resolution, and there was indeed fear that it would do. However, US politicians had expressed special concern over the situation in Sudan generally and Darfur specifically, so there was a desire to find a compromise. The French delegation to the United Nations played a key role in formulating the compromise. Specifically, paragraph 6 of the resolution contains an exemption for nationals, current officials, and peacekeeping troops of states not party to the Rome Statute. This means that while officials of Sudan may be tried, even though the country has not ratified the Rome Statute, officials and peacekeepers from other nonstate parties cannot be prosecuted by the ICC. With this compromise formulation, the United States abstained from voting on the resolution, rather than vetoing it. However, the United States did enter into the record of proceedings a statement recognizing the need for action to be taken, but indicating its preference for an ad hoc regional court, perhaps similar to the hybrid court in Sierra Leone.

Following the referral from the UN Security Council, the ICC prosecutor opened an investigation into the situation in Darfur in June 2005. The prosecutor called for the cooperation of both national and international authorities.

The first case before the ICC on the situation in Darfur is *The Prosecutor v. Ahmad Muhammad Harun ("Ahmad Harun") and Ali Muhammad Ali Abd-Al-Rahman ("Ali Kushayb")*. Harun is the former minister of the interior of the government of Sudan, and Abd-Al-Rahman is the alleged leader of the Janjaweed militias. The Pre-Trial Chamber issued arrest warrants against both men on April 27, 2007. The chamber held that there were reasonable grounds to believe that they were responsible for crimes against humanity and war crimes committed in Darfur in 2003 and 2004, including persecution, murder of and attacks against civilians, forcible transfer, rape, pillaging, destruction of property, inhumane acts, imprisonment, and torture.

The government of Sudan has been reluctant to cooperate with the Court, and the prosecutor has complained to the Security Council about the lack of compliance with Resolution 1593, which explicitly calls for cooperation from the government.

In July 2008, in a groundbreaking decision, the prosecutor requested the Pre-Trial Chamber to issue an arrest warrant for Omar Hassan Ahmad al-Bashir, the president of Sudan, on the grounds that he bears criminal responsibility for genocide, crimes against humanity, and war crimes. The prosecutor alleged that Bashir "masterminded and implemented a plan to destroy in substantial part the Fur, Masalit and Zaghawa groups, on account of their ethnicity."

Uganda

The government of Uganda's referral of the situation in its northern territory offers an example of a government voluntarily referring a situation to the ICC. However, the referral is not as virtuous as it may seem, given that it was designed to initiate proceedings against a rebel group while seeking to avoid investigation of any misdeeds by Ugandan troops.

The current conflict in Uganda is Africa's longest-running conflict. Tensions arose soon after President Yoweri Museveni took power in 1986. In 1987 a rebel group, the Lord's Resistance Army (LRA), was formed from several splinter groups drawn from the former national army. Fighting has resulted in serious human rights abuses against civilians in the north, including summary executions, torture and mutilation, recruitment of child soldiers, child sexual abuse, rape, forcible displacement, looting, and destruction of civilian property. The LRA's signature tactic is to terrorize the population through mutilation: cutting the hands, ears, or lips of villagers suspected of government sympathies.

LRA fighters are drawn largely from abducted villagers, particularly children, mostly between 11 and 15 years of age, though younger children have been taken. According to human rights organizations, children comprise over 85 percent of the LRA's forces. They are used as soldiers, porters, laborers, and sexual slaves. As part of their initiation into the rebel movement, abducted children are forced into committing inhuman acts, including ritual killing and mutilation. They are frequently beaten and forced to carry heavy loads over long distances, loot and burn houses, beat and kill civilians and fellow abductees, and abduct other children. In order to evade capture, thousands of children have become "night dwellers," walking great distances to regroup at facilities run by nongovernmental organizations, as well as on the streets, on shop verandas, on church grounds, and at local factories, and then returning to their villages at dawn. It is estimated that over 30,000 children have been abducted by the LRA. However, human rights groups have documented extensive evidence not only of abuses committed by the LRA, but of many abuses by the Ugandan military as well.

Attacks by the LRA in the mid-1990s forced approximately three-quarters of the Acholi population to flee their homes in Gulu and Kitgum/Pader districts in northern Uganda. It is estimated that the conflict has generated over a million **internally displaced persons**.

Uganda was among the first states to sign the Rome Statute, ratifying it in June 2002. The government of Uganda referred the situation to the ICC in December 2003. It explicitly referred only the situation concerning the LRA, effectively shielding any Ugandan officials from prosecution. The ICC prosecutor, however, replied that he would interpret the referral as concerning all crimes under the Rome Statute that had been committed in the region, not just those by the LRA, and that the investigation would be impartial.

The investigation into crimes committed in northern Uganda since July 1, 2002, formally started in July 2004, with the ICC establishing a field office in Kampala to support the proceedings. In October 2005 the Court issued arrest warrants for crimes against humanity and war crimes for five senior leaders of the LRA: Joseph Kony, Okot Odhiambo, Dominic Ongwen, Raska Lukwiya, and Vincent Otti. Both Dominic Ongwen and Raska Lukwiya have reportedly been killed. In July 2007 the proceedings against Raska Lukwiya were terminated due to his death.

Meanwhile, the Ugandan government engaged in peace negotiations with the LRA. In this context it passed an **amnesty** law, but later amended it to exclude LRA leadership. Amnesties are discussed in greater detail later in the chapter.

The Central African Republic

The Central African Republic signed the Rome Statute on December 7, 1999, and ratified it on October 3, 2001, being among the first states to do so. The conflict in the Central African

Republic began in 2001 when François Bozizé, chief of staff of the Central African Armed Forces (Forces Armées Centrafricaines [FACA]), took up arms after having been dismissed by presidential decree on accusation of an attempted a coup d'état. President Ange-Félix Patassé called on his allies for help, and several groups came to his side in the fighting, including a Libyan military contingent and the Movement for the Liberation of the Congo (Mouvement de Libération du Congo [MLC]), led by Jean-Pierre Bemba Gombo.

Fighting between General Bozizé's rebels and governmental forces began in 2002 and lasted until March 2003, when the rebels took control of the capital, Bangui. Bozizé proclaimed himself president, a position to which he was later elected, in 2005. Patassé went into exile and Bemba Gombo's men returned to the DRC. All combatants perpetrated serious human rights and international humanitarian law violations. Though the conflict ended in 2003, violence continues, with Bozizé's presidential guard reportedly engaging in acts of brutality against the civilian population, particularly in Patassé's northwestern stronghold, provoking large population displacements.

The government of the Central African Republic referred the situation to the ICC in January 2005. The referral included all crimes committed anywhere on the territory of the Central African Republic since July 1, 2002. The decision to refer the case was appealed internally, in view of ongoing national procedures. In April 2006 the highest criminal court of the Central African Republic, the Cour de Cassation, held that its judicial system was unable to carry out effective investigations and prosecutions of the alleged crimes; the national procedures have since been suspended. In order to respect the principle of complementarity, the ICC prosecutor waited for the final decision of the Cour de Cassation before making a determination on the issue of admissibility.

Investigations of the crimes committed in 2002 and 2003 were formally opened in May 2007. The ICC prosecutor announced that the investigations would focus on sexual violence in particular, given that allegations of sexual crimes reportedly far outnumbered alleged killings.

The Pre-Trial Chamber issued an arrest warrant for Jean-Pierre Bemba Gombo, alleged president and commander in chief of the MLC, on May 24, 2008, on two counts of crimes against humanity (rape and torture) and four counts of war crimes (rape; torture; outrages upon personal dignity, in particular humiliating and degrading treatment; and pillage). He was detained by the Belgian authorities and transferred to the Court's detention center on July 3, 2008. Bemba Gombo appeared before the Pre-Trial Chamber for the first time on November 4, 2008.

Reflection on the ICC's first cases

While it is still too early to predict the course of these four cases, whether in terms of specific jurisprudence or political effect, we can draw some conclusions from the actions and debates so far.

Modes of referral: do they affect prospects for a case?

We have seen that governments may refer situations regarding their own territories in a number of ways. This runs contrary to fears that governments would not refer such situations, although it is not entirely reassuring. It is fairly clear that the DRC referred its situation to the ICC under heavy pressure from the Office of the Prosecutor, while Uganda used its referral to trigger investigation of a rebel group it has been battling since 1987, and sought to avoid any investigation into government misdeeds. The Central African Republic's referral appears to be the only one undertaken without coercion, or at least without an open attempt to shield itself.

The fear that the UN Security Council would not be able to reach a consensus to submit referrals to the Court has proven unfounded. US objections to the ICC notwithstanding, the UN Security Council has been able to proceed in the case of Darfur. This might continue to be the pattern, with the United States abstaining from voting, rather than vetoing, where a compromise is reached.

The ICC and conflict resolution

Concerns have been raised about the impact of the ICC on conflict resolution, particularly for countries engaged in conflict or in peace processes. Conducting investigations in ongoing conflict situations presents difficulties both from a practical point of view (e.g. protecting investigators, as well as victims and witnesses) and from a wider political point of view. In this regard, one objection to the ICC is that it functions as an external mechanism for providing justice, similarly to ad hoc tribunals (Chapter 10) and transnational litigation (Chapter 11), and although it is an alternative where states are unable or unwilling to prosecute, it is located far from the victims and affected society. This, critics say, could mean that the Court will not take sufficient account of local needs in the context of transitions, and in particular could disrupt conflict resolution processes or reconciliation efforts. This complicates the relationship between the international prosecutions of the ICC and national peace processes.

Regarding the situation in Uganda, the ICC prosecutor has been prepared to proceed with the investigation notwithstanding ongoing peace negotiations. While the impact of the ICC proceedings could be positive in terms of promoting the consideration of national accountability mechanisms in peace agreements, it could also be negative, with those who may have reason to fear prosecution withdrawing from peace negotiations. In April 2008, Joseph Kony, the leader of the LRA, refused to sign a peace accord unless the ICC arrest warrants against the LRA were removed, paralyzing the peace process. Regarding the situation in Sudan, concerns have been expressed about the impact of the ICC prosecutions on the peacekeeping operations under way in Darfur and elsewhere in the country.

In the other two cases before the Court, concerning the situations in the Democratic Republic of Congo and the Central African Republic, the impact of the ICC prosecutions on **peacebuilding** efforts may be different. In the DRC, initial doubts about the will or ability of the government to offer extensive support to the proceedings, especially given its original recalcitrance to refer the case, have been allayed. In addition, the UN peacekeeping operation in the country, the UN Organization Mission in the Democratic Republic of Congo (MONUC), has explicitly committed itself to helping the government fulfill its obligations within the framework of the ICC process. Any effects on the political stabilization process in the Central African Republic, particularly considering that the referral comes from a government that seized power through a coup and questionable elections, are still unclear.

It is also important to remember that the ICC has jurisdiction only over a small number of serious crimes, and will only focus upon a small number of perpetrators. Thus, the majority of perpetrators are unlikely to be pursued by the ICC, which in the absence of appropriate national judicial procedures could contribute to a perception of **impunity**. The ICC prosecutor has tried to address the balance between international justice, national processes, and reconciliation initiatives by firmly rejecting amnesties but also showing openness to the complementary role that national processes can play. He has also recognized the role of local initiatives in the use of traditional or customary justice mechanisms as retribution, reparation, and reconciliation tools (in Uganda and Sudan), as long as they are not used as an excuse for the perpetuation of impunity. When opening his investigation following the UN Security Council's referral of the situation in Darfur, the ICC prosecutor explicitly stated that traditional African mechanisms are complementary to efforts to achieve local reconciliation.

Key points

- The International Criminal Court (ICC) provides the first permanent forum for international justice since the Nuremberg process following World War II.
- The jurisdiction of the Court is based on the principle of complementarity; it can act only when states are unwilling or unable to prosecute international crimes.
- The crimes under the jurisdiction of the Court are aggression, genocide, war crimes, and crimes against humanity.
- The first cases before the Court are all related to conflicts in Africa.
- The work of the Court is necessarily embedded in the delicate balance between peace and justice when dealing with ongoing conflicts.

Discussion questions

- What are some of the novel aspects of the ICC's powers?
- Consider the three different mechanisms by which investigations can reach the Office of the Prosecutor. What is the impact of each on developing a case for prosecution?
- Consider the four cases currently under the jurisdiction of the ICC. In each case, are there any other accountability mechanisms or even nonjudicial mechanisms such as traditional conflict resolution and reconciliation processes that could have a better impact on peacebuilding?
- Would it be possible to use the mechanisms contained in Article 16 of the Rome Statute in any of the ICC's current cases? How do you think such mechanism may work in the future?

Group exercise

Choose an ongoing conflict, or a conflict that has recently reached a peace agreement, as a potential case for the ICC. Form four groups and role-play the presentation of an expert report before the Security Council (Group 1), the debate within the Security Council (Groups 2 and 3), and the presentation of a report by the Office of the Prosecutor (Group 4).

- *Group 1*: As a group of experts, draft a report on the conflict situation, documenting human rights violations that amount to crimes under the jurisdiction of the ICC and recommending a referral from the Security Council to the Court.
- *Group 2*: As a group of states in the Security Council that are reluctant to proceed to an ICC referral, prepare a report on your grounds for rejection.
- *Group 3*: As a group of states in the Security Council that are in favor of proceeding to an ICC referral, prepare a report on your grounds for support.
- *Group 4*: As the Office of the Prosecutor, prepare a report on the jurisdiction of the Court over the alleged crimes.

Further reading

Abass, Ademola, "The International Criminal Court and Universal Jurisdiction," *International Criminal Law Review* 6, no. 3 (2006): 349–85.

Broomhall, Bruce, *International Justice and the International Criminal Court* (Oxford: Oxford University Press, 2004).

Cassese, Antonio, *International Criminal Law* (Oxford: Oxford University Press, 2008), chaps. 3–5, 15.

Human Rights Watch, "Stolen Children: Abduction and Recruitment in Northern Uganda" (March 2003), http://www.hrw.org/reports/2003/uganda0303/uganda0403.pdf.

Kerr, Rachel, and Eirin Mobekk, *Peace and Justice. Seeking Accountability After War* (Cambridge: Polity, 2007), chap. 3.

Sadat, Leila Nadya, *The International Criminal Court and the Transformation of International Law: Justice for the New Millennium* (Ardsley, NY: Transnational, 2002), chaps. 4, 6–7.

Sriram, Chandra, "Conflict Mediation and the ICC: Challenges and Options for Pursuing Peace with Justice at the Regional Level," report presented at the conference "Building a Future on Peace and Justice," Nuremberg, June 25–27, 2007, http://www.peace-justice-conference.info/download/ws1-sriram%20report.pdf.

Steiner, Henry, Philip Alston, and Ryan Goodman, *International Human Rights in Context*, 3rd edn. (Oxford: Oxford University Press, 2008), chap. 14.

Official documents and sources

Coalition for the International Criminal Court, http://www.iccnow.org.

Human Rights Watch ICC Campaign, http://www.hrw.org/campaigns/icc.

International Criminal Court, http://www.icc-cpi.int.

——, *Elements of the Crime*, http://www.icc-cpi.int/library/about/officialjournal/element_of_crimes_english.pdf.

——, *Rome Statute of the International Criminal Court*, http://www.icc-cpi.int/library/about/official journal/rome_statute_english.pdf.

——, *Rules of Procedure and Evidence* (adopted by the Assembly of State Parties on September 9, 2002), http://www.icc-cpi.int/library/about/officialjournal/rules_of_procedure_and_evidence_english.pdf.

——, update on communications received by the Office of the Prosecutor, http://www.icc-cpi.int/library/organs/otp/otp_update_on_communications_10_february_2006.pdf.

United Nations, *Report of the International Commission of Inquiry on Darfur to the United Nations Secretary-General, Pursuant to Security Council Resolution 1564 of 18 September 2004,* http://www.reliefweb.int/rw/rwfiles2005.nsf/filesbyrwdocunidfilename/hmyt-697tar-un-ici-sud-25jan.pdf/$file/un-ici-sud-25jan.pdf.

——, *UN Security Council Resolution 1593* (referring the situation in Darfur to the International Criminal Court), http://www.iccnow.org/documents/declarationsresolutions/unbodies/1593/sc1593.31march05.pdf.

14 Enduring and emergent challenges and opportunities

This book has provided an introduction to the intersection of two complex and rapidly developing fields of study and policymaking: human rights, and conflict resolution and **peacebuilding**. It has offered an overview of relevant **international humanitarian law** and **international human rights law**, and presented scholarship and debates about human rights and the causes and consequences of conflict, options for **conflict prevention** and conflict resolution, and options for seeking accountability for past atrocities. There are many tensions between the promotion of human rights and the resolution of conflict, but there may also be opportunities for engaging in each in a more complementary fashion. This book has sought to assist students seeking to work in this hybrid area with these analytic tools, as well as with the study of contemporary situations presenting challenges of protecting human rights while addressing conflict. These situations range from largely internal armed conflicts with regional or international dimensions, as in Sierra Leone and the Democratic Republic of Congo, to diffuse and globalized confrontations such as the "global war on terror." Finally, the book has presented a range of critical mechanisms and institutions developed as part of efforts to implement human rights and humanitarian law, generally through criminal accountability, even as conflicts have raged: ad hoc tribunals, transnational mechanisms, **hybrid tribunals**, and the **International Criminal Court** (ICC).

Difficult policy and political decisions must be confronted when seeking to promote justice and resolve conflicts. Though significant challenges remain and will continue to emerge, there are also opportunities for promoting both justice and conflict resolution, rather than choosing one over the other.

Enduring challenges and opportunities

Enduring challenges

Justice versus peace

While great advances in accountability have clearly been made since the early 1990s, beginning with the creation of the ad hoc tribunals for the former Yugoslavia and Rwanda, and continuing through to the negotiation and ratification of the Rome Statute for the International Criminal Court, there remain important tensions between the pursuit of accountability and the pursuit of peace agreements. Contemporary peace agreements continue either to set accountability to one side, as in the case of the Comprehensive Peace Agreement concluded in 2005 to resolve the conflict in Sudan between the northern government, based in Khartoum, and the Sudanese People's Liberation Movement/Army, in the south, or to explicitly include amnesties for one or more parties, as in the case of the Lomé Agreement in Sierra Leone in 1999. The threat or possibility of accountability also continues to hinder the negotiation of some peace agreements, as in the case of negotiations with the Lord's Resistance Army in seeking to end the conflict in northern Uganda, over which looms the shadow of ICC indictments. Objections by individuals and groups who may have committed serious human rights violations during the course of conflict, particularly former combatants, whether governmental or nonstate actors, are likely to continue to impede many **peace negotiations**. They may also pose challenges to peace implementation.

Will and capacity to pursue accountability

A related challenge is that while there may be strong demands for accountability from local populations, or from international human rights groups, there may be limited will at the top political levels to pursue it. Alternatively, there may be a desire by the political leadership to pursue accountability, but relatively limited capacity to follow through, as states emerging from violent conflict generally suffer from decimated infrastructure and limited resources. Even when promotion of accountability comes from the national and international levels, some among the most affected populations at the local level may insist that community-based mechanisms are more effective. If national and local will and capacity are lacking, inter-national venues for accountability may be the only option. However, here too there are problems of will, capacity, and sometimes jurisdiction. As discussed in Chapter 13, the ICC's territorial and temporal jurisdiction is limited. While there has been, to date, one referral to the ICC by the **UN Security Council**, of the situation in Darfur, such referrals are likely to be politically contentious and fairly rare. This means that if the ICC is not an option, and if domestic venues in the countries affected by conflict are not available, then accountability for human rights violations will need to be sought in the domestic courts of other nations, or through the creation of ad hoc or hybrid tribunals. However, in only a few countries are courts prepared to hear cases, whether civil or criminal, for abuses committed in other countries, and this is also politically contentious. Similarly, ad hoc and hybrid tribunals can be costly and require significant political will to create. Nonetheless, such avenues for accountability continue to act as complements to the ICC and may help to fill gaps for the foreseeable future.

The Western imposition objection

As discussed in Chapter 3, the scope and content of human rights obligations remain contested, with some groups and some states claiming that these are Western values, or that they are being imposed by Western states. This objection has been vehemently raised by the government of Sudan in the context of the referral to the ICC of the situation in Darfur; by Robert Mugabe in the context of the electoral dispute in Zimbabwe in 2008; and by a number of African nations in respect to courts exercising **universal jurisdiction** in European countries such as Belgium and Spain over current or former African leaders, with some nations branding the ICC as "an international court for Africa." The objection invokes cultural difference or political power, and will likely continue to be raised for the foreseeable future. However, the degree of deference that this objection should be given is certainly debatable, as it is most frequently invoked by the individuals or regimes who most benefit from it.

Enduring opportunities

While it is difficult to identify any significant, long-standing opportunities for pursuing accountability while pursuing **peacemaking** and peacebuilding, there are a number of emergent and increasingly embedded opportunities, discussed in the next section. Certainly, we now have several decades of practice in domestic **transitional justice** to draw upon, as well as the new wave of international criminal accountability efforts that has emerged since the end of the Cold War. Similarly, embedded practices of peacemaking, **peacekeeping**, and peacebuilding are being carried out by the **United Nations** (UN), the European Union (EU), and other **regional organizations**, as well as bilateral donors and international nongovernmental organizations. The professional and technical expertise of networks of human rights activists and practitioners, as well as conflict resolution advocates and practitioners, offer perhaps the most enduring opportunity.

Emergent challenges and opportunities

Emergent challenges

Pursuit of accountability during conflict

Perhaps one of the most salient emergent challenges involves the growth of efforts to pursue accountability not after a conflict has reached a negotiated agreement or the victory of one side, but while conflict is still under way. This is not an entirely new phenomenon – the **International Criminal Tribunal for the Former Yugoslavia** (ICTY) was created and began to operate prior to the negotiated end to the conflicts in the former Yugoslavia following the Dayton Accords in 1995 – but it is becoming increasingly common. In recent years the courts of countries in Europe have sought to exercise jurisdiction over accused perpetrators in countries where the conflicts had not yet fully terminated, as in the ICC's attempts to prosecute individuals in the Democratic Republic of Congo before the conflict there had ended. The ICC is also investigating crimes committed in Darfur and northern Uganda, and has indicted and sought arrest warrants for suspected perpetrators, even though neither conflict has ended, and in the case of Uganda even despite strong concerns that indictments could impede a peace process.

Human rights and the "global war on terror"

As discussed in Chapter 9, the so-called global war on terror, led by the United States in the wake of the attacks of September 11, 2001, has posed a critical challenge to the protection of human rights and the implementation of international humanitarian law obligations. The US government, under the leadership of George W. Bush, presented this war on terror as a new kind of war, one that is asymmetric and of global reach, in which "the enemy" presents a challenge of such nature and scale as to require preemptive self-defense. In this new type of conflict, it is often argued that human rights can and must be restricted, often in ways that go well beyond treaty derogation provisions for the purposes of public security. In particular, the absolute prohibition upon **torture** came under attack, either through political justifications of necessity, through simply rendering individuals for interrogation to countries that do not respect the terms of the **Torture Convention**, or through redefining the content of torture in ways not justified by the terms of the convention. Similarly, obligations under international humanitarian law have been redefined or incorrectly interpreted by US officials, although some of these interpretations have been judged unconstitutional by the US Supreme Court. While balancing the protection of human rights and the promotion of security is justifiable, and indeed this is why there are provisions in most human rights agreements for some degree of derogation, the war on terror radically shifted that balance in a manner that may be inconsistent with international human rights treaties and international humanitarian law obligations.

Emergent opportunities

New venues

Perhaps one of the most significant emergent opportunities for the promotion of human rights during ongoing conflicts or in postconflict situations is the creation or utilization of new venues for accountability. In particular, transnational accountability mechanisms, through the exercise of universal jurisdiction in countries such as Spain, or civil accountability in countries such as the United States and the United Kingdom, create the possibility of imposing some form of sanction upon human rights abusers who might not otherwise face sanction in their home states. Similarly, the creation of hybrid mechanisms might also offer new opportunities for accountability where previously unavailable. These new venues may be particularly important where purely international accountability is unavailable and domestic accountability is impossible, and can also potentially supplement peacemaking and peacebuilding in countries most affected by conflict and human rights violations.

In situations where the ICC does not have jurisdiction, or the UN Security Council will not refer the situation, or the state affected by the conflict and relevant violations will not initiate a case and the Office of the Prosecutor does not see fit to initiate a case, these mechanisms may help to fill what otherwise might constitute gaps in accountability.

Pursuit of accountability during conflict

Notwithstanding the strong objections of the world's remaining superpower, the United States, to the statute and operation of the ICC, the Court is currently investigating four significant cases. Further, it has even received one case through referral by the UN Security Council, with the United States abstaining. And, perhaps most important, the ICC has been able to do something that most previous mechanisms and accountability processes for gross violations of human rights and international humanitarian law have not: initiate investigations and indictments of high-level perpetrators during ongoing conflict. While such investigations may have the potential to disrupt peace negotiations, they may also constitute a positive incentive for negotiations. Optimists argue that ICC investigations may also have the capacity to prevent or deter violations in the midst of ongoing conflict. Even if the ICC does not manage to arrest suspects, experience suggests that indictments may compel suspects to hide, which may prevent them from committing further human rights abuses. Still, it remains to be seen whether such investigations encourage parties to reach peace agreements or prevent them from doing so, and whether such investigations alter the behavior of combatants and prevent abuses that might otherwise have occurred as conflict continues.

The future

It is of course impossible to predict the future of the vast and rapidly intersecting fields of conflict and human rights. However, we hope that this textbook has provided you with the tools and wherewithal to understand the history of the institutions and mechanisms developed for accountability, and the dilemmas that confront peacemakers. We also hope that it will enable you to develop your own recommendations to respond to particular situations. Further, the political and legal analytical skills that you have gained through your study should enable you to think creatively about future, alternative, options: for legal accountability mechanisms, for peace negotiations, and for sustainable political solutions, which enable weak post-conflict states to address accountability while pursuing peace.

Further reading

Davis, Rachel Benjamin Majekodunmi, and Judy Smith-Höhn, *Prevention of Genocide and Mass Atrocities and the Responsibility to Protect: Challenges for the UN and the International Community in the 21st Century* (UN Office of the Special Adviser on the Prevention of Genocide, International Peace Institute, and Centre for Conflict Resolution, June 2008), http://www.ipacademy.org/asset/file/355/ipigeno.pdf.

Human Rights Watch, *World Report 2004: Human Rights and Armed Conflict*, http://www.hrw.org/legacy/wr2k4/index.htm.

Manikkalingam, Ram, "Promoting Peace and Protecting Rights: How Are Human Rights Good and Bad for Resolving Conflict?" *Essex Human Rights Review* 5, no. 1 (July 2008): 1–11.

Sriram, Chandra Lekha, and Suren Pillay, eds., *Peace vs. Justice? The Dilemma of Transitional Justice in Africa* (Durban: University of KwaZulu-Natal, 2009).

Official documents and sources

United Nations, *Briefings by the High Commissioner for Human Rights to the Security Council and the Peacebuilding Commission* (May 29, 2007), http://www.securitycouncilreport.org/site/c.glkwlemtisg/b.2770455

——, *A More Secure World: Our Shared Responsibility – Report of the Secretary-General's High-Level Panel on Threats, Challenges, and Change* (2004), http://www.un.org/secureworld.

——, *Nuremberg Declaration on Peace and Justice: Annex to the Letter Dated 13 June 2008 from the Permanent Representatives of Finland, Germany, and Jordan to the United Nations, Addressed to the Secretary-General* (July 19, 2008), UN Doc. A/62/885, http://www.peace-justice-conference.info/download/nuremberg%20declaration%20a-62-885%20eng.pdf.

Glossary

African Union (AU) The regional organization that comprises African states. Formerly the Organization of African Unity, it was transformed by a new charter into the AU in 2000.

Alien Tort Claims Act (ATCA) Passed in 1789, this act established the jurisdiction of US federal district courts over "any civil action by an alien for a tort only committed in violation of the law of nations or a treaty of the United States."

amnesty The blocking of criminal action against alleged perpetrators of crimes.

Amnesty International An international organization that advocates and campaigns for the protection and promotion of human rights.

aut dedere aut judicare The principle requiring that a nation try an individual accused of certain crimes, such as genocide, or extradite that person to an appropriate jurisdiction on request.

Common Article 3 An article of identical provisions common to all four Geneva Conventions that requires parties in internal armed conflicts not to engage in specific violations, such as violence and denial of due process to persons not taking part in hostilities.

complementarity The principle that prohibits the International Criminal Court from hearing a case if there is a legitimate legal process under way in a relevant national jurisdiction, or if the accusation has been rigorously investigated and dismissed domestically.

conflict prevention Activities undertaken to mitigate the risk of imminent conflict, or to address deep-rooted causes of conflict.

crimes against humanity Specific acts committed as part of a widespread or systematic attack against any civilian population.

Department of Peacekeeping Operations (DPKO) Part of the United Nations, the DPKO assists UN member states and the UN Secretary-General in their efforts to maintain international peace and security.

Department of Political Affairs (DPA) Part of the United Nations, the DPA is the lead UN actor that supports peacemaking, conflict prevention, and peacebuilding.

diplomacy Efforts by a range of actors, official and unofficial, to promote peaceful settlement of disputes.

Economic Community of West African States (ECOWAS) A regional organization of states in West Africa. Founded in 1975 as an economic body, it now engages in peacemaking and peacekeeping activities through the ECOWAS Cease-Fire Monitoring Group (ECOMOG).

European Convention on Human Rights (ECHR) Drafted in 1950 under the auspices of the Council of Europe, this convention articulates a set of fundamental rights and freedoms that parties are obligated to effect and respect.

European Court of Human Rights   The court that has jurisdiction over claims that rights enshrined in the European Convention on Human Rights have been violated.

Geneva Conventions   A set of four conventions (1949) and two additional protocols (1977):

- *First Geneva Convention*. Addresses the treatment of the sick and wounded in the armed forces.
- *Second Geneva Convention*. Addresses the treatment of the sick and wounded at sea.
- *Third Geneva Convention*. Addresses the treatment of prisoners of war.
- *Fourth Geneva Convention*. Addresses the protection of civilians in armed conflict.
- *Additional Protocol I*. Elaborates obligations and limitations for treatment of victims of international armed conflict.
- *Additional Protocol II*. Elaborates obligations and limitations for treatment of victims of noninternational armed conflict.

genocide   The commission of specific acts with the intent to destroy, in whole or in part, a national, ethnical, racial, or religious group.

Genocide Convention (Convention on the Prevention and Punishment of the Crime of Genocide)   Defines and prohibits genocide, and obligates states to prevent and punish it.

grave breaches   Specific acts committed during international conflict that are designated in each of the four Geneva Conventions as punishable (war crimes).

Human Rights Watch   An international organization that advocates for the protection of human rights.

hybrid tribunals   Tribunals that utilize a mixture of domestic and international staff, and in some cases domestic and international law, to prosecute crimes of international concern that arise from conflict and gross abuses of human rights. Examples include the Special Court for Sierra Leone and the Cambodia Extraordinary Chambers.

impunity   The failure to bring perpetrators of human rights abuses to account.

internally displaced persons   People who have been forced from their homes, usually by conflict or other humanitarian catastrophe, into another part of their country. Because they have not crossed an international border, they are not protected by the provisions of international agreements regarding refugees.

International Bill of Rights   Comprises the Universal Declaration of Human Rights (UDHR), the International Covenant on Civil and Political Rights (ICCPR), and the International Covenant on Economic, Social, and Cultural Rights (ICESCR).

International Court of Justice (ICJ)   The judicial organ of the United Nations, able to adjudicate interstate disputes where it has jurisdiction.

International Criminal Court (ICC)   Established by the Rome Statute, which entered into force on July 1, 2002, the ICC can try individuals under its jurisdiction for war crimes, crimes against humanity, and genocide, and will be able to prosecute the crime of aggression when and if that crime is defined for the purposes of the Court.

International Criminal Tribunal for Rwanda (ICTR)   An ad hoc criminal tribunal created to punish individuals considered most responsible for the 1994 genocide in Rwanda.

International Criminal Tribunal for the Former Yugoslavia (ICTY)   An ad hoc criminal tribunal created to punish individuals accused of committing international crimes, such as war crimes and crimes against humanity, during Yugoslavia's armed conflict and breakup.

international human rights law Includes customary and conventional international legal obligations to respect or protect specific rights of natural persons. In addition to the documents included in the International Bill of Rights, key agreements include the Convention on the Prevention and Punishment of the Crime of Genocide; the Convention Against Torture and Other Cruel, Inhuman, or Degrading Treatment or Punishment; the Convention on the Elimination of Racial Discrimination in All Its Forms; the Convention on the Rights of the Child; and the Convention on the Elimination of Discrimination Against Women.

international humanitarian law Includes customary and conventional international legal obligations that regulate activities during internal and international armed conflict. Key documents include the four Geneva Conventions and their two additional protocols.

jus cogens Obligations that have achieved the status of peremptory norms in international law and from which no derogation is permissible. These include prohibitions on genocide, torture, crimes against humanity, war crimes, piracy, and slavery. Universal jurisdiction may be exercised over those who violate these norms.

nonstate actors Actors that are not state officials or agents of the state; may include multinational corporations, nongovernmental organizations, nonstate armed groups, and terrorist organizations.

North Atlantic Treaty Organization (NATO) Comprises nations of Western Europe and North America that have allied under a treaty of mutual self-defense since the end of World War II. Its membership has grown to involve nations of Central Europe since the end of the Cold War.

nulla poena sine lege A principle of international criminal law meaning "no punishment without law."

nullem crimen sine lege A principle of international criminal law meaning "no crime without law."

Nuremberg Charter (Charter of the International Military Tribunal) The charter that established the tribunal to try accused war criminals in Germany following World War II.

peace negotiation Termination of conflict not through military victory, but through negotiated settlement, whether between states themselves or between states and nonstate armed groups.

peacebuilding Myriad activities undertaken by individual states and the international community to help states consolidate peace and avoid return to conflict.

peacekeeping Use of military and civilian contingents by an external third party, most frequently the United Nations, interposed between parties to a conflict, in an effort to halt fighting or to monitor and implement peace agreements.

peacemaking Reaching a peaceful solution to a conflict through activities such as mediation or negotiation.

proprio motu The power of the prosecutor of the International Criminal Court to initiate a case, if he has jurisdiction.

regional organizations Organizations formed under multilateral agreements to achieve particular regional purposes, often security or economic coordination. Key examples include the African Union and the European Union.

rule of law The accountability of all persons, institutions, and entities, public and private, including the state itself, to laws that are publicly promulgated, equally enforced, and independently adjudicated.

South African Development Community (SADC) A regional organization formed in

1980 to coordinate development projects in Southern Africa. The SADC now also engages in peacemaking and other diplomatic activities.

Special Representative of the Secretary-General (SRSG)   An eminent person appointed by the UN Secretary-General to engage the situation in a particular country, or with respect to a particular topic. SRSGs often head peacekeeping missions.

torture   Defined by the Torture Convention as "any act by which severe pain or suffering, whether physical or mental, is intentionally inflicted on a person for such purposes as obtaining from him or a third person information or a confession . . . when such pain or suffering is inflicted by or at the instigation of or with the consent or acquiescence of a public official or other person acting in an official capacity."

Torture Convention (Convention Against Torture and Other Cruel, Inhuman, or Degrading Treatment or Punishment)   Defines and universally bans torture.

transitional justice   A range of processes and mechanisms to ensure accountability, justice, and reconciliation after conflict or authoritarian rule.

truth commissions   Nonjudicial fact-finding bodies that investigate patterns of human rights abuses during conflict or authoritarian rule.

UN Charter   The international agreement of 1945 that established the United Nations, setting forth the goals of the organization – to prevent war and to promote human rights – and the obligations of states parties.

UN General Assembly   An intergovernmental organ of the United Nations in which all member states are represented.

UN High Commissioner for Refugees (UNHCR)   Was established in1950 by the United Nations General Assembly and is mandated to lead and coordinate international action to protect refugees and resolve refugee problems globally.

UN Secretary-General   Described in the UN Charter as the "chief administrative officer" of the United Nations, the Secretary-General engages in a range of diplomatic activities, including through the offer of his good offices to promote conflict resolution.

UN Security Council   One of the principal organs of the UN, established under Article 7 of the UN Charter, comprising 15 member states, 5 of which are permanent and have the right of veto. The Security Council's primary responsibility is the maintenance of peace and security.

UN Security Council resolution   A resolution passed by the UN Security Council to effect its primary goal of maintaining of peace and security. Affirmative votes from nine member states are required, with no vetoes by the five permanent member states.

United Nations (UN)   Created by the UN Charter in 1945 with the express purpose of saving "succeeding generations from the scourge of war" and reaffirming "fundamental human rights." Key organs include the Security Council, the General Assembly, and the International Court of Justice.

universal jurisdiction   The extraterritorial exercise of criminal jurisdiction over a limited set of international crimes, or violations of *jus cogens* obligations, regardless of the territory in which they were committed.

war crimes   The commission of a range of acts, defined as "grave breaches" in the Geneva Conventions, that are considered violations of the laws and customs of war.

Further reading

Aceves, William J., "*Doe v. Unocal* 963 F. Supp. 880," *American Journal of International Law* 92, no. 2 (April 1998): 979–87.

Adebajo, Adekeye, and Chandra Lekha Sriram, eds., *Managing Armed Conflicts in the 21st Century* (London: Frank Cass, 2001).

Aksar, Yusuf, *Implementing International Humanitarian Law: From the* Ad Hoc *Tribunals to a Permanent International Criminal Court* (London: Routledge, 2004).

Almquist, Jessica, "A Human Rights Critique of European Judicial Review: Counter-terrorism Sanctions," *International and Comparative Law Quarterly* 57, pt. 2 (April 2008): 303–32.

Alston, Phillip, Ryan Goodman, and Henry J. Steiner, *International Human Rights in Context: Law, Politics, Morals* (Oxford: Oxford University Press, 2007).

Ballentine, Karen, and Heiko Nitzschke, eds., *Profiting from Peace: Managing the Resource Dimensions of Civil War* (Boulder: Lynne Rienner, 2005).

Bell, Christine, *Peace Agreements and Human Rights* (Oxford: Oxford University Press, 2003).

Call, Charles T., with Vanessa Wyeth, *Building States to Build Peace* (Boulder: Lynne Rienner, 2008).

Capie, David, and Pablo Policzer, "Keeping the Promise of Protection: Holding Armed Groups to the Same Standards as States" (2003), http://www.armedgroups.org/images/stories/pdfs/keeping%20the%20promise%20of%20protection.pdf.

Cassesse, Antonio, *International Criminal Law* (Oxford: Oxford University Press, 2003).

Crimes of War Project, http://www.crimesofwar.org/thebook/amnesty.html.

D'Amato, Anthony, "Peace vs. Accountability in Bosnia," *American Journal of International Law* 88 (1994): 500–6.

Davis, Rachel Benjamin Majekodunmi, and Judy Smith-Höhn, *Prevention of Genocide and Mass Atrocities and the Responsibility to Protect: Challenges for the UN and the International Community in the 21st Century* (UN Office of the Special Adviser on the Prevention of Genocide, International Peace Institute, and Centre for Conflict Resolution, June 2008), http://www.ipacademy.org/asset/file/355/ipigeno.pdf.

Donnelly, Jack, *Universal Human Rights in Theory and Practice* (Ithaca, NY: Cornell University Press, 2003).

Doyle, Michael W., and Nicholas Sambanis, *Making War and Building Peace* (Princeton: Princeton University Press, 2006).

Duffy, Helen, *The "War on Terror" and the Framework of International Law* (Cambridge: Cambridge University Press, 2005), esp. pp. 332–78, 379–442.

Dunne, Tim, and Nicholas J. Wheeler, *Human Rights in Global Politics* (Cambridge: Cambridge University Press, 1999).

Hirsch, John, *Sierra Leone: Diamonds and the Struggle for Democracy* (Boulder: Lynne Rienner, 2001).

Human Rights Watch reports, http://www.hrw.org.

International Center for Transitional Justice reports www.ictj.org.

International Crisis Group reports, http://www.crisisweb.org.

Ishay, Micheline R., *The History of Human Rights: From Ancient Times to the Globalization Era* (Berkeley: University of California Press, 2004).

Iyob, Ruth, and Gilbert M. Khadiagala, *Sudan: The Elusive Quest for Peace* (Boulder: Lynne Rienner, 2006).

Kaldor, Mary, *New and Old Wars: Organized Violence in a Global Era* (Stanford: Stanford University Press, 2001).

Kerr, Rachel, and Eirin Mobekk, *Peace and Justice: Seeking Accountability After War* (Cambridge: Polity, 2007).

Lutz, Ellen, Eileen F. Babbitt, and Hurst Hannum, "Human Rights and Conflict Resolution from the Practitioners' Perspectives," *Fletcher Forum of World Affairs* 27, no. 1 (Winter–Spring 2003), http://fletcher.tufts.edu/chrcr/pdf/lutz4.pdf.

Macedo, Stephen, ed., *Universal Jurisdiction: National Courts and the Prosecution of Serious Crimes Under International Law* (Philadelphia: University of Pennsylvania Press, 2004).

Manikkalingam, Ram, "Promoting Peace and Protecting Rights: How Are Human Rights Good and Bad for Resolving Conflict?" *Essex Human Rights Review* 5, no. 1 (July 2008): 1–11.

Marks, Susan, "Civil Liberties at the Margin: The UK Derogation and the European Court of Human Rights," *Oxford Journal of Legal Studies* 15, no. 1 (Spring 1995): 69–95.

Martin-Ortega, Olga, "Business and Human Rights in Conflict," *Ethics and International Affairs* 22, no. 3 (2008): 273–83.

Meron, Theodor, "International Criminalization of Internal Atrocities," *American Journal of International Law* 89 (1995): 554–7.

Mertus, Julie A., and Jeffrey W. Helsing, eds., *Human Rights and Conflict: Exploring the Links Between Rights, Law, and Peacebuilding* (Washington, DC: US Institute of Peace Press, 2006).

Nest, Michael, with François Grignon and Eminzet F. Kinsangani, *The Democratic Republic of Congo: Economic Dimensions of War and Peace* (Boulder: Lynne Rienner, 2006).

Nino, Carlos S., "The Duty to Punish Past Human Rights Violations Put into Context: The Case of Argentina," *Yale Law Journal* 100 (1991): 2619–41.

Open Society Justice Initiative reports, http://www.osji.org.

Orentlicher, Diane, "Settling Accounts: The Duty to Prosecute Human Rights Violations of a Prior Regime," *Yale Law Journal* 100 (1991): 2537–618.

Paris, Roland, *At War's End: Building Peace after Civil Conflict* (Cambridge: Cambridge University Press, 2004).

Parlevliet, Michelle, "Bridging the Divide. Exploring the Relationship Between Human Rights and Conflict Management," *Track Two* 11, no. 1 (March), http://ccrweb.ccr.uct.ac.za/archive/two/11_1/bridging.html.

Paust, Jordan J., M. Cherif Bassiouni, Michael Scharf, Jimmy Gurul, Leila Sadat, Bruce Zagaris, and Sharon A. Williams, *International Criminal Law* (Durham: Carolina Academic Press, 2000).

Pugh, Michael, and Neil Cooper, with Jonathan Goodhand, *War Economies in Regional Context* (Boulder: Lynne Rienner 2004).

Ratner, Steven R., and Jason S. Abrams, *Accountability for Human Rights Atrocities in International Law: Beyond the Nuremberg Legacy* (Oxford: Oxford University Press, 2001).

Reno, William, *Warlord Politics and African States* (Boulder: Lynne Rienner, 1999).

Reydams, Luc, *Universal Jurisdiction: International and Municipal Legal Perspectives* (Oxford: Oxford University Press, 2003).

Sriram, Chandra Lekha, *Globalizing Justice for Mass Atrocities: A Revolution in Accountability* (London: Routledge, 2005).

Sriram, Chandra Lekha, *Peace as Governance: Power-sharing, armed groups and contemporary peace negotiations* (London: Palgrave, 2008).

Sriram, Chandra Lekha, and Suren Pillay, eds., *Peace vs. Justice? The Dilemma of Transitional Justice in Africa* (Durban: University of KwaZulu-Natal, 2009).

Sriram, Chandra Lekha, and Karin Wermester, *From Promise to Practice: Strengthening UN Capacities for the Prevention of Violent Conflict* (Boulder: Lynne Rienner, 2003).

Turner, Thomas, *The Congo Wars: Conflict, Myth, and Reality* (New York: Zed Books, 2007).

Wippman, David, and Matthew Evangelista, eds., *New Wars, New Laws? Applying the Laws of War in 21st Century Conflicts* (Ardsley, NY: Transnational, 2005).

Worden, Scott, and Emily Wann, *Special Court of Sierra Leone Briefing: The Taylor Trial and Lessons from Capacity-Building and Outreach* (Washington, DC: US Institute of Peace, August 2007).

Zegveld, Liesbeth, *Accountability of Armed Opposition Groups in International Law* (Cambridge: Cambridge University Press, 2002).

Index

Figures in **bold** refer to boxes and tables, figures in *italic* refer to maps.